Party Pieces

Irish Studies

James MacKillop, *Series Editor*

Other titles in Irish Studies

An Irish Literature Reader: Poetry, Prose, Drama, 2d ed.
Maureen O'Rourke Murphy and James MacKillop, eds.

Irish Orientalism: A Literary and Intellectual History
Joseph Lennon

Joyce and Reality: The Empirical Strikes Back
John Gordon

Joyce and the City: The Significance of Place
Michael Begnal, ed.

Joyce and the Joyceans
Morton P. Levitt, ed.

Navigations: Collected Irish Essays, 1976–2006
Richard Kearney

Reading Roddy Doyle
Caramine White

Trapped in Thought: A Study of the Beckettian Mentality
Eric P. Levy

Women, Press, and Politics During the Irish Revival
Karen Steele

Writing Lough Derg: From William Carleton to Seamus Heaney
Peggy O'Brien

Party Pieces

Oral Storytelling
and Social Performance
in Joyce and Beckett

Alan W. Friedman

SYRACUSE UNIVERSITY PRESS

Syracuse, New York 13244-5160

First Edition 2007
07 08 09 10 11 12 6 5 4 3 2

Title page: (left) Samuel Beckett "conducting a rehearsal." Photograph by John Minihan. Courtesy of University of Delaware Photoservices; (right) James Joyce playing piano. Photograph by Gisele Freund. Copyright © Photo Researchers, Inc.

The paper used in this publication meets the minimum requirements of American National Standard for Information Sciences—Permanence of Paper for Printed Library Materials, ANSI Z39.48–1984.∞™

For a listing of books published and distributed by Syracuse University Press, visit our Web site at SyracuseUniversityPress.syr.edu.

Library of Congress Cataloging-in-Publication Data
Friedman, Alan Warren.
Party pieces : oral storytelling and social performance in Joyce and Beckett / Alan W. Friedman. — 1st ed.
p. cm. — (Irish studies)
Includes bibliographical references and index.
ISBN-13: 978-0-8156-3123-1 (cloth : alk. paper)
ISBN-10: 0-8156-3123-5 (cloth : alk. paper)
ISBN-13: 978-0-8156-3148-4 (pbk. : alk. paper)
ISBN-10: 0-8156-3148-0 (pbk. : alk. paper)
1. Joyce, James, 1882–1941—Criticism and interpretation. 2. Beckett, Samuel, 1906–1989—Criticism and interpretation. 3. Storytelling in literature. 4. Self-presentation in literature. 5. Social interaction in literature. I. Title.
PR6019.O9Z5334414 2007
823'.912—dc22
2007018222

Manufactured in the United States of America

For Liz,

yet once more

Alan W. Friedman is Arthur J. Thaman and Wilhelmina Doré Thaman Professor of English and Comparative Literature at the University of Texas at Austin. He is the author of numerous books and articles on British and American Modernism, including *Fictional Death and The Modernist Enterprise.* His six edited books include *Beckett in Black and Red: The Translations for Nancy Cunard's Negro* and *Beckett Translating/Translating Beckett* (coeditor).

Contents

Illustrations

Acknowledgments

I wish first to express my gratitude to Angela Bourke, Matthew Davies, Carey Harrison, Jeremy Hawthorn, Sean Latham, Ira Nadel, Jahan Ramazani, Charles Rossman, and Michael Wheeler for their careful readings and invaluable criticism of this work in draft and, even more important, for their deep and abiding friendship. Brian Richardson was an equally enthusiastic and insightful reader at a later point in the process. All of them were wholehearted, but not uncritical, supporters at important stages of the work. Other friends and professional colleagues who generously provided me with suggestions, information, and encouragement include George Bornstein, Terry Eagleton, Everett Frost, Luke Gibbons, Lois Gordon, Warwick Gould, Phillip Herring, Declan Kiberd, James Knowlson, Joseph Long, Lucy McDiarmid, F. C. McGrath, Riana O'Dwyer, John Pilling, and Tom Staley. Ivana Slavnic was most assiduous in her meticulous checking and correcting of quotations and citations. I received especially valuable advice and suggestions about dealing with the Joyce material from Michael Gillespie, Michael Groden, Vicki Mahaffey, and Robert Spoo.

The University of Texas at Austin has supported this project by affording me necessary time to research, write, and rewrite. As always, the Harry Ransom Center, under the inspired leadership of Tom Staley, has allowed me easy access to its unique holdings and resources, a marvelous working environment, and permission to quote from two unpublished Beckett letters.

Several chapters have been previously published in different versions and reworked for this book; my thanks to the editors and publishers:

"Beckett's Musicals." *Etudes Anglaises* 59, no. 1 (Jan.–March 2006): 47–59. Special issue on Samuel Beckett. Journal edited by Carle Bonafous-Murat and Ciaran Ross.

"Stephen Dedalus's *Non Serviam:* Patriarchal and Performative Failure in *A Portrait of the Artist as a Young Man.*" *Joyce Studies Annual* 13 (Summer 2002): 64–85. Journal edited by Thomas Staley.

"Party Pieces in Joyce's *Dubliners.*" *James Joyce Quarterly* 36, no. 3 (Spring 1999): 471–84. Journal edited by Sean Latham.

The American Conference of Irish Studies afforded me opportunity to try out various parts of what ultimately became this book at its annual conferences in 1997, 1998, 2003, and 2006.

I am grateful, too, for the kindness of Joseph Strick, who granted me permission to quote from the written text he uses in his film of *Portrait of the Artist* and for the still I use from his film *Ulysses,* and to Sean Walsh, who sent me the unpublished script of his film *Bloom* and has allowed me to quote from it. For illustrations, my thanks go to the following:

BBC: still from *Not I;*

Blue Angel Films: still from the Gate Theatre production of *Ohio Impromptu;*

John Minihan, Riverside Studio London: photograph of Samuel Beckett "conducting" a rehearsal;

New York Times: photograph by Sara Krulwich of *James Joyce's The Dead;*

Pennebaker Hegedus Films: stills from *Rockaby* and *Krapp's Last Tape;*

Photo Researchers, Inc., New York, on behalf of Gisele Freund: photograph of James Joyce playing the piano;

Zenith Entertainment Limited: stills from John Huston, *The Dead.*

At the request of Syracuse University Press, I quote from the following Joyce texts that are in the public domain: *Dubliners* (New York: B. W. Huebsch, 1916); *A Portrait of the Artist as a Young Man* (New York: B. W. Huebsch, 1916); *Ulysses* (Paris: Shakespeare and Company, 1922). Fortunately, these editions are quite similar, respectively, to the Viking Compass *Dubliners* (1962) and *Portrait* (1956), which are based on the Huebsch editions, and to the Random House edition of *Ulysses.* In the few instances where the texts differ substantively, I indicate those differences. For permission to quote from Samuel Beckett's writings, I am obliged to Edward Beckett, trustee of the Samuel Beckett Estate; Faber and Faber Ltd.; and Grove/Atlantic Press.

I am especially grateful to Syracuse University Press for publishing this work in their distinguished Irish series, and particularly to Jim MacKillop, my very supportive series editor, and Glenn Wright, the most assiduous of acquisitions editors, who guided me through many stages of this project, patiently answered all my numerous queries, and remained calm, reassuring, and helpful.

My greatest debt, as always, is to Elizabeth Cullingford (Liz): wife, colleague, severest and wisest critic, and most loving comrade and partner.

Introduction

Party Pieces: Oral Storytelling and Social Performance in Joyce and Beckett explores the tradition of performance pieces in the lives and literary output of two of the greatest and most discussed writers of the twentieth century. This study is predicated on the notion that social performances, particularly "party pieces," are embedded in the fiction of James Joyce and the drama of Samuel Beckett—foregrounded and often parodied in those of the former; less overt, more hostilely treated, and then vanishing but leaving important traces in those of the latter—and central to how they conceptualized their work. My focus is on varieties of performance *within* their texts: on virtuosity and holding forth, communal interaction, compelling or assaulting an audience, and a reciprocal economy of hospitality and hostility in which host and guest perform or fall short by noticeably failing to perform, or even subverting, conventional roles on social occasions such as partying, eating and drinking, and festive celebrations, or as part of everyday activity. Joyce, as often happens with expatriates, sustains and replicates this inherited cultural tradition, valorizing by satirizing, even as it undergoes significant change at home. Beckett's early plays depict party piece performers, necessarily self-parodic in their representations because of reduced, inappropriate, and absurd circumstances and occasions: performance is asserted or demanded by desperate figures in the process of losing not only community but also control, and even a sense of self. In his later plays further depleted figures—"shades"—increasingly inhabit a void where the barest traces, at most, of social intercourse remain; dehumanized, devitalized, disintegrating, on the verge of falling into an abyss of noncommunication and silence, they are, ironically, often wholly trapped in self-consciously "staged" performative roles, whether imposed from within or without.

Occurring within nonformalized social settings, the inherited oral practice takes two main forms. In the first, semiprofessional bards, wandering minstrels, or *seanachies* perform an orature intended to preserve what is being performed, sustain a tradition, or hand it on. Such a calling, Robert Elliott maintains, "was of the highest importance. The poets . . . were prophets, medicine-men, historians, genealogists, lawgivers, encomiasts, 'hard-attackers,' and much else besides."[1] In the second, nonprofessionals perform for the sake of performing, to demonstrate originality, and perhaps also to encourage others to perform. The two modes shade subtly into one another, overlapping and complicating the categories, as preservation and adaptation to changing social and political circumstances contest for priority. And they may look alike to some extent: an evening's social recreation organized by a master of ceremonies (*fear an tí,* in Irish, meaning "householder or host"[2]) who would either introduce a semiprofessional singer or else go around the room eliciting a song or tale from each of those gathered. Entertainment, audience interaction, and reward in the form of food or money would be the likely result in either case, though they might do so in different ways. Oral practice of all kinds had weakened considerably in Ireland by the turn of the twentieth century, but enough remained to inflect the writings first of Joyce and then, in more enervated form, of Beckett, and to make transparent what Walter Ong sees generally as the emergence of "literate thought and expression in terms of . . . and [in] relation to orality."[3]

Party pieces overlap with both traditions, but they are less about preservation than spontaneity, originality, the occasion itself. The anthropologist Roy Rappaport speaks of ritual in a way that suggests *seanachie* practice: "I take the term 'ritual' to denote *the performance of more or less invariant sequences of formal acts and utterances not entirely encoded by the performers.*" Although "Performatives are not confined to ritual," he adds, "performativeness itself may be made possible by ritual."[4] The analogy is especially apt given the long-held theory that theatrical performance—in ancient Greece, medieval England, and elsewhere—derived from "primal ritual." This view was generally accepted throughout most of the twentieth century when the genealogy of drama seemed clear and determined, though Richard Schechner (who considers "play, games, sports, dance and music" equally relevant to theater) and others now deem it "unprovable."[5]

Rappaport, who maintains that the term ritual "encompasses much more than religious behavior," enumerates its features as "performance, formality, invariance, inclusion of both acts and utterances, encoding by other than the performers."[6] Party pieces—whether storytelling, skits, musical performance, or dance—are analogous to ritual in being "performative utterances" (J. L. Austin's term) or "speech acts" (J. R. Searle's),[7] having certain (largely unwritten) rules of form, occasion, decorum, and audience interaction that are expected to be followed. But party pieces are not invariant, rote performances—certainly not within the Irish tradition that helped to produce Joyce and Beckett. According to Samuel Lover, a nineteenth-century storyteller and collector, "The Irish are so imaginative that they never tell a story straightforward, but constantly indulge in episode." Indeed, an oral narrator "would control the length of any story, deciding what might be developed or added, shortened or deleted, depending on the time available, the response of the audience, and his own mood."[8] The folklorist James Delargy concurs: "The tale must be passed on as it has been received, unaltered, not in regard to language, but in form and plot."[9] So invariance with a difference, of a creative sort, is at work in the construction of party pieces for particular occasions and audiences.

Performance itself is a slippery concept since, as Erving Goffman demonstrates in *The Presentation of Self in Everyday Life,* it may be said to characterize every human activity.[10] My attempt here is to narrow the focus to such self-conscious social representation as song, oral narrative, and dance—"party pieces"—that are performed to entertain, inform, or distract an audience (actual or imagined). Ireland has a particularly rich oral performative history that "stretches back unbroken for over twelve hundred years, a literary tradition which in its kind is unparalleled elsewhere."[11] Woods and Köhl suggest that "Ireland may well have some claim to being the richest of the West-European countries in respect of genuine Folk Music."[12] Delargy further argues that "Irish literature, both written and oral, must be studied as a continuous whole. Both oral tradition and written literature have exercised considerable influence one on the other."[13] Neither wholly formal rituals nor recitals within a prepared program nor simply spontaneous—what Vivian Mercier terms the "so-called 'rollicking' type of Irish humour,"[14] like drunks bursting into boisterous declamation—party pieces were often performed at festive gatherings when participants were expected to entertain the assembled group temporarily configuring itself as an audience. They traditionally served to foster an atmosphere of conviviality, fulfill social expectations or requirements, and express or repay hospitality as host and guest perform, for example, welcoming and after-dinner speeches. To accept the performative role willingly, or after minimal persuasion, is usually taken as a sign of generosity, as first Gretta and then Joyce's narrator suggests of Gabriel in "The Dead"; refusal, like that of Bartell D'Arcy, may be deemed churlish. Yet the performance tradition that plays out in Beckett's theatrical works, I will argue, depicts insistence, compulsion, and ultimately refusal.

For party pieces—and the call for them—can be aggressive, defensive, or an imposition, a way of precluding intimate conversation, of cultivating, forcing, or faking a communal circle, or of asserting power.[15] D'Arcy is more the exception than the rule in Joyce and even he is eventually moved to sing, and his singing has a profound transformative effect on his rapt audience. Beckettean performances are almost always cruel, painful, anachronistic, vestiges of an extinguished social world in which party pieces were once appropriate. His performers range from bullies like Pozzo, Hamm, and Voice in *Eh Joe* to reluctant, compelled entertainers or narrators like Lucky, the talking heads in *Play,* and the players in *Quad,* while his audiences are constrained, bribed, assaulted, or, in *Catastrophe,* themselves caught in the coruscating stage light and finally driven from the theater.

The particularities of Joyce's and Beckett's Irish upbringings are apt to this study since it is now generally accepted that both writers are fruitfully viewed within (as well as against) the context of Irish history and culture, perhaps even more than as "international modernists" or continentals.[16] As Luke Gibbons puts it, "These writers' vital contacts with mainland European culture proved productive precisely because they were carrying with them the nightmare of Irish history."[17] And the notion of "Irishness" often played out as deft public performance, with Ireland commonly represented, and self-consciously representing itself, as a nation of gifted talkers, storytellers, performers of party pieces. This tradition has by now been amply demonstrated in "the largest body of collected folktales [and folk music] in the west of Europe":[18] numerous story compendia and collections (for example, those by Thomas Crofton Croker, Samuel Lover, Jeremiah Curtin, William Carleton, Douglas Hyde, Lady Gregory, James Delargy, and Seán O Suilleabháin); Irish music, song, and poetry collected by Edward Bunting, James Hardiman, Thomas Moore, George Petrie, Charles Mangan, among many others;[19] and later folklorist studies such as those of Evans and Zimmermann's comprehensive work, *The Irish Storyteller.*

For Delargy, "Poets and story-tellers in homespun, humble carriers of an ancient culture, preserved until a century ago an oral tradition (*seanchas*) and an oral literature unrivalled in western Europe."[20] Concurring, Vivian Mercier argues that, for the Irish, "cultural interchange at the oral level, in idioms, metaphors, proverbs, folk tales, folk beliefs, has been continuous from the first English invasion down to the present moment."[21] Leerssen finds both continuity and threat in this long tradition of oral deftness: "The peasant's way of reflecting on life is . . . by the rehearsing of old stories. . . . This peasantry-as-folklore-reservoir is always on the verge of diminution or extinction,"[22] and it finally deteriorates into what Anthony Cronin calls the "standing cliché that in Dublin people went to the pubs rather than to their table or desk or easel; and the writer who talked his books away was a recurrent figure in Dublin's own mythology."[23] Luke Gibbons has suggested that "in Ireland, talking is not the cure; it is the problem. The more the Irish talk the worse the problem gets."[24] In this view the creation of home, as both Joyce and Beckett knew, is possible only abroad.

Seán MacRéamoinn describes as commonplace the tourist brochure welcome: "Come to an Irish pub and listen to the great flow of talk, as sweet and as heady as the drink itself." Yet, he maintains, "a verbal emphasis pervades Irish life at all levels" and, further, that "the Irish musical tradition . . . has close links with the dominant verbal culture which it at once sustains and relieves."[25] Writing of Irish subjugation by the British in the early nineteenth century, the cultural historian Paul Johnson risks Arnoldian condescension when he contextualizes Irish indignity and injustice in similar terms: "Much of ordinary Irish life, then as now, was lighthearted, warm, free and easy and fun, lit by flashes of brilliant wit and creative passion."[26] Michel Peillon comments that "Generosity and gift-giving belong, under many forms, to the festive occasion in Ireland," and he details many such occasions as well as the various forms that such generosity takes: "general hospitableness, condescending generosity, expectation of responding to ritualised soliciting or more often nowadays patterns of reciprocal gifts."[27] According to Evans, "The Irish countryman enjoys nothing so much as 'a gathering' of people. . . . That the remarkably large attendances at rural churches and chapels owe something to the social needs of a scattered population is suggested by the phrase, applied to someone who arrives late at chapel: 'he missed the mass but hit the gathering'—he had something worth while for his trouble."[28] The festive occasion alone sufficiently rewards those who make the effort to appear at, and participate in, "the gathering."

Evans expands on this depiction: "There were ceilidhes and spinning parties, and many a clachan had its shanachie (story-teller) and its fiddler or piper . . . who accompanied with folk-tunes. Folk-songs, occupational airs and legendary tales were kept alive in this way."[29] Anthropologist Sharon Gmelch describes a rural population whose lives depended on agricultural rhythms, and whose country fairs provided abundant entertainment: cockfighting, bull-baiting, jugglers, horse-racing, fortune-telling, games of chance, ballad singing and dancing, carnival rides, and theatrical and sideshow performances.[30] Hence an Irish festival is for everyone: "It expands to include all who arrive like some magic boat. . . . people feel no need to include outsiders in any deliberate way because there are no outsiders. If you have come along you are in some way part of the festival."[31]

This portrayal of a natural, communal, performative life, though it minimizes negative aspects of the Irish experience—grinding poverty, intense clannishness, family feuds and other common forms of violence, fierce territoriality—is not merely retrospective, a product of urban/modernist nostalgia and tourist brochures. It appears in numerous contemporary accounts and collections (some of them even post-Famine) that depict a largely rural Ireland, with its subsistent agricultural economy, as an idyllic pastoral ethos comprised of warm, hospitable households filled with happy families and joyful performances, a vision that Eamon de Valera was to enshrine in the 1937 Constitution. For despite Matthew Arnold's patronizing romanticizing of Celticism, it was not so much Irish fondness for "natural magic" that perpetuated an agricultural life close to nature as a lack of fossil fuel and Britain's policy of throttling its embryonic industries in order to keep Ireland a major food supplier. Any people (not just the Irish) lacking print capitalism and electrification are constrained to create their entertainment locally and domestically. When cinema became available (no thanks to Joyce's unsuccessful efforts to establish one in Dublin in 1909[32]), the Irish, like people elsewhere, rushed to enjoy its passive pleasures.

Having helped to end the tradition of party pieces in daily life, Irish cinema often seeks to recuperate its centrality to the country's lost history and culture. Several recent Irish films offer a particularly instructive, and harsh, lens for viewing that past, since they foreground party pieces while recognizing, as Zimmermann puts it, that oral performance "can be sinister when the life of the storytellers is bleak," a situation he exemplifies by citing Thomas Moore's novel, *Memoirs of Captain Rock, the Celebrated Irish Chieftain, with some Account of his Ancestors* (1824): "Certain kinds of Irish storytelling could be connected with interpretations of the past and with contemporary violence. . . . The emphasis is placed on the sinister connotations of Irish storytelling."[33] Neil Jordan's *Michael Collins* (1996) and *The Butcher Boy* (1998) both depict party pieces as central to the representation of Irish culture and to history gone wrong.

Deployed at key moments in *Michael Collins,* party pieces express the characters' political and psychological conditions as well as the transformations they undergo during the course of the movie. Both Kitty Kiernan and Michael Collins perform very differently under greatly altered circumstances at the film's beginning and end. Collins meets Kitty early in the movie when, after being beaten by the Royal Irish Constabulary, he awakens to find her nursing him; in the next scene, Kitty "sings a song by the piano, in the formal way of those days." Her song, the romantic ballad "She Moved Through the Fair," has the haunting refrain, "It will not be long, love, till our wedding day." Collins tries to escape performing "your party-piece," but Kitty, whose song earns her mistress of ceremonies authority, makes a ritual summons: "A noble call is mine and I call on Mick."[34] Collins, who "under persuasion by the party" is constrained to oblige, signals his acceptance with the formulaic "Oh! well do I remember."[35]

His party piece, a west Cork anti-English Famine ballad with the refrain, "And that's another reason why I left old Skibbereen," is especially apt: it is "set in the district where the Famine of the 1840s was particularly vicious."[36] From west Cork himself, Collins returns there at the end only to be killed. In the pub scene the night before his assassination, Collins again performs "Old Skibbereen," this time with gusto and on his own initiative.[37] "He performs," Jordan writes, "to draw attention to himself. So his killers will be drawn towards him. So he can talk to them."[38] And into Collins's death scene, Jordan intercuts shots of Kitty preparing for their wedding, as Sinead O'Connor sings "She Moved Through the Fair,"[39] intercuts that intensify rather than weaken both the shock and the sense of inevitability of Collins's assassination. Recounting old disasters, "Old Skibbereen" comes to signify new ones as well, and the responsibility that Irishmen like Collins (and de Valera) bear for them. For Jordan, "It's not the performance that is important. It's the reality behind the performance."[40] But the film brings traditional Irish performance, underlying reality, and contemporary context together as one.

Jordan's remarkably faithful movie of Patrick McCabe's *The Butcher Boy* (1992) similarly turns on party pieces. Jealous anger turns a celebration—replete with piano playing, singing, dancing, storytelling, drinking, and flirting—suddenly sour. As Francie, the titular character says, "It was all wrong. It was like the moment before a cracked glass shatters. . . . It was the silence around da that made me ice all over."[41] The huge row that his father initiates drives his mother to commit suicide, and the shattered Francie runs off, driven, as Elizabeth Cullingford writes, by "the TV Virgin's rendition of her party piece, 'Beautiful Bundoran,' that sends Francie off on the last and most devastating of his travels."[42] Seeking a happier time, he visits the seaside town of Bundoran, where his parents, "the lovebirds," honeymooned. He stays at the same boarding house, "where there was music in the evenings" and where Benny, like Maria in Joyce's story "Clay," had once sung "I Dreamt that I Dwelt in Marble Halls."[43] Francie images a happy party scene: "Everyone knew them there, all the guests. He used to sing for them in the evenings. It's a pity they never managed to go back. Perhaps they will yet Francis, he [a pedophile priest] says, there's still plenty of time. Indeed there is, I said, it's not often you see a singing skeleton she'll bring the house down."[44]

Unable to retreat into an innocent performative past (either his family's or Ireland's) because it never existed (he learns that, on his honeymoon, his father was drunk daily and abusive to a priest),[45] Francie plunges into madness and horrific violence, only to wind up an institutionalized stage Irish performer, playing the trumpet "just like da. . . . Sometimes they have sing songs in the hall and they ask me for a song. Go on!, they say, you're a powerful musicianor! You're the boy can sing then off I go and before long they're all at it, that's the stuff!" In an echo of Gabriel Conroy's "generous tears" and prospective journey westward at the end of "The Dead," Francie, "with the tears streaming down my face," imagines himself in cleansing snowy mountains at the end of *The Butcher Boy*.[46]

The notion of performance is inherent in modernism as well as in Irish culture. In his preface to "The Nigger of the *Narcissus*" (1908), Joseph Conrad, whose most famous narrator, Marlow, is represented primarily as an oral spinner of yarns to sometimes reluctant audiences, writes of music as "the art of arts,"[47] presumably because of its nonreferential, immaterial, and wholly temporal quality. Conrad is echoing Pater—"All art constantly aspires towards the condition of music"[48]—and Oscar Wilde: "From the point of view of form, the type of all the arts is the art of the musician. From the point of view of feeling, the actor's craft is the type."[49] Joyce was, as Declan Kiberd writes, a "child of Pater and the 1890s;" he "created an art which aspired to the musical condition in which style and subject fuse."[50] Calling music "the catalytic element in the work of Proust," Beckett suggested that "A book could be written on the significance of music in the work of Proust" (*SB4,* 553). A number of such books have, of course, been written about Joyce;[51] studies of Beckett's music have lagged behind work on other subjects, but they too have recently begun to appear.[52]

Beckett's writings, which he increasingly distanced from their Irish originary circumstances as they evolved, emulated what he defined as the condition of music: "other arts . . . can only produce the Idea with its concomitant phenomena, whereas music is the Idea itself, unaware of the world of phenomena, existing ideally outside the universe, apprehended not in Space but in Time only" ("Proust," *SB4,* 553). Music could, therefore, be said to assume a spiritual quality, not in the medieval sense ("the music of the spheres"), but in the sense Virginia Woolf meant when she contrasted Edwardian writers (Bennett, Wells, and Galsworthy, whom she labeled "materialists") with Georgians like Joyce, who were "impressionists" concerned with inner reality and hence "spiritual" writers.[53]

MacRéamoinn writes that "in any consideration of the Gaelic poetic tradition 'singing' is a keyword. Literally from the earliest times down to the present-day, poetry in Irish has been made to be sung"[54]—and often as part of an agenda that transcends the occasion. Noting that many of the operas to which Joyce alludes—for example, *The Bohemian Girl, La Fille du Régiment, Aïda, Lakmé, Il Trovatore*—concern political and class conflict, Allan Hepburn argues that songs taken from them "lose their political valence when casually performed at home. They have no direct influence on lives, however widely they are spread through Dublin culture."[55] Yet the literary deployment of party pieces (including Joyce's use of numerous songs from operas) invests them with moral, social, political, and psychological meaning derived from their new contexts: never casually chosen, their selection and circumstances are matters of identity and perspective as well as taste. When situated within performative media like theater and film, party pieces, like songs and set speeches in Shakespeare's plays, may at first seem to function merely as interludes or plot interrupters: indulged in for their own sakes, and hence suspending, or distracting attention from, the ongoing action. But usually they have the opposite purpose and effect: commenting upon the action they delay, they can serve, like the porter scene in *Macbeth* and the staging of "The Murder of Gonzago" in *Hamlet,* to increase rather than relax tension, as intensifiers and harbingers rather than diversion.

Party pieces are by no means always musical performances, nor are they always expressive of the performer's deeper meaning in the way Woolf suggests, but being temporal they exist at the same end of the expressive spectrum that is occupied by Wilde's and Conrad's notions of music and Wilde's of acting. They represent exactly the sort of ephemerality that Hemingway warned against when writing about bullfighting: "It is an impermanent art as singing and the dance are, one of those that Leonardo advised men to avoid, and when the performer is gone the art exists only in the memory of those who have seen it and dies with them. . . . It is an art that deals with death and death wipes it out."[56] Discussing performance that he calls orality, Ong puts the matter succinctly: "Sound exists only when it is going out of existence."[57] But like the filming of a stage production, performances *in* the text are a way of preserving the ephemeral, as Hemingway did when he wrote about the temporal experiences of fishing, hunting, boxing, bullfighting, and writing.

One useful way of situating the Joyce/Beckett relationship within the Irish context is to suggest that in his fiction Joyce nostalgically, and satirically, dramatizes the expansive tradition in declining transition, while Beckett's plays stage its post-Holocaust demise and disappearance.[58] "Perhaps," as Terry Eagleton suggests, "the drama of Samuel Beckett, which represents and points ironically to the impossibility of representing, is the only fit medium for such subject matter; and indeed those starved landscapes and wasted figures in Beckett are, among other modernist things, instantly recognisable from the bedevilled history of his nation."[59] Beckett himself offered Lawrence Harvey a very similar analysis: "Joyce believed in words. All you had to do was rearrange them and they would express what you wanted. . . . If you really get down to the disaster, the slightest eloquence becomes unbearable. Whatever is said is so far from experience. . . . (There is a danger of rising up into rhetoric. Speak it even and pride comes. Words are a form of complacency.)"[60] Hence, Beckett's lifelong quarrel with words, eloquence, rhetoric.

Both Joyce and Beckett experienced and embodied the continuing oral tradition of social performance in Ireland and embedded it within their writings, even while they felt like uninvited guests in their own home, encountering Ireland in Conor Cruise O'Brien's sense: "The condition of being involved in the Irish situation, and usually of being mauled by it."[61] Endowed with the stereotypical Irishman's gift for the oral and aural (and visually impaired like many of their characters, though Beckett's eye problems came late in life and were minor compared to Joyce's), both were brilliant linguists with university degrees in modern languages who earned their first living as language instructors. This common interest led both of them, for example, to explore the work of Fritz Mauthner, which Beckett read to Joyce. Mauthner viewed language as both basic to all knowledge and yet unreliable and self-referential.[62] Both were superb musicians who often performed in public and created scores of performers within their texts, though Beckett, unlike Joyce, had not contemplated a stage career. Casting and recasting themselves as performers such as Shem and Shaun in *Finnegans Wake* and Pozzo and Lucky in *Godot,* Hamm and Clov in *Endgame,* respectively,[63] Joyce and Beckett were well equipped to play major (absent) roles within (and against) Ireland's performative tradition, and to produce powerful antiphonal responses to the history they inherited.

Party Pieces occasionally discusses productions of Joyce's and Beckett's work, though they are not my focus: numerous excellent studies on that subject already exist.[64] Instead, this book concerns two writers who, for all their radical and iconoclastic approaches to genre, structure, and multilingual expression, remained both alienated from and steeped in the Irish culture of performance, natural rhythm, and expansiveness that infuses much of their writings. Although one of its main characters is a piano teacher, *Exiles,* Joyce's only extant play, is minimally musical: *Carmen* is mentioned (*Ex,* 24), the music from Archie's piano lesson "*is heard faintly*" (31), and Robert plays "*the first bars of Wolfram's song in the last act of* Tannhäuser"(57–58). Perhaps as a consequence, the play is not very performative (either internally or in the theater) and it has a spotty stage history.[65] In contrast, Joyce's fictive texts, as has been amply established with *Ulysses in Nighttown* and *Anna Livia Plurabelle,* and in films like John Houston's *The Dead* and Joseph Strick's *Ulysses,* often gain in beauty, coherence, and authority from being heard, read, dramatized, and filmed, from the interchange of performer and live audience.

Beckett's fiction, as demonstrated by the one-man shows and stage adaptations that he authorized because he trusted Jack MacGowran, David Warrilow, Barry McGovern, and a few others,[66] is both replete with performances and contains extraordinary dramatic potential. MacGowran comments that Beckett's prose is not only musically resonant, but also "strongly dramatic. . . . Beckett has said to me: 'I know that my word on the printed page is difficult to read and assimilate and I know also that it gets added dimension when read and dramatized.'"[67] Beckett had said something similar of *Finnegans Wake* many years earlier: "It is not to be read—or rather it is not only to be read. It is to be looked at and listened to. His [Joyce's] writing is not *about* something; *it is that something itself*" ("Dante . . . Bruno.Vico . . . Joyce," *SB4,* 503).[68] Such comments, truer perhaps of Beckett's work than of Joyce's, licensed MacGowran's staging of Beckett's prose. Yet what I am calling party pieces is not much in evidence in the prose, and limits of space will restrict this study to Joyce's fiction before *Finnegans Wake* and to Beckett's plays.

When asked why "such a small, seemingly backward country as Ireland produced so many great writers in such a relatively brief period of time," Beckett, echoing Joyce's denunciation of English imperialism and the Catholic Church that "have buggered us into existence," said, "When you are in the last ditch, there is nothing left but to sing,"[69] a metaphor for the historic Irish situation that Beckett depicts in *Watt, Waiting for Godot,* and *Happy Days.* Beckett's dramatic characters emerged from the circus, the vaudeville or musical hall stage, or the salon world of social performance, into plays that his American director Alan Schneider called "a kind of theatrical chamber music. In them, sounds and silences, cadences and rhythms, are selected, arranged, pointed and counter-pointed."[70] The play (within the play) is always the thing.

Joyce's fictional characters happen to be performers; Beckett stages performers who happen to be characters—although in later plays like *Play, Not I, Ohio Impromptu, Quad,* and *What Where* they seem to be only, or essentially, performers or even antiperformers, acted upon when they cannot act. The early plays, which retrospectively seem expansive and social, often create slippages of biography, history, and meaning by calling into question the names and identities of the characters, who nonetheless vie for performative priority and center stage dominance, and to avoid being relegated to the passive and anonymous role of audience. Didi and Gogo in *Godot,* like the protagonists of *Krapp's Last Tape* and *Eh Joe,* were conceived as clowns, and they perform, semiprofessionally, skits, games, songs, and verbal riffs to kill time while time kills them. But the fading out, or ebbing, of identity and denomination—and the simultaneous depiction of performative personae losing control of their métier—becomes more and more pronounced in Beckett's dramatic works. Increasingly, his dramatic speakers are either mute or else subvert their own identities and roles by narrating, badly, deflected or disguised stories, thereby calling attention to themselves more as oral storytellers, though ones of deteriorating skills, than as characters.

Human identities are lost as roles usurp the characters who once performed them. Reversing Joyce's pattern in *Dubliners,* whose meanly spirited focus yields to expansive social complexity in "The Dead," Beckett created a stage world ultimately devoid of even the veneer of personal and communal interchange while reducing the inhabitants of that world to failing performers who seem always to have been stuck where they are and yet possess little in the way of identities, relationships, and lives lived in the present. The late plays often depict retrospective, obsessional recreations of "that time" when something (or nothing) happened and keeps on happening through performance that verges on ritual repetition. Little is left, but that little, like Krapp's rerunning of old tapes, occurs often in the late plays, with their refusals to let go of a more vital past, their reiterations, revolvings, and calls for "More." Figures thus stuck because of their inability or failure to move forward become shades of themselves—disembodied voices, mute bodies, metonymic figures—feebler, attenuated, nearly lifeless, yet somehow "stirring still."

The critical responses to these most written about of twentieth-century writers have been invigorated in recent years by increasing focus on their Irishness, politics, textual productions, and relationship to each other, approaches that are all relevant to this study.[71] But *Party Pieces* is the first extended work that interweaves these concerns by foregrounding the performative trope as central to their lives and work. It explores Joyce's fiction and Beckett's plays as presentational enactments that reconfigure performative genres within an oral tradition of Irish self-representation—partly received, partly constructed—of hospitality, expansiveness, and communality as fundamental and integral to the lives and works of these two closely linked writers, though Joyce's emphasis is on their presence, Beckett's on their absence or loss. John Wyse Jackson and Peter Costello, the biographers of Joyce's father, deploy a grand musical metaphor, characterizing the years of John Stanislaus Joyce's life (from Famine to beyond the founding of the Free State, 1849–1931) as a "period of operatic convulsion for the country,"[72] one whose history and culture play out on a stage far larger than seems possible for such a small, marginalized country. My hope is that *Party Pieces* will contribute to an understanding of how Ireland's tiny population, paucity of resources, and vibrant performative tradition are centrally enacted and challenged in the lives and work of Joyce and Beckett, two of its greatest performative artists, who, after lifetimes of being Irish non grata,[73] have become integral to its very sense of itself.

Abbreviations

The following abbreviations are used for citations in the text:

CDDSJ	Stanislaus Joyce, *The Complete Dublin Diary of Stanislaus Joyce*
CSPSB	Samuel Beckett, *The Collected Shorter Plays of Samuel Beckett*
D1	James Joyce, *Dubliners*, B. W. Huebsch edition
D2	James Joyce, *Dubliners*, edited by Terence Brown
ED	Richard Ellmann, *Eminent Domain: Yeats among Wilde, Joyce, Pound, Eliot and Auden*
Ex	James Joyce, *Exiles*
4D	Richard Ellmann, *Four Dubliners*
FW	James Joyce, *Finnegans Wake*
JJ2	Richard Ellmann, *James Joyce*, revised edition
JJQ	*James Joyce Quarterly*
LJJ1, 2, 3	*The Letters of James Joyce*
MBK	Stanislaus Joyce, *My Brother's Keeper: James Joyce's Early Years*
No Author	*No Author Better Served: The Correspondence of Samuel Beckett and Alan Schneider*
OCPW	James Joyce, *Occasional, Critical, and Political Writing*
PA	James Joyce, *A Portrait of the Artist as a Young Man*, B. W. Huebsch edition
SB1, 2, 3, 4	*Samuel Beckett: The Grove Centenary Edition*, 4 volumes
SH	James Joyce, *Stephen Hero*
SLJJ	James Joyce, *Selected Letters*
U	James Joyce, *Ulysses*, Shakespeare and Company edition

Party Pieces

1 "Party Pieces"

Oral Storytelling and Social Performance in Ireland

Joyce liked to recount that Oscar Wilde, whom he referred to as "the singer of the divinity of joy,"[1] told a skeptical W. B. Yeats: "We Irish . . . have done nothing, but we're the greatest talkers since the days of the ancient Greeks."[2] Yeats, who considered that Ireland was distinguished by its tradition of oral poets and singers in contrast to England's practice of producing large novels and histories, certainly thought that Wilde himself was primarily an oral performer: "Only when [Wilde] spoke, or when his writing was the mirror of his speech, or in some simple, faery-tale, had he words exact enough to hold a subtle ear . . . his plays and dialogues have what merit they possess from being now an imitation, now a record, of his talk."[3] In her excellent analysis of Wilde's orality, Deirdre Toomey argues that "Yeats's aesthetic judgement is . . . a mark of an Irish cultural valuing of the oral over the written," and that "Yeats himself manifested a productive tension between extreme endorsement of oral culture . . . and extreme concern with the text."[4]

Traditional Ireland, Zimmermann maintains, "has enjoyed a highly verbal culture, . . . conversation and storytelling have been cultivated there as a game or a fine art."[5] The ancient Irish sagas depict hospitality as a great social virtue, and in poems like *Hills of Holy Ireland,* bards sang "A plenteous place is Ireland for hospitable cheer."[6] In his vast *Handbook of Irish Folklore,* Seán O Suilleabháin, cataloguer and archivist for the Irish Folklore Commission, names the first three "traditional attributes of the Irish people: wit, talkativeness, hospitality."[7] Journeying from home before the era of modern motels and inns could be difficult and dangerous, so that "travel for its own sake," as Roy Foster comments, "was rare and troublesome."[8] Yet the historian P. W. Joyce praises the ancient Irish custom of welcoming travelers, especially in establishing not only guest-houses in every monastery, but also "houses of public hospitality" throughout the country: "All travellers who called, and also certain important persons, such as kings, chiefs, bishops, brehons, etc., when on their circuits, were entertained free of expense. The keeper of one of these houses . . . was held in great honour; and he had a tract of land, besides other large allowances, to enable him to maintain his expensive establishment."[9] From the sixth to the twelfth century Joyce adds, "Hospitality was everywhere enjoined and practised as a virtue, and there was always a welcome from the family of the first private house he [the traveler] turned into."[10] And the guest would repay hospitality with the currency of a traveler: storytelling, a musical performance, or news and gossip from abroad. Medieval Ireland may have lacked hotels with modern conveniences, but it seems to have had the functional equivalent.

A description from 1862 suggests the continuity of such custom despite the intervening travails:

> The kitchen of some country houses in Ireland presents in no ways a bad modern translation of the ancient feudal hall. Traces of clanship still linger round its hearth in the numerous dependants on "the master's" bounty. Nurses, foster-brothers, and other hangers-on, are there as matter of right, while the strolling piper, full of mirth and music, the benighted traveller, even the passing beggar, are received with a hearty welcome, and each contributes planxty [a lively, usually wordless harp tune], song, or superstitious tale, towards the evening's amusement.[11]

Under such circumstances, host and guest conferred blessings upon each other through hospitality and performance.

Similar attitudes and behavior—and party piece performances—were also common among people with far less resources. "The Irish of all classes," P. W. Joyce writes, "like the Homeric Greeks, were excessively fond of hearing tales and poetry recited. . . . every intelligent person was supposed to know a reasonable number of [old tales, poems, and historical pieces], so as to be always ready to take part in amusing and instructing his company."[12] An 1833 governmental commission investigating the condition of the Irish poor reported that they "are more ready to feel for, and to help them [wandering storytellers] according to their means, than any other class, they are never sure but it will be their own case soon."[13]

Zimmermann cites numerous first-hand accounts of communal hearth-side evenings of storytelling by recognized masters of the art and by local residents taking turns as they gather alternately at each other's cabins or in a cabin designated for the purpose. Such ritual storytelling (and music and dancing, though to a lesser extent) is associated not only with special occasions like weddings and wakes, but also with such work as mending of fishing nets and quarrying, with the end of an ordinary day's labor, with the time after private prayer services, with welcoming of visitors (especially if they had a party piece to offer), and with hospitality generally. One outsider in early nineteenth-century Ireland commented that "if the visitor can relate a lively tale, or play upon any instrument, all the family is in smiles, and the young will begin a merry dance, whilst the old will smoke after one another out of the same pipe, and entertain each other with stories."[14] Itinerants who were known as good storytellers had their pick of lodging and had the luxury of choosing to stay where they would receive the most hospitable reception. The traveling man—whether beggar or smuggler, peripatetic schoolmaster or poor scholar, cattle-drover, peddler, tradesman, or farmer, friar, priest, or pilgrim, poet or ballad-singer, piper or harper, fiddler or dancing-master—would repay a night's lodging "with the latest news of fair and market, and the gossip of the country-side and . . . with ballads and songs and stories which he had learnt himself in his home district or had acquired in his travels."[15] According to contemporary accounts (such as those of John Keegan and William Carleton), "those at the bottom of the social pyramid [continued to] sit up half the night in winter, talking and telling stories," a custom that continued well into the 1840s.[16] Gearóid Ó Tuathaigh writes that, in pre-Famine Ireland, "there was a great variety of popular entertainment. Popular poetry and story-telling, survivals of a once majestic Gaelic civilization, still had meaning and an audience in rural communities."[17] But Carleton (writing in 1841) noted that great changes in Irish society have occurred "so rapidly within the last thirty or forty years, that scarcely any one could believe it possible for the present generation to be looked upon in many things as the descendants of that which has immediately gone before them."[18] Yet far greater changes loomed: "The often merry and generally harmless image one had formed of the Irish storyteller had helped conceal a conflictive and darkening background."[19]

Ireland's major nineteenth-century event, the Famine of 1845–52, which Terry Eagleton calls "the most important episode of modern Irish history and the greatest social disaster of nineteenth-century Europe,"[20] had vast political, economic, and demographic ramifications: greatly increased mortality, declines in birth and marriage rates, mass emigration, heightened antipathy toward England (whose policies greatly exacerbated the crisis), urbanization, and modernization. Sir William Wilde (Oscar's father) described the profound cultural dislocation caused by the Famine in terms relevant to this study: "The closest ties of kinship were dissolved; the most ancient and long-cherished usages of the people were disregarded; the once proverbial gaiety and light-heartedness of the peasant people seemed to have vanished completely, and village merriment or marriage festival was no longer heard or seen throughout the regions desolated by the intensity and extent of the famine."[21] In this view the Famine helped to pave the way later in the nineteenth century for nationalist formations like the Gaelic Athletic Association, the Gaelic League (founded on "the necessity for de-anglicising Ireland," primarily through Irish language revival and, beginning in 1897, staging nostalgic *feiseanna,* performative competitions of traditional Irish storytelling, poetry recitations, dancing, and singing), Sein Fein, and the Irish Literary Revival, thereby dividing an ancient, innocent—and performative—Ireland from a contemporary, fallen, political one.

Yet this picture is too simplistic. Centuries earlier the Statutes of Kilkenny (1366) had recognized "the abiding power in Ireland of an ancient literary tradition which was, from the outset, heavily implicated in the world of politics and militarism."[22] Out of fear of that power, the Statutes forbade "the coming of singers, poets, storytellers, rhymers, harpers or any other Irish minstrels among the English settlers, and warned the latter not to harbour them or make gifts to them."[23] In 1534 Henry VIII renewed the edict "that no Yryshe mynstrels, rymours, shannaghes, ne bardes, unchaghes, nor messangers, come to desire any goodes of any man dwellinge within the Inglyshrie, uppon peyne of forfayture of all theyr goodes, and theyr bodyes to prison."[24] And 1776–1815 has been called "probably the most lengthy and sustained period of upheaval in Irish history" and "certainly the period which has left the biggest trace in the record of traditional and popular music and song."[25] Although many of the Irish organizations and societies founded in the nineteenth century proclaimed an apolitical stance, collections like James Hardiman's *Irish Minstrelsy* (1831) reproduced anti-English ballads that allowed "hidden Ireland . . . to reach the ears of the Irish public-at-large in its own voice. . . . it conjured up a most threatening picture: that of a peasantry which was vocal, politically informed and conscious, disaffected and anything but naïve, anything but satisfied with their humble lot in life."[26] Surveying the nineteenth-century tradition of political, and specifically election, ballads, Theodore Hoppen found them ranging from "the poetry of unlimited abuse," which was often millenarian and revolutionary early in the century, to anodyne doggerel and "artificial 'literary' ballads increasingly popular in nineteenth-century drawing rooms."[27] Nonetheless Standish James O'Grady, whom Yeats called "the father of the Irish Revival," predicted that a not very important cultural movement and a not very important political movement would produce a military movement "which would be very important indeed."[28]

The young Padraic Pearse, then, was both following and seeking to revive an ancient tradition when he spent much of the year in which he joined the Gaelic League (1896) wandering in the Gaeltacht (the Irish-speaking area of Connemara) "disguised as a tramp, sleeping in the poorest of the poorest cabins, speaking Irish and collecting old songs and stories, always in search of his soul's Gaelic antecedents."[29] He would, in turn, perform what he had collected, transforming it in the process to serve his political ends.[30] Other nationalists short-circuited this course of action, so that, as a skeptical Declan Kiberd puts it, many "'ancient traditions' of the Irish Revival [like Gaelic football] turn out . . . to be cases of instant archaeology," what Luke Gibbons calls "history . . . staged and contrived," a recreation of the past that can be thought of as another kind of performance.[31]

The Famine disaster assaulted the social and domestic realm, particularly the rundale form of agrarian economy and the village settlements (*cloghans*) where people lived cooperatively, and it undermined the performative interchanges of story, song, and dance that commonly occurred within them. Zimmermann, like Thomas Kinsella and Kiberd, writes of this period in Beckettean phrases: "Contemporary writers described the awful silence and apathy in the countryside during the Great Famine years . . . , and half a century later an old person remembered the situation in Donegal: 'Sports and pastimes disappeared. Poetry, music and dancing stopped. They lost and forgot them all.'"[32]

No danger of "eloquence" or "pride" or "complacency" in "awful silence and apathy . . . disappeared . . . lost and forgot."

Transformations in the personal, familial, and communal configurations of daily life defy easy measure and raise questions about how we can know exactly how the fabric of Irish life was changed by the Famine. Estyn Evans writes that the crisis of the Famine broke "down patterns of behaviour which had continued with little change since prehistoric times"; and he cites and concurs with this post-Famine observation: "The traditions of hospitality were weakened greatly and . . . padlocks made their first appearance at this time."[33] Others argue, however, for a surprisingly unchanged country, one in which, as Walter Ong puts it, "every region preserves massive residual orality."[34] Citing the collections and writings of Jeremiah Curtin in the 1890s, Zimmermann comments that "his investigations confirmed that, contrary to what had been foretold by Wilde and others, oral traditions had not vanished after the Great Famine."[35]

In some ways the tradition had actually been enhanced: Thomas Gallagher's study "shows that virtually every Irish family history has its own Famine episode, and the legends evolving from these episodes have created an important oral tradition. In 1955 a compilation of accounts given by Irish men and women old enough to remember their parents' stories of the Famine was made. It is now housed in the Irish Folklore Department, University College, Dublin."[36] Delargy in the mid–twentieth century was also listening to storytellers who "could bridge the gap of centuries and [speak] the voice of the nameless story-tellers and creators of the heroic literature of medieval Ireland," and he notes one in particular whose mind was "a storehouse of tradition of all kinds, pithy anecdotes, and intricate hero-tales, proverbs and rimes and riddles, and other features of the rich orally preserved lore common to all Ireland three hundred years ago."[37] And Evans himself sometimes writes in the present tense of an enduring Ireland in which the pre-Famine performative tradition continues, if somewhat attenuated, in a communal context of expansive hospitality, conviviality, and intimacy with the cycles of earth and seasons.[38]

On the matter of Irish hospitality, Joyce's brother Stanislaus, writing shortly after the turn of the twentieth century, echoes Portia's characterization of mercy in *The Merchant of Venice* by aligning himself with the traditional view: "Hospitality is not so much a gift as a two-edged pleasure. That was a generous idea of the Italian nobles of the Middle Ages who tried to rival each other in hospitality and prodigality, kept an open table to all comers, and spent large estates in gifts to their dependents" (*CDDSJ*, 95). For Stanislaus, hospitality, like mercy, is twice blest: "It blesseth him that gives and him that takes" (*Merchant of Venice* 4.1.186–87). Yet hospitality, like historic Ireland, has its dark and horrific aspects: it could also be a two-edged sword, one wielded with treacherous intention or one that could be turned against its wielder. P. W. Joyce notes occasions when hospitality was a guise for betrayal and slaughter: people summoned to a feast could not refuse, even when they feared a trap set by their enemies.[39] Hospitality could be used to mask hostility: social interchanges could be perilous rather than convivial, occasions for mutual enjoyment and revelry *or* intimidation and even slaughter.

Similarly, the notion of party pieces can be inverted into the opposite of its image, becoming an aggressive or defensive ritual, a means of causing embarrassment or a way of precluding intimate conversation and of fostering or forcing a communal circle. In a contemporary version of enforced party pieces, less perilous perhaps than such abuses but nonetheless sometimes unpleasant for those who hate to perform socially, speakers at the summer schools that now dot the Irish landscape both deliver lectures (which are not party pieces because they are formal occasions known to planners, performers, and audience in advance) and then are often pressed to perform "spontaneously" at get-togethers that seem to be as integral to the schools as the academic programs. Old hands and those forewarned prepare a song or poem in advance; some canny repeaters have a "signature" piece that they perform (and that is often expected) each time.[40]

Yeats argues, however, that the balance of power sometimes tipped the other way, so that hosts rather than guests were targeted. In early Christian Ireland, he writes, "The bards were the most powerful influence in the land, and all manner of superstitious reverence environed them round. No gift they demanded might be refused them. One king being asked for his eye by a bard in quest of an excuse for rousing the people against him plucked it out and gave it."[41] Subsequent commentators often noted that the poet's powers to bless or curse were so great that they could be successfully wielded to blackmail rich and potent figures.[42] Sometimes audiences—whether guests or hosts—were constrained to play a more active role in the performance than they bargained for, and sometimes at a far greater cost than they anticipated.

Although their familial, social, and religious circumstances differed significantly, Joyce and Beckett were both heirs to this complex Irish tradition of performance; both, too, were alienated and then self-exiled from an Ireland they found constricting and debilitating. They sought to resituate themselves and their heritage not only in contemporary Europe but also within the broader Western culture of literary representation of performance going back to *The Odyssey.* Such linkage was also being made by others: in 1923, the year after the publication of *Ulysses,* the British classicist George Thomson began visiting the Great Blasket, where "the conversation of those ragged peasants . . . electrified me. It was as though Homer had come alive. Its vitality was inexhaustible, yet it was rhythmical, alliterative, formal, artificial, on the point of bursting into poetry. . . . Returning to Homer, I read him in a new light."[43] *The Odyssey,* the great urtext of *Ulysses* and a work that for a time obsessed Beckett, depicts virtually the entire gamut of party pieces, especially within the context of hospitality—both fulfilled and violated. Even in boyhood, Joyce, who was repelled by the heroic militarism of the Irish Cúchulainn, had been "attracted by the warm humanity of Odysseus," though of course Odysseus was, if at first reluctantly, also a military hero.[44] Joyce advised his Aunt Josephine Murray, "If you want to read *Ulysses* you had better first get or borrow from a library a translation in prose of the *Odyssey* of Homer" (*LJJ3,* 174). Taking the hint that Joyce publicly provided in his collaboration with Stuart Gilbert on *James Joyce's Ulysses* (1931), numerous commentators subsequently explored his extensive use, as well as misuse and abuse, of his Homeric model.[45]

Beckett's devotion to Homer is far less transparent, though in 1931, as James Knowlson puts it, "he became totally wrapped up in Homer's *Odyssey,* reading it in Victor Bérard's French translation and recovering, he wrote, 'something of the old childish absorbtion [sic] with which I read Treasure Island and Oliver Twist.'"[46] In 1932, Beckett wrote of seeking in Mallarmé "what I find in Homer and Dante, Racine and sometimes Rimbaud, the integrity of the eyelids coming down before the brain storms of grit in the wind."[47] Beckett, Barbara Hardy suggests, "shows that the choice of one story involves the suppression of others, and refuses to claim reliability for memory or art";[48] so too do Homer and Joyce, whose heroes are highly selective in the stories they tell of their wandering adventures to their Penelopes when they return home to reclaim the hostly and paternal role.

"Hospitality is," as Fritz Senn notes, "very much an Odysseyan theme,"[49] one that had particular appeal to both Joyce and Beckett for its representation not only of social performance (often featuring oral narrative) but also its antithesis: betrayal and violation of domestic space. As in the Irish tradition that Joyce and Beckett inherited and internalized, storytelling, song, and athletic contests are performed throughout *The Odyssey,* usually within the economy of host/guest interchanges. Even more than in medieval Ireland, journeys in ancient Greece were hazardous under the best of circumstances; without the rule of reciprocity between those cast temporarily in the role of host or guest they might have been impossible. Menelaus, Aeolus, and Alkinoos, who warmly receive their guests and provide them with gifts, are among those who enact hospitality as a great social virtue.

The most gracious host in *The Odyssey,* Alkinoos, the king of the Phaeacians, proclaims,

> "Let everyone be easy, host and guest;
> there's more decorum in a smiling banquet!
> . . . . any man with a grain of wit
> will treat a decent suppliant like a brother."[50]

The Odyssey's most significant events in terms of deadly consequences—Odysseus's blinding of Polyphemus, his men's freeing of the captive winds (Aeolus's gift) and their subsequent killing of the Sun God's cattle, and his slaughter of Penelope's suitors—all result from fundamental breaches of the guestly role, and it is Odysseus who commits the initial violation.

He tells the Phaeacians that after leaving Troy he stormed Kikonês without provocation, killed the men who opposed him, took plunder, and enslaved the women (9.42–44). A counterattack cost them many lives, and then Zeus sent a powerful storm against their ships (9.70–71); but Odysseus and his men learn no lesson from this self-induced disaster. When Odysseus subsequently taunts Polyphemus he curses him for inhospitality in the name of the divine guardian of guests:

> "Eater of guests
> Under your roof! Zeus and the gods have paid you!" (9.479–80)

And in revealing his identity, Odysseus alludes to himself as "raider of cities" (9.504), the ultimate violator of the guestly role. Still, Homer keeps the balance of sympathy weighted toward Odysseus by representing the Kikonês episode only in summary rather than by depicting it in detail as he does scenes in which Odysseus's violence is more defensible or those in which Odysseus and his men are wholly victims. Calypso, Polyphemus, the Lestrygonians, and Circe all provoke sympathy for Odysseus by their betrayal of the hostly role, perhaps none more than the Lestrygonians. Their princess waves in greeting to Odysseus's men, who approach in friendship, and then "for greeting / called from the meeting ground her lord and master." Without a word Antiphates "came to drink their blood. / He seized one man and tore him on the spot, / making a meal of him"; finally the Lestrygonians hurl boulders down on the hastily departing ships and spear the crushed men "like fish" (10.111–26).

The antithetical encounter, the perfect meeting of hospitable host and properly grateful guest, would seem to occur when the Phaeacians warmly welcome and regale Odysseus though he is an unknown and now lone suppliant. The special nature of the Phaeacians is hinted at in *Ulysses* when George Russell (Æ) contrasts them with one of Beckett's favorite writers: "France produces the finest flower of corruption in Mallarmé but the desirable life is revealed only to the poor of heart, the life of Homer's Phaeacians" (*U*, 179). Delaying the revelation of his identity for two days and four books of *The Odyssey*, Odysseus finally accedes to the Phaeacian king's request to reveal who he is; but, having courted danger by naming himself to Polypehmus, he does so here strategically and with a double-edged purpose. As Senn puts it, "What he is going to unfold is also a lecture on applied hospitality to his own hosts, who, at this stage, are of good will, although they have remained ominously suspicious and are still sitting on the fence."[51] Odysseus finally repays his warm welcome with an extensive oral narrative that recounts his epic journey since leaving Troy. It is one of the great party pieces in Western literature, but it is far from invariant: Odysseus has presumably told less detailed, because earlier, versions to Circe and Calypso, and he will tell an expurgated version to Penelope after he slaughters the suitors for besieging and abusing his household.

Yet hospitality, like its opposite, betrayal, also contains the risk of fatal consequences. Alkinoos is aware of the danger to his people that their generosity entails, for his father had once said that

> "Poseidon
> holds it against us that our deep sea ships
> are sure conveyance for all passengers.
> My father said, some day one of our cutters
> homeward bound over the cloudy sea
> would be wrecked by the god, and a range of hills
> thrown round our city." (8.564–70)

Nonetheless, the Phaeacians, a trading people who are themselves often strangers in strange lands, value hospitality highly despite its attendant risks. And, impressed by Odysseus's prowess in both word and deed, they perform to excess the hostly role by loading him with treasure and returning him safely to Ithaca. But their generosity is immediately punished, as generosity sometimes is, by Poseidon, who exacts his revenge upon the Phaeacians for aiding the destroyer of his son's sight, the action that climaxes that earlier disastrous host/guest interchange.[52] Again recalling the prophecy, which has now been fulfilled, Alkinoos speaks the hard lesson that represents a fall from expansiveness into a closed, inhospitable society:

> "We make
> an end henceforth of taking, in our ships,
> castaways who may land upon Skhería;
> and twelve choice bulls we dedicate at once
> to Lord Poseidon, praying him of his mercy
> not to heave up a mountain round our city." (13.207–12)

The events of Odysseus's stay with the Phaeacians differ markedly from those occurring in his palace on Ithaca. Not only do the suitors not sing for their supper, but they intend to stay, as Antinoös tells Telemachus, until Penelope does *their* bidding:

> "here are suitors eating up your property
> as long as she holds out. . . .
> we'll never go anywhere else,
> until she takes an Akhaian to her liking." (2.124–29)

Distressed by Telemachus's plight, Athena tells Zeus of the suitors' incessant assault upon hospitality—"that wolf pack of the suitors . . . prey upon his flocks and dusky cattle" (1.93–94)—and pleads to be allowed to turn the tables on them.

In contrast to the suitors, both Telemachus and the swineherd Eumaious instinctively greet strangers by enunciating the economy of hospitality. Telemachus, "irked . . . to think a visitor had been kept . . . waiting," welcomes the disguised Athena:

> "Greetings, stranger! Welcome to our feast.
> There will be time to tell your errand later." (1.121–22)

Similarly, Eumaious tells a beggar, whom he does not know is the disguised Odysseus,

> "Come to the cabin. You're a wanderer too [i.e., like Odysseus].
> You must eat something, drink some wine, and tell me
> where you are from and the hard times you've seen." (14.50–52)

Odysseus responds "in pleasure at this courtesy":

> "May Zeus and all the gods give you your heart's desire
> for taking me in so kindly, friend." (14.57–59)

In Ithaca, the antithetical behavior of Odysseus and the suitors as guests sets the stage for their climactic confrontation when Odysseus, disguised as the lowliest of guests, finally reveals himself as betrayed host avenging the violation of his household by domestic usurpers. The transitional moment occurs when Odysseus, having passed the bow test, quietly says,

> "Telémakhos, the stranger
> you welcomed in your hall has not disgraced you." (21.422–23)

He then reclaims his hostly role, vowing to transform his unwanted guests into a metaphorical meal:

> "The hour has come to cook their lordships' mutton—
> supper by daylight. Other amusements later,
> with song and harping that adorn a feast." (21.427–29)

Appropriately, the last man standing whose fate is in doubt is the minstrel, who begs for his life on the grounds that he served the suitors against his will (which Telemachus corroborates), but also because of what his talent in performance can offer:

> "My gift is song for men and for the gods undying.
> . . . deep in my mind a god
> shaped all the various ways of life in song.
> And I am fit to make verse in your company
> As in the god's." (22.346–51)

Immediate success at home followed by poetic immortality: Odysseus finds the combination irresistible.

Like Odysseus, both Joyce and Beckett felt alienated from their national origins and unwelcome there. Joyce donned the traditional Irish motif of historic betrayal, brought it into his domestic circumstances, and paraded it like a banner throughout his epistolary and literary writings. Beckett entered for a time into a modern version of the ancient host/guest economy that Homer depicts, a world in which salon hostesses held domestic court for contemporary Odyssean notables, as Maud Cunard, for example, did for Yeats, Pound, Eliot, George Moore, assorted artists, politicians, and others. Her ruling authority matched that of Alkinoos: "When the conversation flagged she would call upon her guests to provide their own entertainment by performing parlour-tricks or literally singing for their supper."[53] The forewarned guest came prepared.

Beckett, like Thomas Moore who played the piano in society drawing-rooms of Ireland and England, knew the salon world first hand (he attended Jack B. Yeats's Dublin "Thursdays" for a time during the late 1920s[54]) and indirectly through his close relationship with Maud Cunard's estranged daughter, Nancy. Fletcher and Spurling see the salon as underpropping many of Beckett's plays, and it plays a surprisingly large role in Beckett's writings: antisocial gatherers cavort in *More Pricks Than Kicks; Human Wishes* is set in an eighteenth-century drawing room; and Mme Krap's salon is a central setting in *Eleuthéria* (with overt rudeness displacing the usual polite veneer). Pozzo comes hot from a salon filled with Irish furniture, as his needing to be asked to sit down and to perform testifies, and Winnie in *Happy Days* behaves as though she were presiding over a social gathering. *Endgame*'s Nell and Nagg may be physically confined in dustbins, but their hearts are in their own salons; Hamm and Clov still live in theirs, though it is decayed from what it once was. Henry in *Embers* and Joe in *Eh Joe* have salons in their background; the characters in *Play* have two salons in theirs; and the three women in *Come and Go* are attenuated versions of *Eleuthéria*'s aptly named socialites: Mme Krap, Mme Piouk, and Mme Meck. Mme Krap even speaks of Mme Meck as though she were Winnie playing expansive hostess: "Jeanne sees life and light-heartedness everywhere. It's a permanent hallucination."[55]

But this is not the world Joyce and Beckett chose to inhabit, or assail directly. Instead of wielding Odyssean arms to exorcise their homes and restore a domestic social order, they became self-exiled from their native land: fleeing Joyce's "dear dirty Dublin" and Beckett's "derelict" country whose "charm" consisted of "history's ancient faeces" ("First Love," *SB4*, 236), and then subjecting it to the lancets of their art (*U*, 7). The metaphorical difference is telling. Joyce, as Zimmermann puts it, "through his family and his Dublin pub crawling . . . had received a fund of Irish verbal arts which he later exploited: anecdotes, songs and turns of phrase."[56] Hence, he depicts the urban squalor and poverty of means and spirit he increasingly experienced growing up as a world in which lively interchange is still possible, and to some extent still positive. In contrast, Beckett's recurring Irish image is the bleak landscape or ditch where, according to a *Times* editorial that espoused the British government's attitude toward the Famine, the Irish deliberately placed themselves: "We help all those who help themselves but we do not like throwing money into a ditch."[57] It is in such a ditch that Watt encounters the mystery of the frog's sounds and Molloy ends up, that Estragon spends the night, into which Mr. Rooney expects to fall (*All That Fall, SB3,* 176), and which holds the "bubbling black mud" of burials recollected in *A Piece of Monologue* (457)—and beyond which "there is nothing" ("Fizzle 5," *SB4,* 412).

Irish literary revivalists of the post-Famine generation often shared Britain's vision of Ireland as perpetually pre- or anticapitalist; it was that vision, as much as the country itself, that Joyce and Beckett viewed with hostility, and fled. Neither of them romanticized rural life, or Ireland. Sharing Stephen Dedalus's scorn, fear, and hatred of peasants like the old man with "redrimmed horny eyes" in a mountain cabin in the west of Ireland who "sat, listened, smoked, spat" (*PA,* 251–52), Joyce proclaimed that "no self-respecting person wants to stay in Ireland. Instead he will run from it, as if from a country that had been subjected to a visitation by an angry Jove" ("Ireland: Island of Saints and Sages," *OCPW,* 123). Beckett's Camier contemplates the countryside where Beckett had walked with his father: "It was true countryside at last, quickset hedgerows, mud, liquid manure, rocks, wallows, cow-shit, hovels, and here and there a form unmistakably human scratching at his plot since the first scabs of dawn, or shifting his dung, with a spade, having lost his shovel and his fork being broken. A giant tree, jumble of black boughs, stands between the branching roads" (*Mercier and Camier, SB1,* 466). Unsurprisingly, Beckett found that blasted landscape inhospitable and uninhabitable, though an even more attenuated version of it would serve as *Godot*'s setting.

Although Eyal Amiran maintains that "for Beckett, wandering can be done at home,"[58] Beckett, like Joyce, refused to replicate his characters' failed journeys. Mercier and Camier, like Joyce's Eveline, "did not remove from home, they had that great good fortune. They did not have to face, with greater or less success, outlandish ways, tongues, laws, skies, foods, in surroundings little resembling those to which first childhood, then boyhood, then manhood had inured them" (*Mercier and Camier, SB1,* 383). Both writers could stay home (that is, make their peace with Ireland) *only* by wandering, for, as Kiberd puts it, "the imaginative possession of the Irish landscape seemed possible only to those who were removed from it."[59] Beckett famously said, "I preferred France in war to Ireland in peace,"[60] and left Ireland for France the day after World War II was declared. Perhaps not surprisingly, the *New York Times* report of his receiving the Nobel Prize suggested that Beckett was as French as Shaw was British.[61]

For Ellmann, Joyce and Beckett's removal to live in foreign parts was a symbolic "attempt to proceed from the known to the unknown, to remake themselves in unfamiliar air" (*4D,* 80). Yet like Odysseus, who finally made it back to "One More Strange Island,"[62] both remained obsessed with their island homeland, Joyce more overtly than Beckett. Yeats had written that "no man who deserts his own literature for another's can hope for the highest rank. The cradles of the greatest writers are rocked among the scenes they are to celebrate. . . . There is no nationality without literature, no literature without nationality."[63] Joyce agreed: although he called Ireland "a land almost fabulous in its sorrow and senility,"[64] he nonetheless advised Irishmen to "write what is in your blood and not what is in your brain. . . . I always write about Dublin, because if I can get to the heart of Dublin, I can get to the heart of all the cities of the world."[65] As his father's biographers put it, "The city and its inhabitants never left Joyce's imagination—nor Joyce's imagination it."[66] "In *Ulysses,*" Ellmann adds, "he was confident that he had joined the best possible words (English) to the best possible subject matter (Irish)" (*JJ2,* 505).[67] And to a large extent the words (and music) of this "very Irish book dominated by short oral anecdotes" were derived from traditional Irish performance.[68]

Beckett's Irishness was long ignored or denied, although studies by Harrington, Junker, Eoin O'Brien, and others increasingly depict a Beckett beholden to Irish settings, memories, and traditions. *All That Fall* may be Beckett's one play with a substantially Irish setting, but "Beckett's apparently placeless writings incorporate literally hundreds of shards of Irish scenes and memories, as illustrated most fully in Eoin O'Brien's *The Beckett Country.*"[69] The macrocosm of Joyce's imagination was Ireland writ large; for Beckett the detritus of human history was as likely to be found in Ireland as anywhere else.

Despite their substantial differences of class, religion, and economic circumstances, both Joyce and Beckett inherited, and reacted similarly to, the tradition of Irish performativity that remained vital during their lifetimes even as it intersected with national revival and bloody insurrection. Their self-exile and radical literary innovation distanced them temporally, spatially, and psychologically from Ireland's past and present politics. Yet steeped in traditions they fled, they took with them the complex rhythm of alienation and obsession—and found new ways to represent their performance.

Born a generation later, Beckett had a background that differed from Joyce's in many ways: he came from a Protestant (and Protestant-size) family; his father was stable, responsible, hardworking, and successful at business, and his troubled parental relationship was with his mother rather than his father. He grew up without experiencing the Joyce family's frequent births, moves, and deaths, and downward financial and social spiral. Yet both writers had childhoods in musically talented families, were far more orally and aurally attuned than visual, and were themselves natural and talented performers. And both produced writings that were deeply rooted in the music they heard and performed at home growing up, and in performances they witnessed on the vaudeville stage, in music halls and theaters, and at the circus.

From their earliest days, both Joyce and Beckett were immersed in a culture that rang with music and performance, a culture that saturated their lives and their texts. As John Joyce's biographers write, "The family's earliest roots in the Irish-speaking oral tradition of story-telling and song fed directly into the three great modernist novels that would transform the world's fiction in the twentieth century."[70] Joyce's parents both had fine voices and an interest in opera; often they played the piano and sang together, as he depicts at the beginning of *Portrait of the Artist.* May Murray had piano, voice, and dancing lessons from the age of five to nineteen (*JJ2,* 19–20). Her teachers were well enough known to Joyce for them to serve as models for the Misses Morkan, "the Three Graces of the Dublin musical world," in "The Dead" (*D1,* 262; *JJ2,* 19, 245). Joyce's father was not only a superb tenor, but also "a master of English vernacular and a fine story-teller. His versatility enabled him to adapt his style to all surroundings, whether that of a drawing-room or a saloon. He was full of reminiscences of Irish life of the last half century and his stories were unusually embellished with rare artistry."[71] He embodied, in fact, the duality of the Irish performative tradition: John Joyce "could fascinate indefinitely with stories told with consummate art, one neatly fitting into another. And these stories would be of a perfectly drawing-room character till suddenly, as if taken unawares, he would slip into the coarse vein and another side of his nature and vocabulary be revealed"[72]—a duality depicted fully in his son's writings.

Joyce's own aural talent and performative inclination were manifested early on: he began playing the piano by the age of three; by the age of six he was singing in amateur contests with his parents. Later he composed musical settings for his own poems and those of others.[73] Despite his ironic stance toward Yeats's early poems, Joyce set several of them to music and sang them to friends. Ellmann writes that in June 1935, "pressed to quote something beautiful, he had recited Yeats for two hours. 'Everybody congratulated me on my extraordinary memory, my clear diction and my charming voice'" (*ED,* 34, 53).

Joyce, as Ellmann puts it, "daydream[ed] of himself as Dr. Joyce, poet, epiphanist, and physician" (*JJ2,* 111), and also as stage singer and actor. Mocking his way of speaking as a kind of conversational party piece, "a turn put on" for someone's benefit, his brother Stanislaus "acidly" told him that "if you fail as a poet, you can go on the stage as a patter comedian" (*MBK,* 149).[74] Stanislaus sarcastically comments that Joyce "thought seriously of abandoning his university studies and going on the stage in order to gain a practical knowledge of the production of dramatic works. Beginning with the easiest part of the project, he sometimes took a theatrical paper called, I think, *The Stage* and chose his stage name, Gordon Brown, a choice which bore witness to his admiration for Giordano Bruno" (*MBK,* 121). But even a skeptical Stanislaus was forced to acknowledge his abilities: "Jim's voice, when in good form, has a beautiful flavour, rich and pure, and goes through one like a strong exhilarating wine. He sings well" (*CDDSJ,* 4). Stanislaus adds that Dublin's leading voice teacher was so impressed he gave him lessons "for nothing and advises Jim to take to concert singing as a profession" (*CDDSJ,* 36).

Possessing a remarkable ear and an extraordinary tenor voice inherited from his parents, Joyce did seriously contemplate a stage career (*JJ2,* 150–52, 154–55) and was furious with his father for selling the family piano just at this time, causing a breakdown in their normal relations.[75] He wrote to Oliver St. John Gogarty in June of 1904 requesting the loan of "a decent suit" for his singing engagements, explaining his plan to spend the summer singing "old English songs" to the lute in the south of England (*LJJ1,* 54).[76] As late as August of that year Joyce "was arranging to go away as a travelling actor," but aborted the plan, he wrote to Nora Barnacle, because of thoughts of her (29 August 1904, *LJJ2,* 48)—and also because by that time he had determined that "a poet's job is to write tragedies, not to be an actor in one" (*MBK,* 149). That summer also saw what Ellmann calls "the high point of his musical career" when, like his father before him,[77] he sang in Dublin's Antient Concert Rooms with John McCormack and J. C. Doyle (who were to go on tour with Molly Bloom in *Ulysses*). Nora, along with the reviewers, was enthralled by Joyce's "sweet tenor voice,"[78] which also impressed Triestine reviewers when he performed in 1909.[79] Failing to understand the fuss caused by his writing, which she never read, Nora recognized his musical genius and always thought that "Jim should have stuck to music instead of bothering with writing" (*JJ2,* 168–69).

Joyce, though he continued his singing career vicariously through his son Giorgio, determined to play a very different role in his country's coming of age in a modern industrial world: presciently enacting in his life and in his writings Ireland's transition from an oral to a written culture. In the late 1890s, Yeats wrote that a necessary, if not sufficient, condition for a popular ballad literature to arise occurs when "needful national traditions [are] not hidden in libraries, but living in the minds of the populace. These Ireland has."[80] But as Joyce knew they were also beginning to disappear as Ireland metamorphosed from a largely oral into a largely written culture. So he renounced an oral career for a literate one (though he continued to take voice lessons and sing in concert in Trieste),[81] and found a way of having the best of both: saturated with the music, songs, and other performances of the career not taken, the permanent record that is Joyce's work can be read as a nostalgic (affirming as well as satirizing) recreation of the untrodden path, as well as a means of preserving a way of life that was dying out even as he recorded it.

Party pieces occur frequently in *Dubliners,* and many of its stories turn on a moment of performative interchange as numerous characters sing or otherwise perform, revealing concealed motives, unacknowledged pasts, personal unhappiness, or covert threats. "The Dead," which depicts performance as still integral to a private festive occasion, greatly expands the role of party pieces as indices of moral value and makes song and oral narrative key to its climactic epiphany. In *A Portrait of the Artist,* which weaves some twenty-five songs into the narrative, the Dedalus family, like the Joyces, sang "for hours, melody after melody, glee after glee, till the last pale light died down on the horizon, till the first dark nightclouds came forth and night fell" (*PA,* 190). Although desperate to escape his family's hold on him, Stephen never manages to emerge from the shadow or dominance of his father, a caricature of conviviality, expansive oral performance, and drunken "stage Irish" irresponsibility, a failure that prophecies and insures Stephen's own failure as an artist.

Ulysses, whose lyricism and symbolism Joyce proclaimed and defended,[82] contains allusions to over four hundred songs, many associated with Molly Bloom, a popular soprano, her impresario, Blazes Boylan, and the affair they are having as they prepare to embark on a concert tour. Stephen, the would-be artist, never creates or performs successfully, while Leopold Bloom, ad canvasser and cuckold, proves to have more than "a touch of the artist" about him (*U,* 225). Most performatively textured, *Finnegans Wake,* of which Joyce once said "it's pure music" (*JJ2,* 703), contains allusions to over one thousand songs, including virtually all 124 of the *Irish Melodies* ("tummy moor's maladies" [*FW,* 492.34]) and all of those that appear in Joyce's previous fiction.[83] The *Wake* is also, as Hardy demonstrates, an encyclopedia of narrative forms and themes, of "all conceivable variants of telling and listening"; a vast story of all risings and fallings, beginnings and endings; a Babel "built out of many stories as well as many languages."[84]

Joyce joins and stretches the tradition of Gaelic "singing" by writing an Anglo-Irish prose that seems designed for voice and ear. After abandoning his plan to become a stage performer, he evolved into what Ellmann calls "this indrawn writer" (*4D,* 56), who could be utterly cold and silent "in the face of adulation or hostility" (*JJ2,* 320), averse "to discoursing at large" (*JJ2,* 488), who yet performed often on social occasions. In *Portrait,* Cranly finds it curious that Stephen's mind, which has rejected the priesthood, remains saturated with the religion in which he no longer believes (*PA,* 283), but it would be far more curious if it were not. In fact, Joyce's texts are "supersaturated" with the evidence of two careers not taken: that of the church and that of the stage.

Joyce remained a performer all his life, both within his texts and without, frequently singing and playing both privately and publicly. Ellmann describes numerous occasions when Joyce sang (and even danced) in public: on his first, awkward, meeting with James Stephens, for example, Joyce sang *The Yellow Ale,* a misogynistic drinking song about some of his favorite themes: betrayal, cuckoldry, and death (*JJ2,* 334n). Mary and Padraic Colum write that "A poet in those days was expected to know his own poems and be willing to deliver them. . . . Joyce spoke his verse with deliberateness and precision, but in a naturally beautiful voice that had been cultivated for singing."[85] Joyce, "who had a wide range of ballads, English and Irish,"[86] held forth expansively in Parisian cafés, and often sang both when alone and with others: "On his birthdays, in restaurants, in the homes of friends, in happiness and grief: always Joyce sang."[87] "He would," as Arthur Power tells it, "sing in a light and pleasant tenor voice many Irish ballads in which romance and satire were combined, and which were the secret source of his inspiration."[88]

Not only a form of self-expression, music also served Joyce as a way of releasing tension during times of transition: he refused to pray for his mother on her deathbed, but he played the piano and sang for her,[89] as he did for his brother George when he was dying (*MBK,* 134). He welcomed Giorgio and Lucia into the world with song (the latter a lullaby he composed for the occasion), and he sang a duet with Giorgio at his birthday party in 1939 that also celebrated the publication of *Finnegans Wake.* After war was declared, Joyce sang the "Marseillaise" loudly in a restaurant jammed with delighted French and British soldiers. Shortly thereafter, "Joyce went with Samuel Beckett to retrieve some books from [his now-abandoned] flat, and, extremely nervous, jumped to the piano and sang at the top of his voice for half an hour" (*JJ2,* 715, 727–28). This histrionic self-dramatization was Joyce's cry of protest against a war he considered not only useless and mad, but also a distraction from his new book. Hence, performance expressed and accompanied all that was most important in Joyce's life.

Beckett's performative background and social performances (for example, as piano player at parties) were remarkably similar. His also was a very musical family, and he too was a superb musician. The great Beckett actor Jack MacGowran remarked that Beckett shared a gift for classical music with the rest of his family: "Beckett is a very brilliant musician himself, who plays classics brilliantly on the piano. . . . Beckett's whole background is one of classical music."[90] Beckett's paternal grandmother "was extremely musical and wrote songs herself, as well as adapting pieces for the piano and setting to music various poems"; two of her children were musically gifted, including Gerald, "a talented pianist, who enjoyed playing piano duets with his young nephew Samuel."[91]

Beckett's mother, despite her austerity and rigid sense of propriety, was a social performer: with a "wild sense of humor and great store of impersonations and jokes," she told funny stories at teatime to neighborhood children. She imposed piano lessons and practice on the five children in her charge, with Beckett "the most dedicated and diligent in practicing the piano."[92] Knowlson adds that Beckett's brother Frank "was also a very good pianist, specializing in popular songs, which he used to play to the delight of the extended family. The boys played piano duets together." Sheila Page, Beckett's cousin, said, "Sam used to sing madly with a quavering voice when he played. And we'd all be roaring with laughter out in the hall. But he was very musical."[93] Another cousin, the composer John Beckett, experienced a similar Joycean performance when he "sat down at the piano after the final performance of *Endgame* at the Royal Court Theatre and improvised some hilarious variations on the "Marseillaise," to the delight of Beckett, who responded by singing several bawdy Irish songs."[94] It seems no mere coincidence that when Beckett met Suzanne Deschevaux-Dumesnil, later to become his wife, she was studying the piano and subsequently became a professional; he and a friend played duets against her and her partner.[95] Beckett's nephew Edward, a founding member of the London Festival Orchestra and currently its principal flautist, said that his uncle "was quite a reasonable performer. He played Haydn, Beethoven, Chopin, some Schubert. . . . he could play by ear quite well, vamp out with accompaniment."[96]

Throughout his life Beckett played the piano (and even the tin whistle on which, as he put it, he "used to tweetle"),[97] usually for close friends or when alone; according to Bair, he sometimes used his playing to hide behind. She notes an occasion when, upon coming to dinner at John Calder's house, "He was so nervous about meeting new people that he sat down at the piano and spent the entire evening playing to himself. If anyone tried to engage him in conversation, he pretended to concentrate on his playing and did not answer"[98]—though it is possible that Beckett *was* concentrating. Music, as Knowlson puts it, "was a constant and important ingredient in Beckett's life. His early writing contained many witty allusions to music or musical form. . . . later in his career, he was to use music directly in a number of his plays. Indirectly, he was to draw on his knowledge of musical techniques and terminology, reshaping musical structures and working with repetition and repetition with variation, counterpoint, and changes of key, rhythm, tempo, and pitch."[99] This is an area I explore in chapters 5 and 6 in discussing the structure and rhetorical strategies of Beckett's plays.

Like Beckett himself, actors and directors often responded primarily to the musical rhythm and form of his plays: "His work, particularly his later work . . . turns into word-music as if the whole basis of a sonata was running through his mind as he wrote it."[100] The corollary, for Beckett, was a distrust of language, which pretends to be precise but is not. Knowlson comments that "Beckett's ideas on the inadequacy of language and the superiority of music as an art form, on the relation between the subject and the object in art, and on the notion that rationalism was an aberration and naturalism in art was an impoverishment could flow with so much passion that he was embarrassed by his own fervor, even his wildness."[101] In the conflict between music (or rhythm) and language in Beckett's plays, language loses every time.

Beckett also shared Joyce's devotion to legitimate theater from early on—and then, of course, his became far greater when he assumed the directorship of his own plays. As a young man in Dublin, Beckett, like Joyce, often went to the Abbey Theatre, where he saw many of the plays of the Irish Dramatic Movement and was especially impressed by those of Yeats, Synge, and O'Casey.[102] In Paris, he visited the experimental Théatre Alfred Jarry, where Antonin Artaud challenged audiences to participate as actively and painfully as they do when they visit the dentist.[103] He was also devoted, perhaps even more than Joyce, to such theatrical offshoots as pantomime, vaudeville, and the music hall. Beckett's first theatrical experiences were the annual pantomime at the Gaiety Theatre and Gilbert and Sullivan. He "used to play Sullivan's music on the piano at home; a friend recalled that 'he sang irreverent, ribald Beckett *libretti* in substitution for Gilbert's words.'"[104]

Finally, though he went to the opera and ballet, Beckett was dismissive of such hybrid musical forms and his work differs from Joyce's in offering few references to them. He endorsed vaudeville over opera, which he called "a hideous corruption of this most immaterial of all the arts" in its ability to materialize music; vaudeville "at least inaugurates the comedy of an exhaustive enumeration" (*Proust, SB4,* 553–54). Similarly, he thought that ballet degraded music by subordinating it to the visual: "There are those who can only find satisfaction visually. . . . I can only escape with my eyelids closed." Yet all these performative experiences laid the groundwork for his incorporation of party pieces into his dramatic works and for his increasingly meticulous choreographing of the later plays, including the balletic *Footfalls* and *Quad.* As with Joyce, all the performative modes ultimately played their parts on Beckett's stage.

2 *Dubliners*

"Scrupulous Meanness" Versus Expansive Performance

The text of *Dubliners* is replete with bravura and virtuoso performances—of music, song, and dance; of storytelling, poetic recitation, and extravagant pub talk as well as rhetorical speeches of an occasional nature[1]—derived from the rich Irish performative tradition that Joyce inherited. The performances, many of them party pieces, serve a multitude of purposes, some of which are far from obvious or straightforward. As Allan Hepburn writes, "In *Dubliners,* numerous characters sing folk ballads or operatic arias that belie concealed motives, unacknowledged pasts, personal unhappiness, or covert threats."[2] What Joyce depicts, then, is the range of performative possibilities, but with an emphasis on its negative aspects, its failures, costs, and betrayals, rather than its warmth, vitality, good-heartedness, a tradition very much in decline. Its fullest representation, in "The Dead," foregrounds, laments, and briefly revives that tradition.

Many of the characters in *Dubliners* are performers of one kind or another, or represent themselves as such, but their performative intentions are often more unpleasant, or even threatening, than they seem at first. As Jordan does in *Michael Collins* and *The Butcher Boy,* Joyce problematizes performances, frequently depicting them as awkward, embarrassing, or inappropriate party pieces rather than festive or reassuring; they become moments that epitomize generational, familial, cultural, or political fissures. Joyce's boast to Grant Richards that he wrote *Dubliners* in a "style of scrupulous meanness" (*LJJ2,* 5 May 1906, 132) alludes not only to his writing technique but also to his largely unsympathetic portrayal of the performative tradition, a representation that, however, he modifies and complicates toward the end of the book.

Near the beginning, young boys in both "An Encounter" and "Araby" are humiliated by performative experiences. In "An Encounter," the boy playing truant, who expresses his pleasure musically, patting the stones "with my hands in time to an air in my head"[3] (*D1,* 23), is first drawn to the "queer old josser" (30) he encounters who also seems to be playing an instrument: "always tapping the ground with his stick." The josser, who invokes the Irish oral tradition by asking the boys if they have read Thomas Moore's poetry, offers an oral performance that seems at first to embody two positive features of Irish storytelling: the stranger bearing news of the larger world and the telling of tales to "shorten the road." But the young narrator is soon unnerved by him ("I disliked the words in his mouth"), not so much because he senses physical or sexual danger from the aging pederast, but because his salacious talk becomes an unexpected, eerie, and misplaced party piece: uncannily he seemed to be "repeating something which he had learned by heart. . . . he spoke as if he were simply alluding to some fact that everybody knew, and at times he lowered his voice and spoke mysteriously as if he were telling us something secret which he did not wish others to overhear" (27–29). Like the stories of adult mysteries that the boy in "The Sisters" overhears, this rote performance of social interchange becomes isolating and frightening, rather than engaging and inclusive, because the performer's flaunting of privileged knowledge establishes a narrative authority that both displays and imposes a power hierarchy that the vulnerable listener feels to be threatening rather than reassuring.

The equally impressionable young boy in "Araby" is constrained to endure a commercial scene filled with the oral detritus of a decayed tradition: shouts, appeals, and songs that he finds socially, culturally, and politically degrading. With his aunt, he traversed the unruly streets, hearing "the curses of labourers, the shrill litanies of shop-boys who stood on guard by the barrels of pigs' cheeks, the nasal chanting of street-singers, who sang a *come-all-you* about O'Donovan Rossa, or a ballad about the troubles in our native land" (35). Safely bearing the chalice of his romantic fantasizing amid enemy forces, he feels his body responding like a harp to Mangan's sister, whose "words and gestures were like fingers running upon the wires"; he then sings of his fantasy in lonely isolation rather than joining his companions in play (36, 38).[4] Desperate to set out on his quixotic quest to Araby, he is nearly forestalled by his uncle (modeled on John Joyce[5]), who arrives home late and then begins to perform by rote *The Arab's Farewell to His Steed,* a title adapted from *The Arab's Farewell to His Horse,* a poem by the Irish poet Caroline Norton (1808–77) that was a popular recitation piece in the nineteenth century.[6] As Joyce has it, the boy leaves the kitchen just as his uncle "was about to recite the opening lines of the piece to my aunt," and then strode to the station (39). Barely avoiding becoming an enforced audience, the boy nearly violates the protocols of recitation by leaving in the middle. The American Street Productions film of *Araby* (1997) goes Joyce one better, depicting the violation by showing the boy *sneaking away* as his uncle pronounces, "This calls for a recitation." The boy then runs furiously to the train as his uncle, in a voiceover that pursues him, recites the poem with an increasingly aggressive gusto that seems to lead directly to the boy's epiphany at the tawdry fair: "I saw myself as a creature driven and derided by vanity; and my eyes burned with anguish and anger" (41). He might have done better to stay for the recitation.

Eveline's experience of performance is even more troubling than those of the boys in the first three stories because she is compelled to choose between the life of tedious duty she had promised her dying mother to fulfill and the unknown adventure she desires and fears. Caught between competing storytellers, her abusive father who tells ghost stories (suggesting that the dead have a double hold on her) and a sailor named Frank, who "was very kind, manly, open-hearted" and who "would give her life, perhaps love, too" but about whom she knows little more than his performative nature, she contemplates eloping to Buenos Ayres (45–47). Like Othello, Frank tells tales of distant countries and exotic experiences, and he evinces the power of naming: "He told her the names of the ships he had been on and the names of the different services. He had sailed through the Straits of Magellan and he told her stories of the terrible Patagonians" (46). In addition, he was fond of music and would sing to her; he woos and seems to win her by singing "about the lass that loves a sailor" (45). But "The Lass That Loves a Sailor," a popular song more about drinking than love that raucously promises romance at sea, always made Eveline feel "pleasantly confused" (45).[7] And on the verge of elopement she holds back, presumably because when she comes to it she cannot leave her father, the drunk she knows who, as she quickly recalibrates, "could be very nice," for the mysterious stranger who she fears "would drown her" (46, 48), or worse, since "Going to Buenos Ayres" was Dublin "slang for taking up a life of prostitution"[8] and associated with the white slave trade. Eveline may, therefore, have good reason to recoil from the life into which Frank seeks to seduce her when, like the boys in the earlier stories, she finally rejects an enforced role as audience; for, though Frank shouts for her to come with him, "Her eyes gave him no sign of love or farewell or recognition" as he sails off without her (48). Yet her choice seems likely to doom her to a spinsterhood like Maria's in "Clay" since, in post-Famine Ireland, and as Joyce depicts them, such women rarely had more than one opportunity for marriage.

Disappointment in performance gathers momentum and both political and gendered meaning throughout *Dubliners.* Amid much revelry and music, Jimmy Doyle in "After the Race" makes a long, well-received speech for his supper, though he subsequently "felt obscurely the lack of an audience" (57), and then loses heavily at cards to a young Englishman because he cannot drink and still perform: "He frequently mistook his cards and the other men had to calculate his I.O.U.'s for him" (56–57). In "Two Gallants," Lenehan, "a sporting vagrant armed with a vast stock of stories, limericks and riddles" (59), lives with no apparent means. Like Mick Hart, the original on whom he is based, Lenehan, "insensitive to all kinds of discourtesy" (59), seems to survive on party pieces.[9] First appearing as effusively appreciative audience for Corley's monologue about "a fine tart" (60) who services him in various ways ("Little jets of wheezing laughter followed one another out of his convulsed body" [58]), Lenehan, weary and hungry, hopes that some of the crumbs will fall to him. "His tongue was tired for he had been talking all the afternoon in a public-house in Dorset Street. Most people considered Lenehan a leech but . . . his adroitness and eloquence had always prevented his friends from forming any general policy against him" (59).

Present pickings are slim, however, and Lenehan has eaten virtually nothing all day. He seems literally at his wits' end, drained of bravura vitality: "He knew that he would have to speak a great deal, to invent and to amuse, and his brain and throat were too dry for such a task" (68). Like the boy in "Araby," he seems reduced from performer to instrument, more played upon than playing. Alone, he seems suddenly much older and forlorn, adrift: "The air which the harpist had played began to control his movements. His softly padded feet played the melody while his fingers swept a scale of variations idly along the railings after each group of notes" (67–68). Lacking an audience, Lenehan becomes purposeless, indolent.

As if in mockery of Lenehan, the weary harpist plays Moore's mythically rich poem "Silent, O Moyle" "heedlessly," though the notes "sounded deep and full," on an instrument carved with the half naked figure of a woman, who is also "heedless that her coverings had fallen about her knees" (64–65). Exposing herself to the public for money, the figure is a debased representation of Ireland since "the harp was the instrument of the higher classes, among whom harp-playing was a very usual accomplishment. . . . In very early ages a professional harper was honoured beyond all other musicians."[10] Further, as Leerssen writes, "Moore constantly likens himself, metaphorically, to a bard or, metonymically, to the Irish harp—which once sang of Irish glories, was then silenced, its strings broken by English tyranny, and is now repeatedly taken up again in these melodies. Moore the bard, Moore the harpist or even the personified harp, struggles against silence and against the muzzling effect of the national eclipse."[11] And, Zack Bowen notes, "As the musician idly plucks the melody of the song, which expresses a wish that Erin, still sleeping in darkness, be warmed with the day of peace and love, the image is one of Ireland betrayed and prostituted."[12] At least the harp still sounds in Joyce. In *Rough for Theatre I,* Beckett's blind beggar recalls only that "I once had a little harp," but it never earned him much money (*SB3,* 239).

His body yielding to the sentimentalizing of Ireland's plight, Lenehan at thirty feels "keenly his own poverty of purse and spirit. He was tired of knocking about, of pulling the devil by the tail, of shifts and intrigues" (*D1,* 69). He longs for a domestic life—a good job, a home of his own, a warm fire and good dinner—a life in which he could play the host role and need no longer perform to survive. But his hopes of a change for the better are dashed at the end of the story when his supposed friend Corley, a figure of some authority as the son of a police inspector and someone who conversed often with plain clothes policemen (61), flaunts the gold coin he has managed to obtain from the girl. When Lenehan reappears in *Ulysses,* he is still a maladroit performer: for cigarettes he fawns over the men gathered in the newspaper office as he had over Corley; backing Boylan's horse, he wrongly proclaims Sceptre a certain winner in the Gold cup race; and, playing the court jester role, he proffers a riddle, a limerick, silly jokes, palindromes, and word plays (*U,* 127, 129). Still "on the cadge" (141), he leads the charge to the pub after Stephen proposes the "motion," and later at Barney Kiernan's he plays up to the Citizen by fabricating the story of Bloom's winning money by betting on Throwaway (321).

Mrs. Mooney in "The Boarding House," "a determined woman [who] governed the house cunningly" (*D1,* 74–75), orchestrates the domestic scene that excludes Lenehan. She demonstrates how men a cut above him can be manipulated into a marriage they allow themselves to think they want. The story depicts "music-hall *artistes*" who oblige "*The Madam*" (75) with song and dance at her Sunday nights while Polly Mooney, her daughter, sings flirtatiously "*I'm a naughty girl*" (76). Given "the run of the young men" by her mother, Polly plays the Mimi role from *La Bohème,* going to Bob Doran's room "late one night as he was undressing for bed [to] relight her candle at his" (76, 81). Mrs. Mooney, who has silently watched things develop between them, strategically plays the outraged mother: intervening "when she judged it to be the right moment," questioning Polly awkwardly, not wanting to seem either cavalier or conniving (78), then demanding proper "reparation" from this supposedly worldly man who, she insists, "had simply abused her hospitality" (77–78). Summoned and ensnared by Mrs. Mooney, Doran is too weak and fearful to resist or to see through her performance, and so is trapped and domesticated.

Both Chandler in "A Little Cloud" and Farrington in "Counterparts," either of whom might be Doran in married life or Lenehan if he had gotten what he wishes for, are disoriented and defeated by creative oral narration, whether their own or another's. Embedded passively in his own banal story—married a year, already a father (96–97)—Chandler observes "something vulgar in his friend . . . [a] new gaudy manner," even as he envies the narrative (both experienced and performed) of Ignatius Gallaher, who "had lived, he had seen the world" (94). The encounter provides a shock to Chandler's carefully calibrated existence: "The adventure of meeting Gallaher after eight years, . . . of listening to Gallaher's stories and of sharing for a brief space Gallaher's vagrant and triumphant life, upset the equipoise of his sensitive nature" (98). But an "unfortunate timidity," not unlike Eveline's, and an inability "to assert his manhood" render him, he feels, trapped and bitter, weeping for the loss of the life he imagines he could have lived (99, 105).

In contrast to Chandler, the copyclerk Farrington in "Counterparts" plays the Gallaher role by mimicking everyone from the boss he both scorns and fears to the terrified son he beats (114, 121), and by entertaining the pub crowd with repeated performances of his smart-aleck riposte to his boss, which expands in the retelling from what Jean-Michel Rabaté calls "a spontaneous witticism which was almost a slip of the tongue" ("Could he not keep his tongue in his cheek?" [114]) "into a decisive retort, now seeming a 'smart . . . thing.'"[13] En route to the pub, he mentally rehearses, like Gabriel Conroy contemplating his after-dinner speech, his new party piece: "As he walked on he preconsidered the terms in which he would narrate the incident to the boys" (*D1,* 115). A stereotypical pub performer and wastrel, Farrington, after numerous recountings and rounds of drinks, exhausts his money and himself, even as the Englishman Weathers, "an acrobat and knockabout *artiste*" who takes full advantage of Farrington's folly, stagily protests "that the hospitality was too Irish" (116–17), and then humiliatingly defeats the angry Farrington at arm wrestling.

In "Clay" (whose earlier titles, "Christmas Eve" and then "Hallow Eve," foregrounded party and ritual), the spinster Maria anticipates the performative occasion: "What a nice evening they would have, all the children singing!" (124). Her evening, however, is mostly a series of small disasters. Trying to be sure she gets it right, Maria takes a long time to decide what to purchase for Joe and his wife, until the server sarcastically asks if she wants a wedding cake (127); then, discovering that she had left the present on the tram, "she nearly cried outright" (129); and her vain attempt to make peace between Joe and his brother, Alphy, arouses Joe's anger, which threatens to wreck the occasion (which often happened at Irish gatherings, as *The Butcher Boy* depicts). Finally, Maria's choosing of clay (commonly read as connoting death[14]) in the blindfold game of chance seems to suggest her imminent fate.

Yet her welcome from Joe and his family this evening is a particularly warm one: "Maria had never seen Joe so nice to her as he was that night, so full of pleasant talk and reminiscences. She said they were all very good to her" (131). Perhaps as a polite way of bringing the evening to a close, "Joe asked Maria would she not sing some little song before she went, one of the old songs." Responding to familial hospitality and the spirit of the occasion, Maria "had to get up and stand beside the piano. Mrs Donnelly bade the children be quiet and listen to Maria's song. Then she played the prelude and said *Now, Maria!* and Maria, blushing very much, began to sing in a tiny quavering voice" her party piece, "I Dreamt that I Dwelt in Marble Halls" (131–32), one of the nineteenth-century's most popular sentimental ballads. The song is from Michael William Balfe's *The Bohemian Girl* (1843), the same changeling opera that Frank takes Eveline to in the earlier story (45), perhaps implying that Maria is a version of what Eveline becomes after she refuses to elope with Frank.[15] The opera, as Stephen Watt notes, was "much enjoyed in turn-of-the-century Dublin": from 1888 to 1904, *The Bohemian Girl* was produced thirty-five times in Dublin, which made it one of the city's most popular.[16]

In *The Bohemian Girl,* Maria's song is sung by a young woman who, as a child, was stolen from her castle by gypsies, who raise her as one of their own. Believing her earlier existence to have been only a dream, the singer, in the first stanza, imaginatively recalls riches and high position:

> "I dreamt that I dwelt in marble halls
> With vassals and serfs at my side
> And of all who assembled within those walls
> That I was the hope and the pride.
>
> I had riches too great to count, could boast
> Of a high ancestral name,
> But I also dreamt, which pleased me most,
> That you loved me still the same." (*D1,* 132)

The second stanza, the one that Maria fails to sing, is a preview of the faithful love that, though yet unknown to the young countess, awaits her upon her return to her rightful home:

> I dreamt that suitors besought my hand,
> That knights upon bended knee,
> And with vows no maiden heart could withstand,
> That they pledged their faith to me.
> And I dreamt that one of this noble host
> Came forth my hand to claim;
> Yet I also dreamt, which charmed me most,
> That you lov'd me still the same.[17]

According to Adaline Glasheen, "'every schoolgirl knows' [that] it is bad luck to sing the second verse of this song,"[18] so Joyce's text tactfully omits it as Maria superstitiously repeats the first stanza rather than sing the second. "But no one tried to show her her mistake; and when she had ended her song Joe was very much moved"—to a nostalgia and sentimentality ("there was no time like the long ago and no music for him like poor old Balfe" [*D1,* 132]) that contrast strikingly with his unexplained bitterness toward his brother, and that anticipate the full-scale evocation of the past in "The Dead."

Maria has a generosity of spirit that allows her to participate, even if only occasionally, in a warm family scene at odds with the isolation of most Dubliners. Like Hynes in "Ivy Day in the Committee Room," she receives accolades within her story that, regardless of any intended irony or ambiguity, sympathetic readers can endorse. In contrast, Mr. Duffy of "A Painful Case" follows Eveline in fearfully fleeing intimacy and social intercourse, and withdrawing into himself at the end of his story.[19] Duffy's climactic failure of empathy and expansiveness is anticipated early on when the narrator notes his spartan furnishings and resolute lack of generosity: "He never gave alms to beggars and walked firmly, carrying a stout hazel" (135). The 1983 Radio Telefís Éireann production of the story expands on this hint in a wholly appropriate way: Duffy, though a lover of music for whom operas and concerts "were the only dissipations of his life" (135), refuses the appeal of his colleagues in the bank to play the piano at a benefit in aid of the Royal Hospital even though he is told that "we haven't got anybody else."[20] Under the mistaken delusion of self-sufficiency, Duffy plays his landlady's piano solely for himself, rejecting an appeal from what he considers "Dublin's gilded youth" (135) because, he dismissively asserts, "I'm not a music hall man." As in many of his actions, attitudes, and words, Duffy here anticipates Gabriel in "The Dead," who dismisses "this new generation, educated or hypereducated as it is" (261).

Instead of bodying forth Ireland's expansive performative tradition, Duffy churlishly retreats into the role of passive attendant. As Joyce puts it, Duffy "performed" only two social duties: "visiting his relatives at Christmas and escorting them to the cemetery when they died" (135). His stingy withholding of his musical talent anticipates his subsequent rejection of Mrs. Sinico, whom he meets through their shared love of music but whose proffered emotional intimacy, which he had encouraged at first, he recoils from when it threatens to become something more. Joyce emphasizes Duffy's isolation through class, political, religious, and sexual allusions. He briefly flirts with nationalism by attending "meetings of an Irish Socialist Party," but he discontinued going when the others, all of whom were workmen, turned out to be "hard-featured realists [who] resented an exactitude which was the product of a leisure not within their reach" and who were unlikely to produce a social revolution (137–38). In the story's present, the newspaper Duffy reads is the *Dublin Evening Mail,* a Unionist daily, as opposed to the pub proprietor's *Evening Herald,* a nationalist paper, and he reads of Mrs. Sinico's "squalid" death "not aloud, but moving his lips as a priest does when he reads the prayers *Secreto*" (144, 141), which links him to the ritual of the Mass, but one performed solely for himself.[21]

Duffy is ambivalent toward Mrs. Sinico from the first, drawn to her intelligence, openness, and love of culture, her rapt attention to all he has to say, but fearful of intimacy, her urging "him to let his nature open to the full," to write out his thoughts. Even while feeling himself drawn out of his isolation, he "heard the strange impersonal voice which he recognised as his own, insisting on the soul's incurable loneliness" (137, 139). When Mrs. Sinico passionately reaches out to him, he not only breaks off the relationship but, fearing he might meet her, also stops attending musical performances (139–40). In his initial reaction to Mrs. Sinico's "commonplace vulgar death," Duffy feels revulsion "that he had ever spoken to her of what he held sacred," degraded by "the squalid tract of her vice," determined that "she had been unfit to live" (144), and reassured that he had acted properly in breaking with her.

But her story takes hold of him and impels him to contemplate the loneliness of her life, and his own, as, wandering in Phoenix Park where he and she had walked four years before, he feels her haunting presence. His eyes then fall upon "venal and furtive" lovers who "filled him with despair" because of his self-exclusion "from life's feast." In an epiphany whose language and imagery anticipate the end of "The Dead," he at last confronts his own responsibility and loss: "Why had he withheld life from her? Why had he sentenced her to death? He felt his moral nature falling to pieces" (146). For Joyce, a moral failing is usually an aural one as well. A slowly passing freight train ironically performs only for Duffy's ears the sounds of Mrs. Sinico's haunting presence in "the laborious drone of the engine reiterating the syllables of her name" (146),[22] but the *end* of hearing, which signifies absence and negation, is far worse. The last lines of Duffy's story, severing him from all community and from orality, enunciate his utter isolation: he heard the rhythm "*die away.* He *could not* feel her near him in the darkness *nor her voice touch his ear.* He waited for some minutes *listening.* He could *hear nothing:* the night was *perfectly silent.* He *listened* again: *perfectly silent.* He felt that he was *alone*" (147; my emphasis). The language subtracts and denies: reality, memory, the noise of the train engine, Mrs. Sinico's presence, his own senses, the possibility of human connection. Such absence and silence signify not peace but moral vacuity.

No oral void is permitted in "Ivy Day in the Committee Room," a story dependent upon the performative tradition that has fallen into a debased cultural and political environment. "Ivy Day" is the most dramatic as well as the most political story in *Dubliners,* one that employs dialogue almost exclusively. The narrative voice provides little besides stage directions and cues: for example, Old Jack raking the cinders together and O'Connor rolling a cigarette in the opening scene. Only a few narrative moments go beyond theatrical staging: the description of O'Connor's morning, the "apologetic 'Pok!'" of the corks popping off the bottles of stout, and the final line, the story's only narrative paraphrasing of dialogue. The setting is a small stage upon which the characters enter, perform, and leave, with the unprincipled Henchy trying to control the financial, social, political, and aesthetic interchanges in the scene, determining or falling in with every shift of the conversation, creating a social, political, and financial oral representation of Irish/English relations. His first words are "No money, boys"; he demands coal for the fire; he insists that Ireland should accommodate itself to the new English king who's "a man of the world, and he means well by us. He's a jolly fine decent fellow, if you ask me, and no damn nonsense about him" (153, 154, 166). He first mocks Joe Hynes, then praises him as one who remained loyal to Parnell (168), and finally appoints himself master of the ceremonies that elicit Hynes's poetic elegy and produces a response of "calculated effusiveness."[23] Like Maria in "Clay," Hynes verges on becoming a stock comic figure, but unlike Henchy he retains the dignity of political loyalty as he readies himself for performance: he struggles at first "to remember . . . the piece to which they were alluding," hesitates, takes off his hat, stands, seems "to be rehearsing the piece in his mind," and then recites (168). His sincere doggerel elegizing Parnell inspires a brief, respectful silence, "then a burst of clapping," and finally this cautious and enigmatic literary judgment in the narrator's voice: "Mr. Crofton said that it was a very fine piece of writing" (170). The banal response, the only summarized speech in the story, comports with the political vacuity of the story's present, a time fallen from the vital, romanticized past that Hynes evokes, celebrates, and mourns in his poem's vapid, if genuinely felt, sentimentality. And the form it takes terminates the drama in a manner whose flatness reprises the bathos of Parnell's fall and Irish responses to it.

In "A Mother," as in "The Boarding House," party pieces are artfully wielded as weapons in the domestic and familial field of battle, specifically in the hunt for a husband: when Miss Devlin reached marrying age, "she was sent out to many houses, where her playing and ivory manners were much admired. She sat amid the chilly circle of her accomplishments, waiting for some suitor to brave it and offer her a brilliant life" (171). In a country depopulated by the Famine and emigration, Miss Devlin's siren performance, "when she drew near the limit and her friends began to loosen their tongues about her," finally succeeds as a lure and a trap in the service of social and marital construction, attracting the "sober, thrifty and pious" Mr. Kearny, whom she marries not for love but to spite her friends (171–72). As a mother she trains her daughter Kathleen in her own image: a good convent school, where she learned French and music, and membership in the Royal Irish Academy of Music, with the hope that party pieces might become venture capital.

She overplays her hand, however, when she repackages her daughter for the political market: "When the Irish Revival began to be appreciable Mrs Kearny determined to take advantage of her daughter's [Gaelicly resonant] name" (172–73). She hires an Irish tutor for her, has her exchange picture postcards with Irish friends, and introduces her to the family's musical and nationalist acquaintances. The initial results are gratifying: "Soon the name of Miss Kathleen Kearney began to be heard often on people's lips. People said that she was very clever at music and a very nice girl and, moreover, that she was a believer in the language movement," and she is hired by the *Eire Abu* ["Ireland to Victory"] Society to perform as an accompanist in a series of concerts, climaxing in a nationalist program that includes Michael William Balfe's *Killarney* (from his opera *Inisfallen*), "a selection of Irish airs," and "a stirring patriotic recitation" (172–73, 185–86). But failing to receive the contracted pay for the performances, Mrs. Kearney storms out of the Antient Concert Rooms with her daughter at intermission on the final night, ensuring that "Miss Kathleen Kearney's musical career was ended in Dublin after that" (186). Her marital prospects may also be over since she is still Miss Kearney in "The Dead" when

Miss Ivors names her as her traveling companion for an upcoming excursion to the Aran Islands (242).

In "Grace," the penultimate story in *Dubliners,* Joyce moves toward recuperating performance as a communal act of mutual benefit. The story, as Barbara Hardy demonstrates,[24] depicts public narrative as carefully orchestrated group presentation: a plot designed by the friends of the alcoholic Tom Kernan to entice him to join them on a retreat. Kernan's drunken fall causes him to experience the pub orator's most grievous accident: a partially bitten off tongue that leaves him scarcely able to speak. His long-suffering wife, who sees "a curious appropriateness in his accident," thinks his "tongue would not suffer by being shortened" (*D1,* 200). Distinguished by their performative abilities, the friends band together "to form a 'speech community' that will include the speechless Kernan and thus transform him into a harmless dialogical participant in their ritual of recollection and praise."[25] Jack Power, who had played the accompaniment when the Kernans celebrated their silver wedding anniversary, devises the plot and officiates at its enactment. Martin Cunningham, who has a face like Shakespeare's (*D1,* 200; also *U,* 93), is entrusted with the narrative lead as a speaker known to have "secret sources of information" (*D1,* 202). M'Coy, who "had been at one time a tenor of some reputation" (201), chimes in, like Henchy in "Ivy Day," eager to participate in the performance: "Mr M'Coy, who wanted to enter the conversation by any door, pretended that he had never heard the story" (204). Even the late-arriving Mr Fogarty "was not without culture" (212). Although Kernan initially thinks that his guests are planning an evening at the opera and then listens "with an air of calm enmity" (208) as they discuss making a retreat, he not only acquiesces as Cunningham orchestrates an elaborate theological discussion (one full of misstatements), but he enters fully into the spirit of the occasion and then submits to their wiles, perhaps partly to regain performative authority through rehearsed confession: "I'll just tell him my little tale of woe. I'm not such a bad fellow—" (218). The evening's success is measured by Kernan's ignorance that he has played unwitting audience to a carefully constructed and enacted party piece. Cunningham's performative skill is so compelling that Joyce grants him an encore in the "Hades" chapter of *Ulysses.*

Joyce, who considered Ireland's expansive performative tradition to be still very much alive in a Dublin that was, as Mary and Padraic Colum put it, "oral as no other [city] in Western Europe was" (57), regretted his failure to give it its proper due in the early stories of *Dubliners.* Reconsidering his "style of scrupulous meanness," he wrote to Stanislaus that he had "been unnecessarily harsh" toward Dublin and chided himself for having underplayed the city's "ingenuous insularity and its hospitality. The latter 'virtue' so far as I can see does not exist elsewhere in Europe" (*LJJ2,* 134, 166). Terence Brown maintains that "Dublin's musical vitality is the only aspect of civic life in the city to which Joyce seems able to extend any kind of approval" (*D2,* xxv), yet mostly the early stories approve it only grudgingly, often finding more threat than pleasure in performance. "The Dead," however, is musical and social in its very conception, taking its theme from Thomas Moore's song, "Oh, Ye Dead!"[26] which was "a party piece of Joyce's."[27] The story, as Leerssen puts it, demonstrates the "ongoing presence of Irish verse and song as a performed, oral medium" as a still powerful factor in Joyce's work.[28] Further, as Clive Hart reminds us, "'The Dead' plainly focuses on hospitality in the ordinary sense of that word. Despite the darker parts of the story, the party, with its central dinner scene (rendered much less good-humoured in the film . . .), has the liveliness and appealing richness of a Christmas scene from Dickens."[29]

Far more than the other stories in *Dubliners,* "The Dead" offers a balanced representation of performance as still integral to a private festive occasion, greatly expands the role of party pieces as indices of moral value, and makes song and oral narrative key to its climactic epiphany.[30] Mary Jane plays the piano and Aunt Julia sings in response to their guests' insistence; Bartell D'Arcy's rude refusal to sing for the assembly (and then his singing only for himself) is a breach of hospitality; Gabriel Conroy pays for his supper—"under this hospitable roof, around this hospitable board" (*D1,* 260)—with an expansive and elegiac after-dinner speech based on John Joyce's oratorical style (*MBK,* 28). It is especially noteworthy that the speech climaxes the dinner scene since, as Kevin Barry writes, "Food, in 'The Dead', is a custom of civility: it is plentiful, varied, ceremonious and generously shared"[31]—qualities largely absent from the preceding pages of *Dubliners.* And the story, and book, end with Gretta's account of Michael Furey's life and death, a narrative she seems to have spent all her married life rehearsing but *not* telling.

One purpose of "the Misses Morkan's annual dance" (*D1,* 224) and epiphanic dinner is to promote the music school of "the Three Graces of the Dublin musical world" (262) and the piano lessons that Mary Jane gives.[32] Hence, "listening to music is one of the major themes of 'The Dead.'"[33] Performance, of dance and oral narrative as well as music, is another. The story is structured as a series of host/guest performative interchanges, an emphasis nicely replicated in the Richard Nelson/Shaun Davey musical production, *James Joyce's The Dead,*[34] which, unusually, places most of the performers with their backs or quarter-profiles to the audience, so that what is mostly seen are not the performances, but the other characters: seated, facing forward as a stage audience, reacting to the performers.

It is a matter of economic survival as well as hospitality that the occasion should go well. The party is comprised almost entirely of musical performers, teachers, students, and aficionados—who find nothing exceptional in Mr. Browne's account of how the gallery boys of the old Royal Theatre "would sometimes in their enthusiasm unyoke the horses from the carriage of some great *prima donna* and pull her themselves through the streets to her hotel"

1. Performance in *James Joyce's The Dead,* Belasco Theater, New York (singing for their fellow performers, rather than for the audience: Daisy Eagan, left, Emily Skinner, and Marni Nixon with other cast members). Photograph by Sara Krulwich. From *New York Times,* 27 Feb. 2000, 7. Courtesy of the *New York Times.*

(*D1,* 255–56). The guests make repeated appeals for music throughout the evening, but elicit a series of strikingly *in*appropriate responses. One piano is closed up, its top functioning as a sideboard (234). On the other piano "Mary Jane was playing her Academy piece, full of runs and difficult passages. . . . the piece she was playing had no melody for him [Gabriel] and he doubted whether it had any melody for the other listeners" (238). Mary Jane's piece, as Terence Brown points out, would have been "prescribed by the Royal Irish Academy of Music to test the technical proficiency of musicians and teachers of music" (D2, 308 n25). More suited to a performance at the Antient Concert Rooms, like the one in "A Mother," it is as inappropriate to its occasion, a festive evening at a private home, as is the Old Josser's performance in "An Encounter." And it drives everyone but Aunt Kate to alternative activities, though all rush back to applaud enthusiastically as Mary Jane finishes playing (*D1,* 240).

Then, after Mary Jane (235), Gretta (245), and others have tried and failed to persuade Bartell D'Arcy to sing, the elderly spinster Aunt Julia, in yet another inapt performance, sings "Arrayed for the Bridal," referred to in John Huston's film of *The Dead* as "one of her favorites from her concert days." It is, as Norris notes, "fiendishly difficult" to sing:

> Arrayed for the bridal, in beauty behold her,
> A white wreath entwineth a forehead more fair;
> I envy the zephyrs that softly enfold her, enfold her,
> And play with the locks of her beautiful hair.[35]

The music for the song comes from Vincenzo Bellini's opera, *I Puritani* (*The Puritans,* 1835), the historical context of which is Cromwell's victory over the British monarchy, which was followed by his invasion and suppression of Ireland. The song is personally as well as politically infelicitous: the visually oriented Gabriel later recalls not Aunt Julia's singing itself, but the "haggard look" of mortality that she evinces during her performance (*D1,* 286), and he envisages her arrayed not "for the bridal," but for death. (In *Ulysses* the narrator of "Ithaca" confirms that she is dying [623].) As with Maria in "Clay" and Kitty Kiernan in *Michael Collins,* death's imminence counterpoints and subverts the musical performance of eros.[36]

Finally, the professional singer Bartell D'Arcy, though entreated throughout the evening (*D1*, 271), disdains hospitality by ungraciously refusing to sing until, most of the guests having departed, it suits his own mood. Afterward, he responds rudely to the praise that his singing receives: "'Can't you see that I'm as hoarse as a crow?' said Mr. D'Arcy roughly" (271). Yet despite himself his party piece becomes the most important event of the evening: he performs it for its precisely appropriate audience and it initiates the story's climax and resolution. D'Arcy's singing momentarily immobilizes Gretta on the stairs, and the "grace and mystery in [Gretta's] attitude as if she were a symbol of something" provokes Gabriel, like Browning's Duke of Ferrara in "My Last Duchess," first to transform his wife into an imagined picture that, with unintended irony, he calls "Distant Music," and then to respond lustfully to his aestheticized image of her.[37] As Gretta listens to D'Arcy singing "The Lass of Aughrim" "in the old Irish tonality" (270), Gabriel translates her link to orality into the visual, with which, tellingly, he is much more comfortable. As he soon learns to his dismay, he is equally removed from both the song she hears and the past it evokes for her.[38]

Joyce deepens the irony by having Gabriel repeat the phrase "distant music" several pages on, but instead of singing or love, what Gabriel hears are his own posturing words that he had once written to Gretta ("Like distant music these words that he had written years before were borne towards him from the past" [275])—posturing because, as he admits to himself in the hotel room, he had never loved any woman (287). Just as he has idealized what he now sees as his foolish lust (283), so he has idealized rather than loved the wife of whose origins he is ashamed and whom he has kept from returning to her native Galway since their marriage; no wonder she has never trusted him enough to tell him about Michael Furey before this night. Their contrasting responses in the stairway scene dramatize the disconnection between them: for Gretta, though she cannot remember the name of the song, the music rouses memory since Michael Furey used to sing "The Lass of Aughrim" to her; for Gabriel, the imagined painting stimulates his longing to master "her strange mood" (270, 272, 279). The stairway scene is stereotypically gendered: Gabriel's gaze and imagination reify his wife as symbolic and sexual object, yet the aurally attuned Gretta is far more sympathetic than the visually oriented and marginalized Gabriel, who "could hear little save the noise of laughter and dispute on the front steps, a few chords struck on the piano and a few notes of a man's voice singing" (269). She is also a more compelling figure than Gabriel, perhaps because we experience the banality of his thoughts directly but can only speculate about what has transfixed her.

In *Cinema and Ireland,* Kevin Rockett, Luke Gibbons, and John Hill argue that, although it "contains some of the most visually arresting passages in [Joyce's] writing, . . . 'The Dead' is strangely resistant to screen adaptation." They suggest that the Huston film of the story, which Kevin Barry calls both "one of the most tactful readings of Joyce's 'The Dead'" and "also a strong *mis*-reading,"[39] is overly dependent on visual imagery and "seemingly throwaway details. . . . During the long dinner party everyone goes through their paces but the night is stage-managed to the last. Party-pieces and the stilted conversation of role-playing are the most that can be achieved by way of self-expression."[40] Huston's film does take its cues from Joyce's story when it makes three significant changes that give even greater prominence to party pieces; the results are a mixed success, but one that helps to illuminate and tease out the performative nature of the story.

The film's first major change concerns Aunt Julia, whom Joyce, in one of the rare successful performances in *Dubliners,* has sing in a voice "strong and

2. Gretta on stairs listening to Bartell D'Arcy sing "The Lass of Aughrim" while Gabriel looks up at her. John Huston, *The Dead.* Courtesy of Zenith Entertainment Limited.

clear in tone, . . . with great spirit," hitting "even the smallest of the grace notes," causing her willing listeners to experience a favorite Joycean image of transcendence: "To follow the voice, without looking at the singer's face, was to feel and share the excitement of swift and secure flight" (*D1*, 247). Aunt Julia's assured performance is especially poignant since it occurs only six weeks after the papal edict of 22 November 1903 that ejected her (and all other women) from the church choir after thirty years of service, and shortly before her death.[41] Margot Norris persuasively argues that the social occasion helps to explain Mary Jane's silencing of "Kate Morkan's protest of the pope's politically oppressive act [in turning 'the women out of the choirs that have slaved there all their lives' (*D1*, 249)] and her outrage at the injustice inflicted on her sister."[42] In contrast to Joyce's representation of her, the film's Aunt Julia, as if intended to provide an aesthetic justification for the pope's action, sings extremely badly: "thin, cracking, and quavery, . . . neither in tempo nor in tune"[43]—which makes the enthusiastic reaction of Gabriel and the other guests hypocritical and banal.[44]

Second, the film adds a character named Mr. Grace (a punning personification of "the grace notes" [*D1*, 247] taken from Aunt Julia?) who recites Lady Gregory's prose version of "The Grief of a Girl's Heart" (which he calls *Broken Vows*), an Irish tale of a girl betrayed by love, which deepens the significance of D'Arcy's singing the thematically similar "The Lass of Aughrim."[45] (Huston nicely foregrounds "The Lass of Aughrim" by having a harp play the melody at key moments in the film, most notably the beginning and end, and by having Frank Patterson's D'Arcy sing not uncertainly and hoarsely, as Joyce has it [270], but beautifully and movingly, the reverse of the film's treatment of Aunt Julia.) The connection between the recitation and the ballad is strengthened by Grace's naming of his source, since Lady Gregory's dead husband, the author of the notorious Gregory Clause in the Poor Law Act of 1847 that caused the eviction of thousands of destitute peasants during and after the Famine, shares his name with the betrayer of "The Lass of Aughrim."[46] And third, the film radically alters the setting, timing, audience, and meaning of Gabriel's story of his grandfather's horse.[47]

Clive Hart, who served as a consultant on the movie, comments on the first two of these changes: he objects to the altered singing of Aunt Julia (whom Norris calls "perhaps the truest and greatest artist in 'The Dead'"[48]), but finds merit in the Grace character and his recitation, though he acknowledges that "Joyce would have hated the introduction into his story of a passage of Celtic revival literature—especially . . . from a writer [Lady Gregory] for whom he had so little respect."[49] About the first of these changes Hart convincingly argues that "if Julia sings badly, [Gabriel] is guilty of a shallow insincerity when he speaks of how her singing 'must have been a surprise and a revelation to us all tonight.' . . . The film's transformation of this statement of honest praise into empty clichéd rhetoric seriously undercuts Gabriel's use of the vital thematic word 'revelation.'"[50] Having Aunt Julia sing badly—quavering, lacking in grace notes, barely holding the tune—the film contradicts not only the story but also what Leopold Bloom recalls in *Ulysses* ("Great song of Julia Morkan's. Kept her voice up to the very last" [*U*, 155]), and it makes Gabriel's praise dishonest, renders his use of the word "revelation" an act of bad faith, and makes him less sympathetic as Gretta's audience at the end of the story than Joyce seems to intend.[51]

Huston's creation of the Grace episode has the opposite effect since, as Hart suggests, "A recitation at a party of this kind was entirely to be expected."[52] A ballad well known in the West, Lady Gregory's translation of the Irish love-lament "Donal Og," "The Grief of a Girl's Heart" reinforces Gretta's role, as does, by contrast, its theme of faithless love. Huston's camera underscores the story's East/West dichotomy and Gretta's centrality by moving between her and Gabriel when Grace recites:

> You have taken the east from me,
> You have taken the west from me.

The film shows Gretta "*almost as if she were in a trance. Though her gaze is inward, an enigmatic beauty pours from her like that of a fine unsentimental picture of the Annunciation,*" and Gabriel "*slightly baffled*" by her expression.[53] The scene anticipates subsequent similar depictions of Gretta in the film: she lapses into a reverie at the dinner table when music plays after Aunt Kate praises a singer named Parkinson for having "the purest tenor voice that was ever put into a man's throat" (*D1*, 256); she is immobilized and haloed on the stairs, listening to D'Arcy sing, a figure of "grace and mystery" that Gabriel reads symbolically (270); she wears a distracted look in the cab ride back to the hotel; and Gabriel looks on in the hotel room while she listens to the even more distant music with which the dead Michael Furey continues to serenade her.

The film further foregrounds the theme of faithless love by having Lily enter the scene in the midst of Mr. Grace's recital and have her remain there, framed and lit by a doorway, until he finishes. This scene visually valorizes Lily's earlier bitter assertion that "—The men that is now is only all palaver and what they can get out of you" (227), especially if one accepts Kevin Whelan's view that Lily, like the girl in Grace's recitation, is "pregnant and abandoned."[54] Yet both "The Grief of a Girl's Heart" and "The Lass of Aughrim," unlike Gretta's tale of Michael Furey, suggest that men were no better in the past than they are in the present, a view that D'Arcy self-servingly endorses when he says "I presume there are as good singers to-day as there were then" (256). In the film, Grace's narrative initiates the thematic process that leads to D'Arcy's singing of "The Lass of Aughrim" and Gretta's account of Michael Furey's death. As Grace's audience, the entranced young female guests largely determine the success of his party piece: their applause, rousing Gretta from her trance, responds, as Hart notes, "fully to the recitation, which powerfully shifts the focus of 'The Dead' from Gabriel to Gretta. That shift of focus was doubtless always necessary," he adds, for Gretta "is, as far as we know, the only person in 'The Dead' who has a story worth the telling."[55] (Whelan would presumably argue that Lily does too.) Party pieces, then, can serve as an oral bridge to the film's altered dramatic center, especially since Parkinson's voice, Grace's recital, and D'Arcy's singing similarly mesmerize Anjelica Huston's Gretta, who is culturally sophisticated rather than, as Joyce's Gabriel recalls his mother patronizingly saying of her, "country cute" (*D1,* 239). They thus contextualize and deepen Gretta's narrative, which then takes its place as the last in a performative series of sexual and political betrayals, and then return us to the story with a renewed appreciation of Gretta's central role in it.

In contrast to Mr. Duffy in "A Painful Case," Gabriel is depicted in "The Dead" as a willing player, albeit a poor one, of many parts.[56] As if enacting multiple auditions, Gabriel constantly retreats into awkward performativity, trying "to cover his agitation by taking part in the dance with great energy" (243), and then nervously reviewing his speech while longing to escape from the stifling confines of the party into what, as the goloshes episode indicates, has never been his natural element: the cold and solitude outside. Full of self-doubt, he fears that he will "only make himself ridiculous by quoting poetry to them which they could not understand. They would think that he was airing

3. Lily in doorway listening to Mr. Grace perform "The Grief of a Girl's Heart." John Huston, *The Dead.* Courtesy of Zenith Entertainment Limited.

his superior education. He would fail with them just as he had failed with the girl in the pantry. He had taken up a wrong tone. His whole speech was a mistake from first to last, an utter failure" (229). Gabriel's dis-ease results in part from his being psychologically and emotionally distanced from surroundings that are supersaturated with the appeals and interchanges characteristic of an oral and performative culture. Walter Ong generalizes about those in Gabriel's situation: "We (those who read texts such as this) are for the most part so resolutely literate that we seldom feel comfortable with a situation in which verbalization is so little thing-like as it is in oral tradition."[57] Gabriel relates awkwardly to all those who are closer to that orality: the semi-educated Lily, who is "done schooling this year and more";[58] his "two ignorant old" aunts, one of whom, unlike Joyce, became a professional singer but then was barred from church choirs by papal edict; the nationalist Miss Ivors, who wears a "large brooch which . . . bore on it an Irish device and motto" and who wants Gabriel to accompany her to the Aran Islands in order to experience Irish as a living language (he is willing to "go visiting together" [243] with her only within the context of the dance which, to mask his discomfort, he performs energetically); and Bartell D'Arcy, the tenor with the "lovely voice"; and Michael Furey who, according to Gretta, "was going to study singing only for his health. He had a very good voice" (284). Both D'Arcy and Furey sing to her but not to him (227, 247, 240, 243, 235, 284).

Although he is a teacher, Gabriel's primary professional identity in the story is that of a reviewer (and presumably a good one since even Miss Ivors likes his "review immensely" [242]) for *The Daily Express* (a Unionist newspaper for which Joyce also wrote), an occupation that gives him an inflated sense of literary pretentiousness. Hence, his instinct is to quote, inappropriately, from great writers in his speech and to tell Gretta that his conversation with Miss Ivors lacked substance, for twice he says that he and Miss Ivors had "no words" (245). He keeps the exterior world at one remove by wearing goloshes, viewing it through gilt-rimmed glasses that "screened his delicate and restless eyes" (228), glimpsing his reflected "face whose expression always puzzled him when he saw it in a mirror" (281), watching the falling snow through the window, and learning about the weather through the mediation of print: "Yes, the *newspapers* were right: snow was general all over Ireland" (287–88; my emphasis).[59]

Yet Gabriel, like the boy in "Araby" responding like an instrument to the words and gestures of Mangan's sister, resonates to the music he does hear. Though Mary Jane's piano piece "had no melody for him," her recital acts as an overture for Gabriel's thoughts: for as her hands race over the keyboard, Gabriel's mind darts as quickly about the room, viewing pictures suggestive of death (the balcony scene from *Romeo and Juliet,* the two murdered princes from *Richard the Third*), then thinking of his aunts, his own mother's lack of musical talent (which he inherits), his brother, and finally his mother's "sullen opposition to his marriage." As Mary Jane concludes her piece, "playing again the opening melody with runs of scales after every bar," Gabriel's scattered thoughts also wind down, and "while he waited for the end the resentment died down in his heart" and he joins in the enthusiastic clapping of those who returned, while Mary Jane blushes in embarrassment and flees the room (239).

Gabriel's speech is also a metaphoric musical occasion, although he alters a phrase he had contemplated using—"*a thought-tormented music*" (246)—to "a thought-tormented age" (261). As the dinner draws to an end, everyone prepares for this year's version of Gabriel's annual piece: conversation gradually ceases, guests resettle into their chairs, coughing starts and stops, "and then a few gentlemen patted the table gently as a signal for silence." When Gabriel, like the conductor of an orchestra, stands motionless before his audience, their patting of the table, like opening applause urging him to commence his performance, "at once grew louder in encouragement and then ceased altogether." And then, just prior to his speaking, a musical prelude sounds: he hears a piano "playing a waltz tune and he could hear the skirts sweeping against the drawing-room door" (259). Despite Gabriel's unease and his subsequent denigration of the speech as foolish (286), it is an effectively delivered and enthusiastically received homage to the princely "tradition of genuine warm-hearted courteous Irish hospitality, which our forefathers have handed down to us and which we in turn must hand down to our descendants" as well as to the "great singers of the past . . . whose fame the world will not willingly let die" (261–62). Consciously or not, Gabriel here assumes the traditional role of the Irish poet as "the cultural guardian of the Gaelic heritage, whose task it was to guarantee historical continuity, to legitimize the present in terms of the past."[60] Extolling a romanticized past over a fallen present, Gabriel's rhetoric of generosity praises "those qualities of humanity, of hospitality, of kindly humour which belonged to an older day," while chastising "this new generation, educated or hypereducated as it is," that, having grown up in the social context consequent upon famine, mass emigration, the Gaelic revival, and urbanization, seems to him to have elevated antisocial rudeness to a virtue in the dubious cause of nationalism (*D1,* 261).

Yet Gabriel's performance is highly ironized by the troubled history of Irish hospitality: Vincent Pecora, for one, maintains that "the socially embedded attitude toward hospitality and generosity that Gabriel invokes in his speech becomes in the end nothing more than the codified expression of the myth of self-sacrifice, of grateful oppression, lying at the heart of Joyce's Dublin."[61] Gabriel's posturing is also exposed by his earlier fear that he would "only make himself ridiculous by . . . airing his superior education" (229), by his uneasy fit with his Irish environment, and by the absence of the particular audience, Miss Ivors, at whom his criticism of contemporary Irish politics is primarily aimed. Such ambiguity in the representation of Gabriel's speech anticipates the ambiguity of the story's ending.

Huston is less politically subtle than Joyce, and the ending of the film more final, less ambiguous, than the story. Huston's Miss Ivors urges upon Gabriel the need to depend upon "ourselves alone" (from the Irish for "Sinn Fein"), then departs not for home but to attend a political meeting at which "James Connolly's speaking."[62] Mr. Grace, sounding like Mr. Casey in the Christmas scene in *Portrait,* mournfully, and irrelevantly, evokes Parnell, "my dead king," at the dinner table and angrily denounces his betrayers. Rockett, Gibbons, and Hill deem it especially noteworthy that the film's ending links imagery of death ("the lonely churchyard on the hill" [*D1,* 288]) with "the silhouetted remains of round towers and monastic ruins, emblems of a golden age in nationalist history."[63] Gabriel had earlier stiffened at Miss Ivors's declaration that Gretta was from Ireland's West ("—Her people are, said Gabriel shortly" [*D1,* 242]), and his refusal to go west with Miss Ivors and Gretta represents, among other things, a rejection of Ireland's past, and future. At the end of the film, however, the iconographical "signs of a new beginning, harbingers of a political and cultural awakening," express Gabriel's "own repressed cultural identity," and provide, they maintain, "a glimpse of Joyce's political as well as his personal unconscious."[64] Yet these supposed "signs of a new beginning" are cinematically conclusive: imagery of ancient ruins and crosses in graveyards may serve to valorize Gabriel's Irishness at last, but the movie's omission of the thought (whether Gabriel's or the narrator's) that "the time had come for him to set out on his journey westward" (*D1,* 287) seems to leave Gabriel rooted in a dead Celtic past, with no way of partaking of "a political and cultural awakening," let

4. Cemetery at Oughterard. End of John Huston, *The Dead.* Courtesy of Zenith Entertainment Limited.

alone a personal one. The story's end concerns the incertitude of continuing; the film's is all about ending.

Political concerns also inflect the film's third striking performative change. Joyce has Gabriel, fresh from the triumph of his speechmaking, still sufficiently ecstatic to launch into his raucous narrative, one he seems to have told successfully many times before, of the "late lamented Patrick Morkan" and the strange antics of his horse Johnny at the "sight of King Billy's statue" (266–67). In contrast to his character's prior and subsequent failures, Joyce made this storytelling a second successive performative success for Gabriel, one acclaimed by the departing guests' raucous laughter that largely occludes the political significance of the horse's slavish circling of the hated English king's effigy. Yet Gabriel's acting out seems to validate Miss Ivors's "West Briton" charge: "Gabriel paced in a circle round the hall in his goloshes amid the laughter of the others" (267). Overtly using the anecdote to deflate Gabriel in advance of the final scene, Huston has the storytelling occur *after* rather than before Gretta hears D'Arcy singing, in the cab ride to the hotel rather than at the Morkan doorstep, and within the strained Gabriel/Gretta relationship rather than as a successful end-of-party piece. The film thereby turns Gabriel's story against him personally as well as politically: his self-conscious, hesitant recounting

5. Celtic tower, not really round. End of John Huston, *The Dead.* Courtesy of Zenith Entertainment Limited.

fails to establish intimacy with his wife, who seems scarcely aware of him and who responds to its telling with distracted, distanced nods and awkward half smiles. This reaction of Gretta's, which is far more disconcerting than her missing the narrative entirely as she does in the story by being offstage, underscores the reciprocal and emblematic nature of party pieces: performer, audience, occasion, and substance must all cohere for success to occur. Lacking a responsive audience, Gabriel's narrative (as inappropriate as bawdy humor in a formal setting) falls flat in the film, thus anticipating the greater failure—of both his irony toward Michael Furey and of his lust—to connect with his wife. The film, in fact, considerably underplays both Gabriel's irony and his lust, thereby flattening and weakening his character.

As Joyce's Gabriel soon learns, D'Arcy's singing "The Lass of Aughrim," a song of seduction, abandonment, and death, evokes for Gretta a call from the world of shades that echoes the one made by Michael Furey on the night he caught "his death in the rain" (285).[65] "Trembling with desire to seize her," Gabriel carefully stage-manages the lighting and mood of the hotel seduction scene (277–78). But, as Kershner puts it, his imagination, while "highly theatrical [is,] despite his claims to literary sophistication, . . . theatricality of a low order."[66] Gabriel longs to play the master of revels: first by recounting to her their intimate life as his memory has illuminated it ("He longed to recall to her those moments, to make her forget the years of their dull existence together and remember only their moments of ecstasy") and then by reenacting what, in some versions, Lord Gregory does to the lass: "to crush her body against his, to overmaster her" (*D1*, 275–79).[67] But Gretta's hitherto secret story, reversing Scheherazade's in evoking rather than forestalling death, trumps both her husband's story and his lust, reverberating beyond Gretta's memory of dead passion and into Irish national identity: for "the vast hosts" of the summoned dead (287) whom Gabriel's soul imaginatively approaches presumably include not only Michael Furey but also those who died in the ballad (the babe and then the lass, plus Lord Gregory in some versions), as well as the battle dead of Aughrim in 1691, which competes with the Boyne as the site of the worst defeat in the Jacobite war against Williamite rule[68]—perhaps "the most disastrous battle in Irish history"[69] and, as Roy Foster puts it, "the last great pitched battle in Irish history."[70] Not only Michael Furey, but Aughrim and its dead lie in Gretta's native county, Galway, to which she longs to return.[71] Gabriel, as we have seen throughout "The Dead," is still circling King Billy's statue like his grandfather's glue factory horse.

The language and imagery at the end of "A Painful Case" sound again on the last pages of "The Dead," yet their rhythm and meaning become strikingly different as Gabriel responds far more positively than Mr. Duffy to the unspoken appeal for understanding.[72] Gabriel speaks to Gretta in the hotel room with two voices, one that is full of "dull anger" (*D1,* 281), ironic and cold. But despite himself another voice breaks through: "A kinder note than he had intended went into his voice. . . . He tried to keep up his tone of cold interrogation but his voice when he spoke was humble and indifferent." Caressing her hand, he speaks sadly, "shy of intruding on her grief" (281–85). He thus expresses empathy for his wife that leads shortly to his epiphanic vision of blindness and self-absorption, a vision that occurs, Joyce hints, before it is too late. Critiquing his own party performance, Gabriel now sees "himself as a ludicrous figure, acting as a pennyboy for his aunts, a nervous, well-meaning sentimentalist, orating to vulgarians and idealising his own clownish lusts, [a] pitiable fatuous fellow" (283)—but one perhaps capable of changing.

Early in the last scene, Gretta calls Gabriel "a very generous person"; and at the end "generous tears filled Gabriel's eyes" in sympathetic and imaginative response to the taps upon the window pane, a summons from Gretta's, his, and Ireland's dead (280, 287).[73] The verbal echo is crucial if Gabriel is to be afforded the possibility of embodying and recuperating Ireland's open-hearted tradition of hospitality. As Hart puts it, the story "celebrates the hospitality possible in a human consciousness, in the human spirit. Gabriel, the most reliable man at the party—by implication the most dependable of hosts in social circumstances—finds that he must learn to be more than reliable, to be a good host in other more vital ways. If he is to be a loving and understanding husband, he must welcome, in his spirit, the ghost of his wife's dead lover."[74] It may well be that through his generous tears Joyce's Gabriel too at last hears the distant music "in the old Irish tonality" (*D1,* 270). Such "a strong affirmation of Gabriel's potential value"[75] is lost when the movie's Gretta calls her husband "responsible" rather than "generous."

Although Joyce had, in "The Soul of Ireland," dismissed the West of Ireland as "a land almost fabulous in its sorrow and senility" (*OCPW,* 74), "The Dead" implicitly not only rewrites the "scrupulous meanness" of the earlier style of *Dubliners* but also reconceives, renders ambiguous, and makes peace with the Ireland of Connacht. After Gretta falls asleep, Gabriel, exhausted from the passion of memory and narrative rather than of sex, reconsiders her story sympathetically: "So she had had that romance in her life: a man had died for her sake" (*D1*, 285), a thought that leads Joyce's Gabriel, but not the film's, to "generous tears" and to resolve, finally, "to set out on his journey westward" (287).[76] Whether the West connotes Gretta's origins, Ireland's distant past, the Irish literary revival, the contemporary politics of Miss Ivors, death, or all of these, this resolution comes to represent Gabriel's last best hope of ceasing to live in bad faith. Realizing at last "how poor a *part* he, her husband, had *played* in her life" (285; my emphasis), Gabriel has begun to imagine a possible new repertoire that he must enact if he is ever again to perform successfully for his most intimate audience: "she who lay beside him" (287).

3 Stephen Dedalus's *Non Serviam*

Patriarchal and Performative Failure in *A Portrait of the Artist as a Young Man*

In *A Portrait of the Artist as a Young Man,* which as his brother Stanislaus says is "almost autobiographical, and naturally as it comes from Jim, satirical" (*CDDSJ,* 12), Joyce further complicates the moral valance of performance that he depicts in *Dubliners.* He does so primarily by parodying the figure of the artist as public entertainer (which he does with increasing expansiveness in *Ulysses* and *Finnegans Wake*) and by fictionalizing his relationship with John Joyce not as it was—tolerant and amicable for the most part—but defined by Stanislaus-like bitterness toward his father, who is far more performative than paternal. Commenting on the autobiographical gap, Roger McHugh suggests that in Joyce's creation of Stephen Dedalus, "His sense of humour and his gay tomfoolery are little to be seen";[1] according to Stanislaus, "People like Jim easily" (*CDDSJ,* 146), unlike himself. No one, in or out of Joyce's fiction, ever calls his protagonist "Sunny Stephen."[2]

Where Gabriel Conroy in "The Dead" evokes John Joyce's oratorical style in praise of hospitality, both *Portrait* and *Ulysses* recreate him as the stage Irishman he seems to have played all his life. According to Stanislaus, John Joyce "was quite unburdened by any sense of responsibility" toward his large family (*MBK,* 50), but "even Stanislaus had to admit that his father had the stage skill and temperament to make an audience friendly towards him: he was perfectly at ease on the boards. In fact he shone in the limelight."[3] John Joyce, as Bernard Benstock puts it, "carved out for himself a Dublin reputation as a drinker, storyteller, and pub tenor."[4]

Joyce's father reincarnated one of Jeremiah Curtin's folk-tale sources: "Earning money, with plenty to eat, and nothing whatever to do but tell lying stories to the gentleman [Curtin] from morning until night."[5] Simon Dedalus is a caricature of conviviality, one whose excesses of public performance (of story, song, drink, and foulness of mouth) are not only unremunerated except for instant acclaim, but utterly displace familial, economic, political, and religious obligations. Even more than Bartell D'Arcy, Simon embodies performance as self-serving and ungenerous, to the point of being mean-spirited and patriarchally aggressive, wielding it as a weapon against his son. He reprises the traditional storyteller who "routinely disparaged his sons when they had the temerity to retell his stories in his presence or to try to help when he stumbled over a phrase or passage. The excellence of a son's rendering did nothing to lessen Johnny's ferocity, for it was his family leadership—most fully realized in occupational mastery—that he defended."[6] Stephen reacts with growing hostility toward his father and all he represents, a reaction that seems necessary for his attainment of independence, but that ultimately inhibits his own growth as an artist since it negatively characterizes not only patriarchy but also performance and artistry.

As his earliest recollection of his brother, Stanislaus describes "a dramatic performance of the story of Adam and Eve, organized for the benefit of his parents and nursemaid," in which Joyce "was the devil. What I remember indistinctly is my brother wriggling across the floor with a long tail probably made of a rolled-up sheet or towel" (*MBK,* 3)—Joyce's first recorded Luciferean moment, and with his parents cast as Adam and Eve before the fall. Saturating all his texts with evidence of the career not taken, Joyce embodied the performative above all in his representation of John Joyce, who was not only a singer but had also starred as a comic performer in college theatricals (*MBK,* 24–25). Joyce and his father, who had objected to his son's elopement with Nora, seem to have communicated best through music, and it was through music that they ultimately made peace. On Joyce's visit to Ireland with Giorgio in 1909, his father played and sang for him. In response to his father's quizzing him, Joyce identified the aria as one sung by Germont to his son in Verdi's *La Traviata:* learning that his son's beloved is dying, Germont expresses his remorse for having treated them cruelly (*JJ2,* 276–77). And so John Joyce accepted Nora, and father and son were reconciled through the mediation of performance. But in his fiction Joyce radically reinflects the father/son relationship, denying Stephen his Nora and omitting the benign paternal performance and reconciliation.

Joyce's self-representation in *Portrait* enacts or evades a series of performances from the first. Stephen's earliest memories, like those of Stanislaus, are of performances, three of which occur on *Portrait*'s opening page when his five physical senses, along with his sense of rhythm, begin to operate. All three performances are predicated on domestic order, and identity, that is soon destabilized. An inveterate storyteller as well as singer, Simon begins both the novel and the novel's focus on oral narrative with "Once upon a time and a very good time it was . . . ," asserting a traditional Irish formulaic opening[7] that soon degenerates into family discord and a defining role for Stephen as the story's central figure, "a nicens little boy named baby tuckoo."[8] A lyrical song, "Lilly Dale," the first of some twenty-five songs embedded in the text, immediately follows the story:

> O, the wild rose blossoms
> On the little green place.[9]
> He sang that song. That was his song.
> *O, the green wothe botheth.* (*PA*, 1)

The song subsequently reappears when Stephen conflates its elements into the fanciful green (or Irish) rose that he longs to discover "somewhere in the world" (*PA*, 8, 71); and then, failing that, in the world of his imagination into which he increasingly retreats: "I desire to press in my arms the loveliness which has not yet come into the world" (297). In the third of *Portrait*'s opening performances, Stephen's mother "played on the piano the sailor's hornpipe for him to dance [while] Uncle Charles and Dante clapped" (2). The young Stephen later recalls such scenes of ephemeral musical and familial harmony—performative scenes that Joyce and Nora recreated for their young children in their Trieste home[10]—as more substantial than Simon's place in the world: "He thought of his own father, of how he sang songs while his mother played and of how he always gave him a shilling when he asked for sixpence and he felt sorry for him that he was not a magistrate like the other boys' fathers" (24). The expansive paternal performance, which displaces worldly and familial responsibility for Simon, soon degenerates into "a long and incoherent monologue" about his fallen fortune (72). Stephen's response is increasingly condescension and alienation rather than the "filial piety" (or even sympathetic audience) expected of him (108).

Like Joyce, Stephen himself comes to play numerous performative roles—storyteller, essayist, actor, singer, piano player—and often to the applause of schoolmates, teachers, priests, and family. The initial mood of benign performance, however, is transformed by Stephen's imagination. Lying ill in the infirmary he envisages his own funeral, repeating over to himself the song "Dingdong! The Castle Bell!": "How beautiful the words were where they said *Bury me in the old churchyard!* . . . He wanted to cry quietly but not for himself: for the words, so beautiful and sad, like music. The bell! The bell! Farewell! O farewell!" (22). But such self-indulgent performance is quickly countered by accusations and imperatives—beginning with Dante's demand that he apologize (presumably for his friendship with the Protestant Eileen), followed by submit, obey, admit, confess, pray, repent, commune, sign, conform (the list is lengthy[11])—and by Stephen's growing resistance to all such imposed speech acts. At first he accepts the roles that others want him to perform: according to his father, "He was baby tuckoo" (1); he does not reveal that Wells pushed him into the cesspool because "His father had told him . . . never to peach on a fellow" (4, 19); he says the grace before the Christmas dinner, cued by his father's "Now, Stephen" (28); and, urged on by his classmates, he resolves to tell the rector of the injustice he had experienced (62).

Soon, however, Stephen determines that he could be happy only when he was far beyond all who call or demand of him (93)—whether the call is to the religious life, or to empathize with the "recurrent note of weariness and pain" he hears in his siblings' voices, or to mind the mocking cries of his friends or Davin's appeal to join the Nationalist cause. Heron and Wallis demand that he admit to his relationship with Emma, but quick-witted Stephen, who "knew that the adventure in his mind stood in no danger from their words . . . , began to recite the *Confiteor,*" and the successful performance causes Heron and Wallis to laugh "indulgently at the irreverence" (86). Wandering nighttown "like some baffled prowling beast," Stephen awaits "a sudden call to his sinloving soul" (112, 115), but soon after the retreat and his confession he finds himself able to resist when "he felt his soul beset once again by the insistent voices of the flesh" (176). His bathing friends cry out to him from the water, but he "parried their banter with easy words" (195). As Joyce has it in *Stephen Hero,* only one imperative is to be heeded: "He would suddenly hear a command to be gone, to be alone, a voice agitating the very tympanum of his ear. . . . He would obey the command and wander up and down the streets alone" (*SH,* 30–31). Joyce, as he commonly does, deflates Stephen's self-aggrandizement, following the transcendent call of a "voice from beyond the world" with his friends' mockingly summoning up his name and destiny:

> —Hello, Stephanos!
> —Here comes The Dedalus! (*PA,* 195)

The repeated "alone," a word Joyce often attaches to Stephen, expresses all that lies in opposition to communal engagement generally, including the performance of party pieces.[12]

My argument here is that Stephen's flight is essentially negative: *from* his father and all that he embodies—familially, culturally, politically, historically, and performatively—rather than toward his goal of artistic creation. Given Simon's oppressive and destructive presence, such a flight seems necessary for Stephen's survival; but, like his mother's haunting presence in *Ulysses,* it leaves him no scope for independent thought, creativity, or performance. In 1912, when Irish Home Rule was approved, Joyce prophesied that the celebration would be an uneasy one: "There will be a shade at the feast: the shade of Charles Parnell . . . The shade of the 'uncrowned king' will weigh upon the hearts of . . . the new Ireland" (*OCPW,* 193, 196).[13] That prophecy plays out during *Portrait*'s Christmas dinner scene, a site of political, religious, and family conflict and animosity rather than the party peace that the occasion and Mrs. Dedalus demand. Joyce crystallizes Simon's failure by having him precipitate and preside over this domestic disaster, Stephen's first and last communal dinner. Such rituals ended early for Joyce as financial ruin and domestic disharmony precluded proper family meals, which may have been just as well given *Portrait*'s account of his father's performance as host and initiator of the crisis. Whatever Joyce may be satirizing in "The Dead," his representation of hospitality there seems genuine, and Gabriel's after-dinner speech in praise of both the tradition and its current manifestation largely unironic. Gabriel's performance goes unchallenged because his antagonist, the nationalist Miss Ivors, has already left the Morkan party. In *Portrait,* Dante remains to rise to Simon's bait.

Stephen's performance of grace at the beginning of the Christmas dinner unwittingly sets the stage not for the party piece that might have been expected (and that Gabriel performs during the analogous moment in "The Dead"), but for its opposite: a fierce confrontation between guest and host. When Simon introduces the topic of religion and politics ("—That was a good answer our friend made to the canon. What? said Mr Dedalus" [*PA*, 30]), Dante violates the guest role by aggressively defending the clergy who had denounced Parnell from the pulpit and attacking both her host and his dwelling: "—There could be neither luck nor grace, Dante said, in a house where there is no respect for the pastors of the church" (33). Though Mrs. Dedalus and Uncle Charles plead that political conflict should be avoided on this day of all days, the host/guest conflict escalates as Simon, shifting into a performative gear that he must know will further antagonize his guest, first croons "like a country singer" and then "began to sing in a grunting nasal tone":

> *O, come all you Roman catholics*
> *That never went to mass.* (35)

Dante insists that what she calls morality supersedes not only politics but the spirit of the occasion, and she lays claim to defending Stephen's youthful innocence: "—O, he'll remember all this when he grows up, said Dante hotly—the language he heard against God and religion and priests in his own home" (34). Her assault triggers both Simon's savage denunciation of the clergy who turned on Parnell and Casey's account of spitting tobacco juice into a heckler's eye, a story of minor triumph that Dante turns back against its narrator. Refusing to play the passive role of sympathetic audience, Dante affirms the clergy who denounced Parnell and then storms out; Casey, breaking down in pain and despair, "sobbed loudly and bitterly" (41). Dante is right about the impact the occasion has on Stephen, though not in the way she means: Stephen's climactic *non serviam*—"I will not serve that in which I no longer believe whether it call itself my home, my fatherland or my church" (291; also 281)—represents a pox on all the houses that would claim him.[14] Lacking both voice and an alternative expressive outlet after pronouncing grace on the graceless, Stephen, having learned a lesson in withdrawal and survival in the domestic realm presided over and betrayed by his father, begins his retreat from the furor into "silence, exile, and cunning" (291).[15] Simon's most intense passion is expended in mourning for another defeated patriarch, a lesson Stephen transmutes into the artistic principle of withdrawal that comes to define his ultimate alienation and failure.

Shortly after the Christmas dinner fiasco, Stephen experiences a second disaster with graceless patriarchy when he is pandied for neither doing his schoolwork (owing to having accidentally broken his glasses) nor explaining this lapse to the satisfaction of Father Dolan, the sadistic personification of Catholic authority. The blows Stephen receives are as much to his naïveté as to his hands, for he believes that his "schoolboy story,"[16] since it's a truthful recounting of his innocence, should persuade even a skeptical audience. Hence, Stephen feels guilt—a mixture of "shame and agony and fear"—when Father Dolan trumps his story: "—Hoho! The cinderpath! cried the prefect of studies. I know that trick" (*PA*, 54, 53). Stephen seems less shocked by the physical hurt he suffers than by the flogging that offends both his sense of justice and his narrative sense (a true story should be believed), and it casts him in the role of guilty victim ("scarlet with shame" [55]) that he rejects as inappropriate since he has done nothing wrong. The prefect had also assailed his sense of identity by twice asking him his name: "Why could he not remember the name when he was told the first time? Was he not listening the first time or was it to make fun out of the name? The great men in the history had names like that and nobody made fun of them. It was his own name that he should have made fun of if he wanted to make fun. Dolan: it was like the name of a woman that washed clothes" (59–60). In contrast to Dolan, the sympathetic rector, Father Conmee, both hears Stephen out and knows who he is without having to ask: "Your name is Dedalus, isn't it?" (62). Even this early Stephen finds special meaning in his "strange name," which "seemed to him a prophecy . . . of the end he had been born to serve" (196)—an identity that intensifies his isolation.

The interaction with Dolan seems, retrospectively, a harsh response to a failed rehearsal. Recounting the pandying incident to the rector and being assured that he will receive no further punishment, Stephen feels "happy and free" in part because he has regained narrative authority and thinks that he can now reclaim the initiating role: "He would not be anyway proud with Father Dolan. He would be very quiet and obedient: and he wished that he could do something kind for him to show him that he was not proud" (64). Yet Stephen's desire to enact such condescension proves unsatisfiable because his initial view is accurate: as Joyce depicts them, the Church's representatives (even Father

Conmee, as his subsequent mocking account of the affair reveals [75–76]), are powerful patriarchs, often arbitrary in their wielding of authority, as likely to be wrong as right.[17] Perhaps in consequence the episode remains just below Stephen's consciousness, susceptible to resurfacing in an instant. In the "Aeolus" chapter of *Ulysses*, Myles Crawford urges Stephen to write the book of Dublin, "Give them something with a bite in it. Put us all into it, damn its soul. Father, Son and Holy Ghost and Jakes M'Carthy." Like Father Dolan, Crawford claims to be able to read Stephen: "You can do it. I see it in your face," and in an instant Stephen is back on his knees before his abuser: "See it in your face. See it in your eye. Lazy idle little schemer" (*U*, 130).

Shaped and repressed by forces more powerful than himself, the young Stephen finds that his richest experiences are vicarious, imagined or envisioned rather than actually performed: his own death and funeral (*PA*, 22); witnessing the return of Parnell's body to Ireland (25); his patronizing of Father Dolan (64); embracing the role of the dark avenger out of *The Count of Monte Cristo* (68); being damned forever in hell during the retreat; serving in the mysterious role of priest (183); attending his English lecture (206); playing the piano and singing to Emma (although this last may be a memory rather than an imaginative construct [257]). He takes solace in the romantic future that surely awaits him, a future that is far more vivid than the past he remembers only dimly (104): "The hour when he too would take part in the life of that world seemed drawing near and in secret he began to make ready for the great part which he felt awaited him[,] the nature of which he only dimly apprehended" (68). Yet his forays into the world are unsatisfactory and brief; his retreats from it come sooner, and deepen, as a sense of foreboding repeatedly "dissipated any vision of the future" (70). He founds "a gang of adventurers," but soon decides "that he was different from others. He did not want to play. He wanted to meet in the real world the unsubstantial image which his soul so constantly beheld" (68–71).

The terrifying threats of the retreat drive Stephen to confession, but its seemingly life-transforming impact soon dissipates. And rather than serving as "the angel of mortal youth and beauty, an envoy from the fair courts of life" who will "throw open before him in an instant of ecstasy the gates of all the ways of error and glory," as Stephen would have it, the "birdgirl," like Emma on the tram, becomes something he can imaginatively capture and make into what he will so long as no direct contact occurs: "His cheeks were aflame; his body was aglow; his limbs were trembling. . . . Her image had passed into his soul for ever and no word had broken the holy silence of his ecstasy" (199–200). The masturbatory fantasy Stephen experiences here anticipates what occurs during the only fruitful creative act that Joyce affords him, when Stephen's "soul had passed from ecstasy to languor" during his writing of the villanelle (262).

Stephen retains "his habits of quiet obedience" (93), never allowing his "turbulent companions to seduce him from his habit of quiet obedience" (181), well into adolescence, even as he becomes increasingly alienated from a domestic space that initially nurtured performance. The phrase "He was sitting" (which appears three times in less than two pages [74–75]) emphasizes Stephen's self-willed isolation, his failure to enter into the spirit of these several occasions. The third time occurs at a children's party where, "though he tried to share their merriment, he felt himself a gloomy figure amid the gay cocked hats and sunbonnets." Constrained to perform his party piece before he can escape into himself, "when he had sung his song and withdrawn into a snug corner of the room he began to taste the joy of his loneliness" (75). Joyce elides the party piece itself, as he does the tram poem, revealing nothing of what Stephen performs, or how it is performed, or what response it receives.[18]

Such narratival amnesia comports with Stephen's alienation from the party and his aloofness from others that plays out in the tram scene with Emma, which follows immediately. Here his pride of self-sufficiency causes him *not* to "catch hold of her . . . and kiss her," although (or because) he thinks that that is what she wants and expects. Instead, he suppresses his racing heart, rejects the gift she offers, and stands listlessly (76–77). Then through a mounting series of negatives that reprises Mr. Duffy's failure in "A Painful Case"—"There remained *no* trace of the tram itself *nor* of the trammen *nor* of the horses: *nor* did he and she appear vividly" (78; my emphasis)—he transmutes the experience that did not happen into a work of art, which is also elided, that Joyce mocks by depicting the creative process as the performance of a series of clichéd gestures.

First, Stephen sits "at his table in the bare upper room for many hours. Before him lay a new pen, a new bottle of ink and a new emerald exercise." He then begins mechanically, writing at the top of the first page "From force of habit . . . the initial letters of the jesuit motto: A.M.D.G." and a Byronic title, “To E—— C——,” with “an ornamental line underneath” (77). He inappropriately concludes, again presumably from force of habit, with the initials of another Jesuit motto: “L.D.S.” For all the evocations, however, it is neither God nor some poetic forebear but Stephen himself who solipsistically both inspires and serves as recipient for the art of this creative act, whatever it may actually be: subsequently “he went into his mother’s bedroom and gazed at his face for a long time in the mirror of her dressingtable” (78), as if awaiting applause. Stephen’s narcissism replays that of his father, who, in preparation for his entry onto the Christmas dinner stage, “looked at himself in the pierglass above the mantelpiece, waxed out his moustache ends . . . and still from time to time he withdrew a hand from his coat tail to wax out one of his moustache ends” (26). Effacing both Stephen’s art and artistry, Joyce also effaces the would-be artist by exposing him as simultaneously subject and object of his own gaze, a creature of his mother’s vanity mirror whose best and only audience is himself.

At school Stephen’s major performative accomplishment is not a party piece but starring in the Whitsuntide play as “a farcical pedagogue” (81), which he finds embarrassing: “He felt no stage fright but the thought of the part he had to play humiliated him” (94). Heron, his friend and rival, challenges him to deviate from the script and send up the rector instead, which he can apparently do well: “Go on, Dedalus, he urged, you can take him off rippingly” (84). But unlike Joyce, who on the analogous occasion offered a “cheeky mimicry of the ‘pedantic bass’ of the Belvedere Rector,”[19] Stephen adheres to his text, heeding “the voice of the plump young jesuit which bade him speak up and make his points clearly.” Momentarily forgetting himself, he enters fully into the occasion and the part he plays: “Another nature seemed to have been lent him. . . . For one rare moment he seemed to be clothed in the real apparel of boyhood . . . he shared the common mirth.” And the play comes unexpectedly alive: “The play which he had known at rehearsals for a disjointed lifeless thing had suddenly assumed a life of its own. It seemed now to play itself, he and his fellow actors aiding it with their parts” (94–95). Yet when the performance ends and the audience breaks apart, separating into its discrete individuals, he flees his waiting family, especially “his father’s questions,” in “pride and hope and desire,” which quickly decline into “wounded pride and fallen hope and baffled desire” (96).

Although he returns physically, the book's next scene, the trip to Cork that climaxes Simon's economic and social decline, underscores Stephen's psychological distance from Simon as both failed father and impoverished storyteller, as well as his refusal to play the audience role Simon demands of him: "He listened without sympathy to his father's evocation of Cork and of scenes of his youth, a tale broken by sighs or draughts from his pocket flask" (97). Simon's self-indulgent and drunken nostalgia, which causes Stephen a succession of embarrassments (107), deepens his isolation, cold aloofness, and sense of merely drifting through life (107–8), and leads ultimately to his mocking dispraise of Simon to Cranly (284).

Making a rare gesture of filial empathy just before Simon's humiliating bankruptcy auction, Stephen compliments his father's singing of the self-referential song, "'Tis Youth and Folly/Makes Young Men Marry": "That's much prettier than any of your other *come-all-yous*" (98–99).[20] At this latest low point in his life, however, Simon reacts by boasting to his pub audience that he's a better man than his son, and offers to prove it by outperforming him: "I'll sing a tenor song against him" (107).[21] The young Stephen had, when challenged, vaguely denoted his father "A gentleman" (3); Simon elaborates on the notion, insisting on the linkage between performance and gentlemanly (and nationalist) status: "When I was a young fellow. . . . I mixed with fine decent fellows. . . . One fellow had a good voice, another fellow was a good actor, another could sing a good comic song, another was a good oarsman or a good racket player, another could tell a good story and so on. We kept the ball rolling anyhow and enjoyed ourselves and saw a bit of life. . . . But we were all gentlemen, Stephen—at least I hope we were—and bloody good honest Irishmen too" (102). Stephen later parodies this passage, amalgamating and embellishing all the roles, glibly enumerating his father's "zigzag career"[22] as a succession of unsuccessful performances or auditions: "—A medical student, an oarsman, a tenor, an amateur actor, a shouting politician, a small landlord, a small investor, a drinker, a good fellow, a storyteller, somebody's secretary, something in a distillery, a taxgatherer, a bankrupt and at present a praiser of his own past" (284).[23]

In *Ulysses,* Bloom too sees Simon primarily as performer, though he spins it more positively: "It's the droll way he comes out with the things. Knows how to tell a story too" (*U,* 145). According to Bloom, Simon "Could have made oceans of money" by singing (263), but he prefers to proffer his talent for drinks in the Ormond bar: "—I have no money but if you will lend me your attention I shall endeavour to sing to you of a heart bowed down" (262). Simon's roleplaying supersedes or becomes his reality perhaps because, as Joyce puts it in *Stephen Hero,* he is such a good audience for himself that he "was quite capable of talking himself into believing what he knew to be untrue" (*SH,* 110). Disgusted with his father's boasting and profligacy, Stephen is his sullen and reluctant audience only until he manages to effect his escape.

The most extensive oral performance in all of Joyce's writings is the preacher's melodramatic, mesmerizing sermon on hell and damnation at the retreat, and it casts Stephen in the receiving role of enforced audience. He internalizes and personalizes a call that scares him nearly witless: "Every word of it was for him. Against his sin, foul and secret, the whole wrath of God was aimed" (*PA,* 131; also 142, 157). Reduced to cowering self-abasement, weeping "for the innocence he had lost" (160), and finally confessing his sins under duress and with extreme embarrassment, Stephen voices what he had physically enacted: "His sins trickled from his lips, one by one, trickled in shameful drops from his soul festering and oozing like a sore, a squalid stream of vice. The last sins oozed forth, sluggish, filthy. There was no more to tell. He bowed his head, overcome" (166). He receives, in response, the church's "grave words of absolution," its "token of forgiveness," and its injunction to cease committing sins of impurity that are, uniquely, deemed "dishonourable and unmanly" (167). But Stephen soon learns that the sins of his past remain in the present (rising up against him, like Bloom's in "Circe" [*U,* 503–4]), and must be recounted repeatedly: "with humility and shame," he must "confess and repent and be absolved, confess and repent again and be absolved again, fruitlessly" (*PA,* 177–78). The part of abased confessor, having been learned well, seems to be his to perform in perpetuity—until he rejects the entire Catholic script.

Joyce depicts such Catholic dramas as the mass, sermon, and confession as ritual party pieces: occasions to perform assigned parts before a designated audience in order to reaffirm shared belief or to earn the accolade of (spiritual) approval. But he drains meaning from these performances, often turning them into occasions of pain, absurdity, or mockery. Stanislaus, who broke with the church earlier and more fully than his brother, but saw drama become a thing of supreme importance for him, "what the Mass had been" (*MBK,* 87), provided Joyce with the basis for his parody of the confessional: "You should never do that, my child. You should never eat meat on holy days . . . days of abstinence. You should always observe the rules of our Holy Mother, the Church. Our Holy Mother, the Church, makes these observances for the good of our souls . . . and eh . . . you should be careful, for the future, always to keep the observances of our Holy Mother, the Church . . . and eh . . . never to eat meat on days of abstinence especially among Protestants. . . . Is there anything else, my child?" (*CDDSJ*, 14 September 1904, 102).

In his obsessive devotion and abstemiousness after his confession, Stephen unwittingly enacts Stanislaus's parody. Playing the role to the hilt, Stephen dedicates each day to spiritual mystery, hallows himself anew every morning, begins each day "with an heroic offering of its every moment of thought or action for the intentions of the sovereign pontiff and with an early mass," lays out his daily life "in devotional areas" while constantly saying the rosaries (*PA*, 170). Further, having vicariously suffered the torture of "every sense of the flesh . . . and every faculty of the soul" (139), he reverses the book's opening expansiveness by mortifying his senses one by one—including that of rhythm, since Joyce has him, while mortifying his senses after his anguished confession, neither sing nor whistle (163)—until penitent and penance seem to become as indistinguishable as Yeats's dancer and dance (170–76). Yet ultimately the path of excessive denial leads to its obverse, and soon "the insistent voices of the flesh . . . began to murmur to him again during his prayers and meditations" (176).

All his life Stephen has felt himself beset by insistent voices (and "calls," appeals, and summonses) that challenge and prescribe roles for him, voices that become increasingly strident and "hollowsounding" as the book progresses. He hears "the constant voices of his father and of his masters, urging him to be a gentleman above all things and urging him to be a good catholic above all things"; he hears another voice "urging him to be strong and manly and healthy"; "yet another voice had bidden him to be true to his country and help to raise up her language and tradition." A "worldly voice would bid him raise up his father's fallen state by his labours," while "the voice of his school comrades urged him to be a decent fellow, to shield others from blame or to beg them off and to do his best to get free days for the school" (93). Davin's "simple" invocation of the Irish tradition of patriotic storytelling and his appeal to the

Nationalist cause "touched Stephen pleasantly"[24] (rather than deeply), as does Davin's unique use of his christian name (or, rather, the "homely version": Stevie). Listening to his friend's story of crossing the hills one night and encountering a young, half naked seductress (a traditional embodiment of Ireland, like the one on the Irish harp in "Two Gallants" [*D*, 65]) calling the stranger to her bed, Stephen patronizingly thinks of Davin as a young peasant with "the attitude of a dullwitted loyal serf" who "worshipped the sorrowful legend of Ireland" and whose "nurse had taught him Irish and shaped his rude imagination by the broken lights of Irish myth." Like his father at the Christmas dinner, Stephen then offers his inappropriate audience a counter-narrative, shifting his focus from the political to the personal and aesthetic by performing "the verses and cadences of others which were the veils of his own longing and dejection" (*PA*, 209–10). Upset by Stephen's tales of his sexual adventures, Davin can only respond that he wished Stephen had not told him (237).

The summons to the priesthood that Stephen receives (182–83) at first seems the definitive call that will exclude all others, a means of escaping failed patriarchy by becoming "father" to himself. In his initial response to the "voice of the director urging upon him the proud claims of the church and the mystery and power of the priestly office" (188), Stephen remembers how he had often imagined himself acting out the greatest role of all: "He had seen himself, a young and silentmannered priest, entering a confessional swiftly, ascending the altarsteps, incensing, genuflecting, accomplishing the vague acts of the priesthood which pleased him by reason of their semblance of reality and of their distance from it" (183–84). But the call to the priesthood, like the earlier imperatives, becomes just one more in a series of external appeals to perform that he rejects. Stephen has long recognized that "Nothing moved him or spoke to him from the real world unless he heard in it an echo of the infuriated cries within him. He could respond to no earthly or human appeal" (103–4). Further, his obsessive devotion at the beginning of chapter IV seems to have exhausted that vein in him so that, in response to the call to the priesthood, he merely "wondered vaguely" about the possibility, contemplates "the remoteness of his own soul from what he had hitherto imagined her sanctuary, at the frail hold which so many years of order and obedience had of him," and determines that his "destiny was to be elusive of social or religious orders." Coming to view this call as but the latest and greatest of traps, "he knew now that the exhortation he had listened to had already fallen into an idle formal tale." Convincing himself that he rejects the priesthood for the "snares of the world" (187–88), Stephen becomes both mock priest and false altar in the religion of his art (202–3), performing at the opening of Section V a parodic, self-indulgent mass that represents his final break with the church.

But Stephen has increasingly shifted his focus away from action in the world and onto language, to words and names (most of which seem "queer" when he dwells on them), and then more to their rhythms and sounds than to their meanings. At first, words are his way into the world: "Words which he did not understand he said over and over to himself till he had learned them by heart: and through them he had glimpses of the real world about him" (67–68). The linkage is disturbing at times, however, as when he finds the word *Foetus* carved in a desk in the classroom where his father had attended school: "It shocked him to find in the outer world a trace of what he had deemed till then a brutish and individual malady of his own mind" (101). And the word assumes a haunting presence that momentarily undermines his self-confidence: "The letters cut in the stained wood of the desk stared upon him, mocking his bodily weakness and futile enthusiasms and making him loathe himself for his own mad and filthy orgies" (102).

Word and deed similarly fail to cohere in the scene with the prostitute. When she demands a kiss, his lustful, longing body, as it had on the tram, fails to perform and remains stiffly withheld. This time, however, the word does become flesh as "she bowed his head and joined her lips to his. . . . It was too much for him. He closed his eyes, surrendering himself to her, body and mind, conscious of nothing in the world but the dark pressure of her softly parting lips" (114). Yet this fleeting contact quickly becomes parodic: an excess of sensual indulgence followed by an excess of sensual denial.

Stephen is intrigued by the multiple meanings of "belt" (3) and "suck" (whose "sound was ugly" [6]), by Athy's punning name (23), by Vincent Heron's having "a bird's face as well as a bird's name" (84). He is uncertain whether it is the words "cold and hot" on the faucets or the water that comes out of them that produces the sensations of chill and warmth (7). In isolation he contemplates himself, his name, and his place in the universe (12; he does so again while walking alongside his father [101]), and also all the "different names for God in all the different languages in the world" (12). The rector's winy breath makes him feel ill during his first communion, but the "word was beautiful: wine" (49). A similar dichotomy occurs when he cannot summon up any of his childhood's vivid moments. "He recalled only names. Dante, Parnell, Clane, Clongowes" (104). And so, too, with his rejection of the priesthood: what he opts for is the music of words: "the poise and balance of the period itself . . . he drew less pleasure from the reflection of the glowing sensible world through the prism of a language manycoloured and richly storied than from the contemplation of an inner world of individual emotions mirrored perfectly in a lucid supple periodic prose" (193–94). And rather than experience directly the Dublin that he traverses on his way to the University, Stephen's imagination sets up a screen, envisioning the "rainladen trees" as figures out of the plays of Hauptmann. Tidal flats evoke "the cloistral silverveined prose of Newman"; provision shops "recall the dark humour of Guido Cavalacanti"; a stonecutter's work summons up "the spirit of Ibsen," and "a grimy marine dealer's shop" the lovely lyrics of Ben Jonson (204–5).

Stephen is, in fact, doubly removed from the reality around him since he considers the language in which he experiences it to be secondary to him. In their interchange early in chapter V, the English dean of studies not only raises that most awkward of questions for Stephen—"You are an artist, are you not, Mr Dedalus? said the dean," a question Stephen fails to answer—but also unwittingly triggers Stephen's introspection concerning his very ability to think, speak, and create in the language of the colonizer: "—The language in which we are speaking is his before it is mine. How different are the words *home, Christ, ale, master,* on his lips and on mine! I cannot speak or write these words without unrest of spirit. His language, so familiar and so foreign, will always be for me an acquired speech. I have not made or accepted its words. My voice holds them at bay. My soul frets in the shadow of his language" (216, 221). For Stephen, language—which further confuses by using the same words both in literature and in the marketplace (219)—becomes a means not of engaging or creating the world but of defining his distance from it, and doubly so since he has no more interest in either Irish or Ireland than does Gabriel Conroy.

The dean's question seems definitively answered in the negative when, during his only attempt to write a poem in *Ulysses,* Stephen imagines a Berkeleyan equivalence between the objects of the visible world and his own scribbling: "Who ever anywhere will read these written words? Signs on a white field. . . . veil of space with coloured emblems hatched on its field" (*U,* 48). Between solipsism ("Signatures of all things I am here to read" [37]) and irrelevance ("There all the time without you: and ever shall be, world without end" [38]), Stephen cannot decide whether the artist's task is to recognize the inherent fixity of objects or to fix them himself, as Menelaus wrestled with Proteus and refused to let go until the demigod assumed and retained a single form. Despite his love of foul odors and fascination with bodily fluids (the narrator of "Ithaca" says he has not washed himself in eight months [625–26]), Stephen keeps himself at a remove from the reality of experience that he claims to encounter a million times and out of which he fails to create. Joyce himself escaped Stephen's dilemma by embracing these contradictions: dividing his aesthetic perspective between Stephen and Bloom, Joyce yoked together the material and the mythic by capturing or recreating the details of a Dublin day while infusing every detail with rich metaphoric meaning.

The most poignant and seductive appeal made to Stephen occurs when, upon returning home after the summons to the priestly vocation, he confronts "the faint sour stink of rotted cabbages . . . from the kitchen gardens. . . . He smiled to think that it was this disorder, the misrule and confusion of his father's house and the stagnation of vegetable life, which was to win the day in his soul" (*PA,* 188). But when actually there, Stephen cannot long romanticize, or endure, life in "his father's house" where, as Stanislaus recalls it, domestic performance sought to fill the cultural and economic void of Ireland's present: "They all used to sing. The singing of sentimental ballads was a backwash of that ebbing wave of romanticism, in which poetry and all it is wont to express had degenerated, Tommy Moore assisting, to a drawing-room accomplishment" (*MBK,* 15–16).[25]

Stephen's siblings, like the Joyces, "would sing so for hours, melody after melody, glee after glee, till the last pale light died down on the horizon, till the first dark nightclouds came forth and night fell" (*PA,* 190). The song they sing, Moore's "Oft in the Stilly Night," serves as metaphor as well as performance.[26] It contrasts "boyhood's years" of innocence, hope, and love with present cheerlessness, loss, and death, leaving the speaker

> like one who treads alone
> Some banquet hall deserted;

> Whose lights are fled, whose garlands dead,
> And all but he departed.

Stephen hears the implicit plea in his siblings' voices as he listens "with pain of spirit to the overtone of weariness behind their frail fresh innocent voices. Even before they set out on life's journey they seemed weary already of the way." Empathy briefly prompts Stephen to sing with them, but he soon flees their implicit appeal to share their fate as both the song, with its "recurring note of weariness and pain," and the domestic scene recapitulate the family's downward spiral caused by his father's wastrel behavior. This flight of Stephen's—"walking rapidly lest his father's shrill whistle might call him back" (*PA,* 190–91)—prepares for the climactic scene on the beach, which follows almost immediately, and his utter alienation from others that culminates verbally in his reiterated negative credo: "*non serviam:* I will not serve" (134, 281, 291), which for Stephen also means "I will not perform."

Fantasizing a meeting with Mercedes out of Dumas' *Count of Monte Cristo,* Stephen had imagined that in a "moment of supreme tenderness he would be transfigured. He would fade into something impalpable under her eyes and then in a moment, he would be transfigured. Weakness and timidity and inexperience would fall from him in that magic moment" (71). Yet Joyce uses Stephen's self-aggrandizing to ironize and deflate the moment of transfiguration even before it happens, and he does the same thing with the scene on the beach. Just before it occurs, Stephen's musings turn to his sense of a special destiny, to which a "voice from beyond the world was calling [him]" (195): to "create proudly out of the freedom and power of his soul, as the great artificer whose name he bore, a living thing, new and soaring and beautiful, impalpable, imperishable" (197; Stephen again invokes Daedalus on 196, 264, and 299). But even as he imagines his soul transcending his earthly existence, he is recalled to himself by the mocking voices of his rude and "characterless" friends repeatedly crying out vulgar Latinate variations on his name:

> A voice from beyond the world was calling.
> —Hello, Stephanos!
> —Here comes The Dedalus! . . .
> —Come along, Dedalus! Bous Stephanoumenos! Bous Stephaneforos! (195)

Their cries anticipate, recast, and undercut the visionary scene, which follows almost immediately, that he characterizes as setting him on the path of artistry: "to triumph, to recreate life out of life!" (200).

Such rhythmic counterpointing is characteristic of Joyce's treatment of Stephen. His lecture to Lynch on aesthetics is drearily set and assailed by their surroundings: "A crude grey light, mirrored in the sluggish water, and a smell of wet branches over their heads seemed to war against the course of Stephen's thoughts" (242). It is punctuated by a "long dray laden with old iron [intruding] the harsh roar of jangled and rattling metal" (245), by Donovan's "benevolent malice" (247) as he recounts exam results, and by the rain that provokes Lynch's mocking inquiry: "—What do you mean . . . by prating about beauty and the imagination in this miserable Godforsaken island?" (252). Stephen is also on shaky ground substantively; as Norris notes, "Joyce's object in mixing the Ibsen theory with that of Aquinas is to discredit Stephen's grasp of Ibsen."[27] Later, Stephen's romantic fantasy of Emma—"it was her body he smelt: a wild and languid smell: the tepid limbs over which his music had flowed desirously and the secret soft linen upon which her flesh distilled odour and a dew"—yields to the reality of a louse crawling on his neck (*PA*, 275), what Beckett in *Rough for Radio II* calls "Vermin in the lingerie" (*SB3*, 319).[28]

Stephen's encounter with "the birdgirl," like the earlier tram scene with Emma, is most striking for his transforming it into a nonoccurrence. As director of the mise-en-scène, Stephen transmutes the girl into an abstraction, "a strange and beautiful seabird" that "Long, long . . . suffered his gaze." He then flees from any possible contact in order to sustain the ideal form, beyond action, beyond language: "Her image had passed into his soul for ever and no word had broken the holy silence of his ecstasy" (*PA*, 199–200). It is not, as Stephen would have it, the world's "misrule and confusion" that he embraces, but his aestheticized retreat from it. Stephen's self-deceit complements the hypocrisy and misogyny that Norris discerns in him.[29] Having closed his ears to all extrinsic calls, Stephen determines that his destiny lies beyond the hearing of such voices (93), heeding instead a confused inner music, "his throat throbbing with song" in response to "the call of life to his soul" to create and perform in "the fair courts of life" (194–200). And yet it is precisely in those courts that Stephen, unlike Joyce, refuses, or finds himself unable, to live and to create. The party pieces that Stephen performs early on enact positive aspects of the culture he inherits, and seem to set the stage for achievement to come. But by representing Simon as a caricature of both conviviality and irresponsibility, and transforming Stephen's relationship to his father from his own to that of his embittered brother Stanislaus, Joyce depicts Stephen as not only alienated from all the forces that would claim him, but also culturally and spiritually deprived, cut off from both creative resources and an artist's necessary audience even as he claims to embrace them.

The pattern of willful self-isolation and posturing that his friends repeatedly note in chapter V begins with Stephen's definitive break with Simon, who execrates him as a "lazy bitch." Stephen's response is merely semantic, mocking the rhetoric of Simon's curse: "He has a curious idea of genders if he thinks a bitch is masculine" (203). But the calls continue, and they continue to take their toll: "His father's whistle, his mother's mutterings, the screech of an unseen maniac were to him now so many voices offending and threatening to humble the pride of his youth" (204). Though he occasionally feels the need "to find himself still in the midst of common lives" (205), he responds with ever greater self-assertion and detachment, taking pleasure in provoking his friends' repeated charges that recapitulate his aloofness from them and all others. McCann says, "—Dedalus, you're an antisocial being, wrapped up in yourself" (206); Davin: "—You're a terrible man, Stevie, . . . always alone" (236); Cranly: "—Have you never loved anyone?" (283) and "—alone, quite alone. . . . Not only to be separate from all others but to have not even one friend" (292). The isolating refrain only feeds its provoker's proud "spirit which had always made him conceive himself as a being apart in every order," as one who exults in being "alone and young and wilful and wildhearted" (187, 199).

Stephen's main counter to this drumbeat is his solipsistic, masturbatory villanelle ("He too was weary of ardent ways" [260]), which Bowen calls "the microcosm and artistic epiphany of the entire novel,"[30] and which Joyce undercuts by having Stephen write it on the inside of a cigarette packet.[31] While writing it, Stephen romanticizes a scene he recalls when he performed for Emma, who begged "him to sing one of his curious songs. Then he saw himself sitting at the old piano, striking chords softly from its speckled keys and singing . . . to her . . . a dainty song of the Elizabethans, a sad and sweet loth to depart, the victory chant of Agincourt, the happy air of Greensleeves" (257).[32] But as the memory ends he rebuffs her friendly advances, disdainfully and jealously turns from her, and with "rude brutal anger routed the last lingering instant of ecstasy from his soul" (258). So only through self-deception can Stephen believe that, with the villanelle, he "had written verses for her again after ten years." And fearful of being ridiculed by having his poem "read out at breakfast amid the tapping of eggshells" (261), Stephen is unwilling to risk offering it to Emma or the world: he recites the poem only in private and only to himself. His apprehension that his work will be disvalued, that his writing will be derided, feeds Stephen's artistic paralysis.

Joseph Strick's film of *Portrait* does make the poem into a performative occasion, but its Stephen comes off even worse than he does in the novel. He recites an abbreviated version of the villanelle to a bewildered Emma who says, "It's lovely Stephen. I don't understand it, but the music of it is lovely." In response to Emma's feeble critique Stephen contemptuously proposes, in a moment taken from *Stephen Hero*, that he and she "live one night together . . . and then . . . say goodbye in the morning and never . . . see each other again!" In *Stephen Hero* Emma, trying to disengage herself from him, "murmured as if she were repeating from memory: —You are mad, Stephen" (*SH*, 198). The stunned, insubstantial movie Emma simply flees without a word, leaving Stephen looking utterly foolish.

Seamus Deane argues that Stephen's final creation, his diary, affirms his achievement of artisthood: he "takes over the telling of his own story, finally replacing the words of others with his own words, ultimately achieving eloquence after beginning in baby lispings and mispronunciations."[33] Kevin Whelan similarly represents Stephen as "finally achiev[ing] eloquence and narrative self-sufficiency only at the cost of leaving [his] communit[y]."[34] And Strick's film of *Portrait* visually endorses this assessment by showing Stephen—answering the call of the birds (and "of the hawklike man whose name he bore" [*PA*, 264])—sailing away from Dublin toward Paris at the end, having begun both the journal and the journey that seem to promise artistic success.[35]

Yet despite its occasional honesty and self-awareness, Stephen's solipsistic diary, written solely for the audience of himself, represents more self-aggrandizement on its writer's part, and Joyce's Stephen, perhaps handicapped by his sense that English remains both familiar and foreign to him, "an acquired speech. I have not made or accepted its words" (221), never achieves either eloquence or narrative self-sufficiency. Stephen's presumably unintended pun, in determining "to forge in the smithy of my soul the uncreated conscience of my race" (299), suggests that at some level he knows that his rhetoric is counterfeit, posturing rather than substantive. And despite telling Davin that "the shortest way to Tara was *via* Holyhead" (296), he never embarks. He remains fixed in place because, as Joyce told Frank Budgen, "He has a shape that can't be changed."[36] Stephen may stand at Dún Laoghaire pier but he gets no further, and there, or within short walking distance, he still is when we next see him in the Martello Tower at the beginning of *Ulysses* (or as Richard Rowan in *Exiles*): still proclaiming his independence and artisthood, still creating nothing, still ensnared by the forces that begot, reared, and misshaped him. Stephen's Paris, like Hamlet's England, exists only offstage, requiring an imaginative leap on our parts if we are to accept the reality of an intervening journey out and back. Like Tennyson's Ulysses forever posing and declaiming on the dock at Ithaca, Joyce's Stephen remains in a state of penultimacy, poised for what never happens: the journey to "encounter for the millionth time the reality of experience" (299) and the artistic career that, despite all evidence to the contrary, he has convinced himself lies just beyond.

4 Vying for Artistry in *Ulysses*

The Stephen Dedalus who resurfaces in *Ulysses* is located exactly where he was at the end of *Portrait of the Artist* and still bitterly entangled in the nets of "nationality, language, religion" that he had determined to soar beyond (*PA*, 238). From the beginning of *Ulysses* to its end he is world-enmeshed and -weary: "I am a servant of two masters, Stephen said, an English and an Italian. . . . And a third, Stephen said, there is who wants me for odd jobs" (*U*, 20).[1] Though he had vowed to dedicate himself to the religion of art and to "the fair courts of life" at the end of chapter IV of *Portrait* (*PA*, 200), Stephen's artistic career, like his life, is a nonstarter. His situation is one that Victor Turner calls liminality, more particularly "outsiderhood": the condition of "voluntarily setting oneself apart from the behavior of status-occupying, role-playing members" of a social system.[2]

As Stephen repeatedly acknowledges to himself, *Ulysses* offers even less evidence than *Portrait* of his creative or vital powers at work. Recalling the scene of narcissism in *Portrait* when, after writing his first poem, he stared at himself at length in his mother's vanity mirror (78), Stephen self-mockingly contemplates his performative failure: "You bowed to yourself in the mirror, stepping forward to applause earnestly, striking face. Hurray for the Goddamned idiot! Hray! . . . Books you were going to write with letters for titles. Have you read his F? O yes, but I prefer Q. Yes, but W is wonderful. O yes, W. Remember your epiphanies written on green oval leaves, deeply deep, copies to be sent if you died to all the great libraries of the world, including Alexandria?" (*U*, 40–41). Later in the same chapter he again thinks "of the alphabet books he was going to write" (48), but that he has not.

Ulysses begins with a performance, but it is not Stephen's; he is not even present in the scene, or the book, until Buck Mulligan summons him to serve as audience. Mulligan, the better performer, reminds Stephen of his failure to pray for his mother on her deathbed when she asked him, and then derisively declaims lines from Yeats's "Who Goes with Fergus?" that Stephen, like Joyce, had put to music and then sung to his dying mother: "Fergus' song: I sang it above[3] in the house, holding down the long dark chords. Her door was open: she wanted to hear my music. Silent with awe and pity I went to her bedside. She was crying in her wretched bed. For those words, Stephen: love's bitter mystery" (9). So the song, whose words Stephen murmurs to an uncomprehending Bloom after he is knocked down by Private Carr at the end of "Circe" (558, 564), is associated with personal and performative failure: Stephen's *non serviam;* his mother's weeping despair for her son; her death and continued haunting presence ("You sang that song to me. *Love's bitter mystery*" [540]); and Mulligan's usurpation of cėnter stage.

Many poems swirl around in Stephen's head, but he manages to write only one in *Ulysses:*

> On swift sail flaming
> From storm and south
> He comes, pale vampire,
> Mouth to my mouth. (127)

As if exhausted by momentous achievement, Stephen stretches out on the strand like the god of creation: "*Et vidit Deus. Et errant valde bona*" (48). Yet "Proteus" depicts Stephen's materiality more than his spirituality: he urinates on the sand as if performing a poem ("a fourworded wavespeech: seesoo, hrss, rsseeiss, ooos. . . . spent, its speech ceases") and then picks his nose (49). Further, like Stephen's Wildean comment about the cracked looking glass of a servant serving as a symbol of Irish art that Mulligan, either missing the allusion or assuming that Haines will, thinks Stephen can fob off on Haines for money (7),[4] this poem is derivative rather than original (what *Finnegans Wake* calls "stolentelling" [*FW,* 424.35]), a pastiche (though Stephen seems not to know it) of the last stanza of a keening poem, "My Grief on the Sea," from Douglas Hyde's *Love Songs of Connacht.* In it a woman left behind in Ireland mourns for a lover who is "On board of a ship Voyaging to America"; in her grief she summons up a vision of him in the final stanza:

> And my love came behind me—
>   He came from the South;

His breast to my bosom,
His mouth to my mouth.[5]

As if to underscore the inside joke at Stephen's expense, Joyce has Stephen "write" the parodic or plagiarized poem in "Proteus" (*U,* 47–48), the chapter of metempsychosis, but not reveal it until "Aeolus" (127), where it becomes just one more bit of windy Irish rhetoric.

Although employed as a teacher in "Nestor," Stephen behaves more like the class clown or hired entertainer, performing on cue from his limited repertoire of party tricks. Having confused his students by defining a pier as "a disappointed bridge," Stephen acts out the implicit advice of the major seventeenth-century Irish poet, Dáibhí Ó Bruadair: "When I see how people set no value on poetic wit, and when to run in steps of sages brings to no one any joy, when the heroes of the Fenians stand no longer up erect, an empty jingle is the only poetry which suits my mind."[6] Stephen envisions himself reprising the aphorism before a more receptive audience: "For Haines's chapbook. No-one here to hear. Tonight deftly amid wild drink and talk, to pierce the polished mail of his mind. What then? A jester at the court of his master, indulged and disesteemed, winning a clement master's praise" (*U,* 25).[7] Yet, unlike Farrington in "Counterparts," even that humiliation will be denied him since he is not invited to the evening's festivities at George Moore's.

Responding to his students' plea to tell them a story, to entertain rather than teach them (25), Stephen asks a nonsense riddle (which he parodies and then parses in "Circe" [520–21]), a riddle that he sings in *Bloom,* Sean Walsh's film of the novel.[8] Unsurprisingly, his riddle mystifies his students:

The cock crew
The sky was blue:
The bells in heaven
Were striking eleven.
'Tis time for this poor soul
To go to heaven. (*U,* 27)

His answer ("The fox burying his grandmother under a hollybush" [27]) only baffles them further, but his thoughts link it to an image of guilt over his failure to bury and mourn his mother (28), making the riddle a veiled personal confession. And Stephen alludes explicitly to the classroom as a site of performance when, in "Oxen of the Sun," he refers to his teaching salary as "tribute . . . for a song which he writ" (373). Stephen's other performative turns include "*A Pisgah Sight of Palestine* or *The Parable of The Plums*" and his much-anticipated, and far-fetched, critique of *Hamlet* as autobiography in "Scylla and Charybdis." Although, as Shari Benstock notes, Stephen has refused prior to June 16 to participate in the social exchange of storytelling,[9] "Aeolus" locates him in the windy cave of rhetoric, site of oral performance. Interrupters attempt to clear performative space for themselves: Lenehan offers a riddle and then palindromes (127, 132); the wind god Myles Crawford, like the musician in "Two Gallants," plays a debased "HARP EOLIAN!" by smartly twanging a piece of "dental floss . . . between two and two of his resonant unwashed teeth" (123). The chapter also offers three speeches that move backward in time toward Ireland's mythologized past until it links up with Israel's, a theme of many Gaelic poets. The speeches unfold as a kind of traditional party piece competition: "Gather round the fire, do ye, and let everybody tell his story after his own way; and let the rest hearken, whether they like it or not, until 'tis over, and then tell their own, if they think 'tis better."[10] Ultimately drawn in, Stephen offers his parable as the fourth in this performative series.

The first speech, which Stephen misses, is City Councilor Dan Dawson's grandiloquent extolling of Irish natural beauty—"*note the meanderings of some purling rill as it babbles on its way, fanned by gentlest zephyrs tho' quarrelling with the stony obstacles, to the tumbling waters of Neptune's blue domain, mid mossy banks*"—which Ned Lambert reads out in snippets from the newspaper (*U,* 119–21) to the derisive responses of his anguished listeners who deem the speech pretentious, tourist-board rhetoric. Zimmermann comments that "storytelling is a social transaction," requiring performer and audience collaboration; quoting the folklorist Kevin Danaher, he adds that "'A poor storyteller soon lost his audience and, moreover, earned scorn and contempt as one who had set himself above his station as an expert in an art beyond his talent.'"[11] Ned's reading of Dawson's speech provokes *second-hand* "scorn and contempt" from his rebellious audience (aimed more at Dawson than at Ned's reading): "That will do, professor MacHugh cried from the window. I don't want to hear any more of the stuff"; "Bombast! the professor broke in testily. Enough of the inflated windbag!"; "O! Mr Dedalus cried, giving vent to a hopeless groan. Shite and onions! That'll do, Ned. Life is too short" (119–21). Only the discreet Bloom, who understands the difference between oral and written appeals, silently acknowledges the basis of Dawson's popularity: "All very fine to jeer at it now in cold print but it goes down like hot cake that stuff" (122). Delargy agrees with this distinction: "The thick growth of alliterative adjectives would roll trippingly on the tongue of a practised story-teller, and have the effect of impressing his illiterate audience, to whom, a thousand years ago as to-day, high-flown rhetoric had a charm and an ever-new appeal."[12] But not for the bulk of the audience gathered in "Aeolus."

The seedy barrister J. J. O'Molloy next declaims from "One of the most polished periods I think I ever listened to in my life" (*U*, 134): the defense by Seymour Bushe in the Samuel Childs murder case (Childs was accused of murdering his brother; Joyce attended the October 1899 trial [*JJ2*, 91–92]). Bushe's rhetoric evokes Renaissance glory generally and, in particular, its legal principles derived from "Roman justice as contrasted with the earlier Mosaic code, the *lex talionis*" (*U*, 134). This time Bloom is absent and it is Stephen who responds silently, if embarrassedly—"His blood wooed by grace of language and gesture, blushed" (135)—perhaps because he disdains such rhetoric or because it is beyond him.

In the third piece, Professor MacHugh performs "impromptu" Joyce's version of what he, and Yeats, viewed as "the greatest extempore speech ever made":[13] John F. Taylor's oration (delivered at a meeting of the Law Students' Debating Society, 24 October 1901) in defense of Irish language revival, home rule, and national freedom. The speech culminates in a popular Irish analogy: a vision of Moses defying Pharaoh, leading the Israelites out of Egypt, and descending from Sinai "*bearing in his arms the tables of the law, graven in the language of the outlaw.*" This time all of the audience—like the one listening to Hynes's elegy for Parnell in "Ivy Day in the Committee Room"—is awed and silenced. "That is oratory, the professor said, uncontradicted" (*U*, 137). Joyce had no interest in involving himself in a movement of Irish cultural nationalism that Yeats and others saw as "recourse to the unspoilt freshness of ancient Ireland [that] could signal an escape out of the seemingly inevitable process of decay, decrepitude and cultural entropy,"[14] but he takes it seriously enough to represent it at some length, whether at face value or parodically.[15] For Beckett such an Ireland has disappeared and left only its detritus behind.

Stephen contemplates entering the oratorical competition as MacHugh launches into Taylor's speech: "Noble words coming. Look out. Could you try your hand at it yourself?" (*U,* 136). Deciding to risk it, he implicitly equates himself with Moses when he declares that he has a vision too and then prods himself into performance: "On now. Dare it. Let there be life" (139). As Shari Benstock notes, Joyce provides the parable's details from Stephen's experience, and thereby hints at the workings of his creative imagination: the two "*Frauenzimmer*" he sees on the strand in chapter 3 become "Two Dublin vestals . . . elderly and pious, [who] have lived fifty and fiftythree years in Fumbally's lane" (139), where he recalls an encounter he had with a prostitute (47, 139); and he hears a voice crying "Eight plums a penny! Eight for a penny!" just before he enters the newspaper office (92).[16]

Stephen also adopts the Ireland/Israel analogy from Taylor's speech, but instead of bringing down the tablets from Mount Sinai, Stephen's Moses is stranded on Mount Pisgah, viewing the Promised Land he never enters. And like the plumstones that the two "Dublin vestals" spit out, Stephen's pointless parable falls on arid ground both times he tells it. In "Aeolus" he emits a nonverbal final punctuation that gives momentary pause to his nonlisteners as they head for the pub: "He gave a sudden loud young laugh as a close. Lenehan and Mr O'Madden Burke, hearing, turned, beckoned and led on across towards Mooney's" (142). Myles Crawford then dryly asks if he is finished and where they got the plums (142, 143), revealing that he has been no more an attentive audience than the others since Stephen had just said that they bought them from a girl as they entered Nelson's pillar (139). Professor MacHugh, Stephen's one attentive listener, discerns no moral in his parable, but he is amused by Stephen's throwaway reference to Nelson on his pillar as a "onehandled adulterer" and laughs appreciatively at Stephen's title (142, 143). Later that night Bloom, an Irish Jew who embodies rather than stages the Ireland/Israel analogy and an ever tactful host and audience, simply ignores the parable when Stephen narrates it to him (638): perhaps he's had enough plumstones for one day since, regarding Boylan's tryst with Molly, Bloom had thought, "he gets the plums, and I the plumstones" (359). As for Stephen's *Hamlet* performance, it is a much larger, more self-aggrandizing, and therefore riskier effort and, consequently, a far greater failure when it too falls on unreceptive ears.

Rejecting all work, even literary (599), Stephen opts instead for the role of performing seal that he learned from his father's example and authority. His tedious and self-undermining presentation in "Scylla and Charybdis"—a party piece that Mulligan's cry of pain indicates he has heard before (17)—is prepared for by his "*Terribilia meditans*" in "Proteus" (45) that serves as a kind of rehearsal. Reincarnating Menelaus wrestling with Proteus, Stephen himself assumes various guises: Aristotle, Jacob Boehme, Bishop Berkeley, Lessing, among others, imagining himself as philosopher, theoretician, and mystic as he strolls along Sandymount Strand. Curiously perhaps, Stephen, though analogized to Byron and Shelley in *Portrait* and boasting in "Scylla and Charybdis" that he would have been banished from Plato's commonwealth (178), fails to envision himself here in the role of poet. In fact, recalling his rejection of the priesthood he thinks, "Cousin Stephen, you will never be a saint" (40), a line that also assails his artistic pretension since it echoes Dryden's famous putdown, "Cousin Swift, you will never be a poet."

Stephen's first step, or acting direction, in "Proteus" is to contemplate the "ineluctable modality of the visible"; he then searches for meaning and performative clues in the "signatures of all things I am here to read" (37). Narrative shifts in the first four lines of the chapter's second paragraph dramatize Stephen's role as Protean performer: "Stephen closed his eyes to hear his boots crush crackling wrack and shells. You are walking through it howsomever. I am, a stride at a time. A very short space of time through very short times of space" (37). In the first three of these sentences, the narrative voice shifts from third person to second to first; the fourth sentence implies the first-person voice of Stephen. This declension underscores not only his Protean quality in the chapter, but also his self-consciousness as a performer of multiple roles. The second and third sentences also enact a minidialogue between Stephen as self-referential actor and Stephen as investigator of the quotidian world. A structurally analogous interchange between voices in his head occurs shortly thereafter when Stephen imagines, but then rejects making, a visit to his mother's family (39), in part because he anticipates that his uncle will sing to him an aria about family decline: "Houses of decay, mine, his and all" (40).[17] A far more elaborate and barbed inner dialogue plays out during his *Hamlet* performance in "Scylla and Charybdis" (discussed below).

Stephen self-mockingly recalls playing the part of the Wildean dandy in Paris: "My Latin quarter hat. God, we simply must dress the character. . . . Just say in the most natural tone: when I was in Paris, *boul'Mich'*, I used to" (41). He had gone into exile with grand intentions: "You were going to do wonders, what? Missionary to Europe after fiery Columbanus" (42),[18] and to achieve recognition: "For that are you pining, the bark of their applause?" But he has become one with history's failed pretenders, vicariously living their lives (45), assuming the tragic role by dint of dressing for the part by wearing his "Hamlet hat" (47). Hardly an aesthetic achievement, Stephen's shadowy performance in "Proteus" fails to enact his definition in *Portrait* of art as "the human disposition of sensible or intelligible matter for an esthetic end" (*PA*, 242). Rather, he can be seen as rehearsing on the sidestage of Sandymount Strand for his much-anticipated pièce de résistance in the library.

Stephen's autobiographical reading of *Hamlet* has a self-serving purpose: to impress the assembled literati by outdoing them at their own game and to demonstrate that Shakespeare, triumphing over squalid circumstances, transformed personal betrayal into artistic achievement, as Stephen presumably means to do. Yet the autobiographical fallacy is a trap, one that creates contradiction: Stephen views Ann Hathaway's seduction of Shakespeare as "the original sin that darkened his understanding, weakened his will and left in him a strong inclination to evil" (*U*, 203), while also insisting that a "man of genius makes no mistakes. His errors are volitional and are the portals of discovery" (182). Stephen himself fails this test of artistic genius since he is haunted by "errors, boasts, mistakes" (475), which stifle rather than liberate creativity. Further, Stephen's lecturing here, like his disquisition on aesthetics in chapter V of *Portrait*, reflects his priorities: he spends far more time talking about art than creating it.

Like Gabriel Conroy preparing for his after-dinner speech, Stephen takes pains to establish the dramatic occasion in the library scene. His imagined curtain rises—"Lifted."—and he self-consciously constructs the appropriate setting and mood: "—It is this hour of a day in mid June, Stephen said, begging with a swift glance their hearing" (180). As with "The Parable of the Plums," he chivvies himself along as he seeks to engage his audience: "Local colour.

Work in all you know. Make them accomplices" (180). And still, in Cranly's phrase, "supersaturated with the religion in which you say you disbelieve" (*PA*, 283), he formulaically invokes the Jesuit muse to assist his public meditation, "Composition of place. Ignatius Loyola, make haste to help me!" (*U*, 180), just as he had invoked the Jesuit motto when writing his first poem in *Portrait* (*PA*, 77). He coaches himself on how best to ingratiate himself with his audience—"Smile. Smile Cranly's smile" (*U*, 176) and "Flatter. Rarely. But flatter" (200)—while mentally entreating their sympathetic engagement: "See this. Remember"; "Listen"; "Bear with me" (184, 186). He then muses on the meaning of his performance, both for them and for himself: "What have I learned? Of them? Of me?" (206). Stephen works hard to make his performance interactive: "Speech, speech. But act. Act speech. They mock to try you. Act. Be acted on," he urges himself (203). And when the moderate John Eglinton offers a compromise theory of Shakespeare's relationship to his work—"—The truth is midway, he affirmed. He is the ghost and the prince. He is all in all"—Stephen, echoing his earlier admonition to himself, hastens to agree: "—He is, Stephen said. The boy of act one is the mature man of act five. All in all. In *Cymbeline*, in *Othello* he is bawd and cuckold. He acts and is acted on" (204).

Despite, or perhaps because of, the malleability Stephen demonstrates here, an internal voice critiques his performance as it unfolds: "I think you're getting on very nicely. Just mix up a mixture of theolologicophilolological"; "What the hell are you driving at? I know. Shut up. Blast you. I have reasons"; "Are you condemned to do this?" (196, 199). Finally, tired of his own voice, Stephen silently repudiates the elaborate theory of creativity he is presenting (203, 205), thus subverting the paradigm of artistic accomplishment he ostensibly seeks to establish. What his parable of familial sundering and reconciliation (185, 187) does seem to emphasize is his unacknowledged need, and failure, to achieve with Simon the kind of rapprochement that Joyce eventually achieved, through music, in his postelopement reconciliation with John Joyce: "Paternity may be a legal fiction" (199), but "—A father, Stephen said, battling against hopelessness, is a necessary evil" (198). Stephen's later punning comment to Bloom—that he left his father's house "To seek misfortune" (575)—rings with the truth of the confessional. His tedious exposition ends up bemusing his audience rather than amusing or persuading them, winning little praise, and provoking Eglinton's dismissive comment, "a French triangle," and Mulligan's mockery. Immediately after he finishes, Eglinton pointedly reminds Mulligan of Moore's party that evening (while ignoring Stephen [206]), even as Stephen allows Mulligan to haul him off to buy drinks. Following dejectedly (206), Stephen, like Prufrock hearing the mermaids' song, recalls watching the birds for augury of his artistic vocation near the end of *Portrait,* an augury that has proved false: they do not prophecy for him. Again surveying the sky from the library steps, he sees no birds this time, and arrives at a sense of deflation: "Cease to strive" (209), he counsels himself, which may well signal the end of his artistic ambition.

Whatever Stephen's underlying motives for exposing himself in this curious performance, what seems to be uppermost in his mind is the vague possibility of making money, which becomes something of a leitmotif of his. In *Portrait* he counters MacCann's insistence that he add his name to a testimonial for universal peace by asking to be paid for signing (*PA,* 229). He similarly asks Haines, a satirical depiction of an English folklorist collecting quaint Celtic lore, whether he would make any money from the book he wants to make of his sayings. When Haines laughs dismissively, Mulligan chides Stephen, "You put your hoof in it now," implying that, though doing what Mulligan had advised in touching the wealthy Haines for money, Stephen has given offense to the "Sassenach" and that such offense still matters (*U,* 16, 7, 9). In "Scylla and Charybdis," John Eglinton tells Stephen he is "the only contributor to *Dana* who asks for pieces of silver," and spurns him by saying he should not expect payment for his *Hamlet* theory since he does not believe in it himself (205). His last try—"For a guinea, Stephen said, you can publish this interview"—elicits only Mulligan's "honeying malice" (205). A would-be bard lacking both traditional patronage and the mendicant's skill, Stephen continually undermines himself as both moneymaker and artist, following the path of failure trod by public cadgers like Lenehan, in both *Dubliners* and *Ulysses,* and his own pub-performing father.

Mulligan repeatedly blunts Stephen's potential authority and authorship. "He fears the lancet of my art," Stephen thinks, "as I fear that of his" (*U,* 7), but Mulligan's besting of him goes even further: though he urges Stephen to play poor old Ireland and the English cultural tourist as he does (16), Mulligan also usurps Stephen's performative role. What Bowen calls "Mulligan's debunking parody of Stephen's priestly posture" at the opening of "Telemachus,"[19] reprises, elaborates on, and surpasses in wit and dramatic quality the paler version that Stephen enacts at the beginning of chapter V of *Portrait*. Unlike Stephen, Mulligan expansively tells jokes (for example, about God as "the collector of prepuces" [*U*, 13]) and performs several songs, beginning with Yeats's "Who Goes with Fergus?" (9), a song, as his mother's ghost reminds him (540), identified with Stephen. Mulligan also sings "On Coronation Day," "For old Mary Ann," and "The Ballad of Joking Jesus,"[20] all in chapter 1 (11, 13, 18–19).

In "Scylla and Charybdis," Mulligan trumps Stephen's *Hamlet* performance by recounting a mock interview with "the bard Kinch at his summer residence" in nighttown; singing parodies of Burns's "John Anderson My Jo" and Yeats's "Baile and Aillinn"; criticizing Stephen's (that is, Joyce's) hostile review of Lady Gregory's *Poets and Dreamers;* and then, usurping the Moses role, reading "his tablet: *Everyman His Own Wife/or/A Honeymoon in the Hand/(a national immorality in three orgasms)*" (206–8). Moore's failure to invite Stephen to the evening's festivities (while including Mulligan) and Russell's exclusion of him from his anthology of young Irish poets may be not aberrations or personal snubs (as Stephen wants to believe), but reasonable judgments of their respective qualities and achievements as artists and entertainers (185). As the actions of the old milk woman in "Telemachus" suggest (she "bows her old head" to Mulligan; "me she slights" [14]), Stephen is, as Mulligan calls him, a "dreadful bard" (6) and an equally bad performer, the result, Mulligan tells Haines, of his Catholic upbringing: "—They drove his wits astray, he said, by visions of hell. He will never capture the Attic note. . . . He can never be a poet. The joy of creation. . . ." He laughingly adds, "He is going to write something in ten years" (239).

Stephen consistently thwarts all possibility of having an artistic career, even while repeatedly mocking himself for doing so. It is uncertain whether Stephen will help the patronizing Englishman Haines, whom he impresses with his verbal felicity, to make a collection of his sayings, but their interchange inaugurates a pattern for Stephen, who does no writing or publishing on his own. In "Aeolus," Stephen delivers Deasy's letter for publication, but ignores Myles Crawford's challenge to write *Dubliners* or *Ulysses*: "Give them something with a bite in it. Put us all into it, damn its soul. Father, Son and Holy Ghost and Jakes M'Carthy" (130). In "Scylla and Charybdis" Stephen similarly ignores Lyster's suggestion that he present his *Hamlet* theory to the public (188). And in "Eumaeus," when Bloom praises Simon's singing of "M'appari" from *Martha,* "which . . . he heard, or overheard . . . yesterday, a privilege he keenly appreciated, from the lips of Stephen's respected father, sung to perfection," Stephen, referring to himself, says that he does not sing it (615), and then changes the subject. Ever pragmatic, if unwittingly patronizing, Bloom, recognizing the talents of both father and son, suggests that Stephen, with his "phenomenally beautiful tenor voice," could have a musical career and still "have heaps of time to practise literature in his spare moments"; but the only response he receives are "three smoking globes of turds" from a nearby horse (616, 618).

Curiously, even the few performances that Joyce allows Stephen are absent from Joseph Strick's film of *Ulysses,* which, whatever its other virtues, omits much of the novel's cinematic quality.[21] As if to underscore Stephen's artistic and performative failure, Strick allows him only a single party piece, one demanded of him by Buck Mulligan at the lying-in hospital and that he turns into a crude, and feeble, attack on his tormentor. Joyce sets the scene, which Mary Lowe-Evans calls "a parody of the Last Supper where the apostles become drunken bachelors,"[22] by having the inebriated Punch Costello roar out "Étienne chanson" ("Stephen song"), a parody of "The House That Jack Built" that depicts the act of creation as making a place for drink:

> *Behold the mansion reared by dedal Jack,*
> *See the malt stored in many a refluent sack,*
> *In the proud cirque of Jackjohn's bivouac.* (376)

The macrocosmic response to Costello's drunken song literalizes Stephen's remark to Deasy in "Nestor" that God is "a shout in the street" (34): "A black crack of noise in the street here, alack, bawled, back. Loud on left Thor thundered: in anger awful the hammerhurler. Came now the storm that hist his heart. . . . But the braggart boaster [Mulligan] cried that an old Nobodaddy[23] was in his cups it was muchwhat indifferent and he would not lag behind his lead" (376–77).

In Strick's film the scene is both made more dramatic and reconfigured to focus on the Stephen-Mulligan antagonism. As self-appointed master-of-ceremonies, Mulligan first transforms the drunken revelers into an audience: "Shut your bleeding gobs won't you?", and then mock-seriously performs a bawdy song before he patronizingly introduces the tipsy Stephen: "The priestified bard will now perform for your particular entertainment. Right old son." With an anatomical skeleton hanging on the wall over his shoulder seeming to serve as audience, Stephen sings in plain chant his version of the Benediction Hymn, "*Adoro te,*" directing the last line at Mulligan:

> *Adoro te devote*
> *Latens Deitas*
> *Jesu Christ figuris*[24]
> Stick it up your arse.

The immediate response, an intensified version of the mocking, applause-like rain at the end of Stephen's lecture to Lynch in Strick's film of *Portrait,* is a huge thunderclap (which Stephen, like Joyce, fears) and that Mulligan, reversing the meaning of the hymn's first two lines ("O Godhead hid, devoutly I adore thee"), interprets as a revealed godhead of sorts: "Jesus, the old cod upstairs. Have a care Stephen. It's Nobodaddy himself. He's jabbering over the roofs." Thus, Strick's Mulligan caustically links performance (Stephen's if not his own) with divine retribution.

Sean Walsh's *Bloom* also depicts little in the way of Dedalian party pieces. It offers a much shorter version of the drunken hospital scene, with Stephen performing a parodic mass, "Now drink we, for this is not my body, but my soul's

6. Stephen sings with anatomical skeleton as background audience. Joseph Strick, *Ulysses.* Courtesy of Joseph Strick.

embodiment," and receiving "loud, drunken agreement" when he declares for the pub: "upon the utterance of the word . . . Burkes!" In the classroom he tells the students his confusing definition of a pier and dismays them with his riddle when they ask for a story. He also briefly performs his *Hamlet* theory in the library, drunkenly plays a pianola in the brothel, and "recites an Irish song to Bloom" at 7 Eccles Street.[25] Like Strick, Walsh finds, and bodies forth, little evidence of Stephen's being on the threshold of a successful artistic career.

Joyce's Stephen enters the nighttown world of "Circe" chanting "*with joy the introit for paschal time*" (*U,* 410). This echo of Mulligan's parodic mass at the book's opening continues the competition for the blasphemy prize between Stephen and his "Usurper" (23). As a coda to his speech on aesthetics in *Portrait,* Stephen tells Lynch that he considers the rhetorical strategies of Socrates, Aristotle, and Shakespeare to be their way of expressing the sexual repression and frustration they experienced in their domestic lives (411). At Bella Cohen's brothel an equally frustrated Stephen declaims with impressive drunken nonsense (474); summons up as the eight beatitudes his drinking companions from "Oxen of the Sun" (479); and muses on playing the piano: "Play with your eyes shut. Imitate pa. . . . Minor chord comes now. Yes" (486).[26] Bowen suggests that the questing Bloom hears piano music that he shrewdly judges to be Stephen playing: "A man's touch. Sad music. Church music. Perhaps here" (449).[27] When, following the music, Bloom enters Bella Cohen's, his hunch is confirmed: Stephen, standing at the pianola, with two fingers "repeats once more the series of empty fifths" (*U,* 474). But in both Strick's movie and the book, Stephen refuses the call of Florry, one of the prostitutes, to "Sing us something. Love's old sweet song." He responds like the churlish Bartell D'Arcy of "The Dead": "No voice. I am a most finished artist. . . . Spirit is willing but the flesh is weak" (487). Stephen's motivation here is ambiguous: is he rejecting the specific song—which is associated with Boylan's seduction of Molly and ultimately with the reunion of Molly and Bloom—or the performative invitation? Does being a most finished artist mean that he considers himself complete and self-contained, and therefore in no need of performing or creating in order to be an artist? Or is he finished *as* an artist before he has even begun? Either way his self-assessment and nonperformance here undermine the notion, shared by many critics, that, by the end of *Ulysses,* he is on his way to becoming its author.

Stephen's few performances within the performative "Circe" are mainly clownish turns that reinflect his Icarian role and earn him contempt and dismissal. After being called "a spoiled priest. Or a monk" by Florry and a "cardinal's son" by Lynch, Stephen imaginatively plays a drunken prelate, mocking the role he had rejected in *Portrait* but that has remained repressed within him and emerges here. He refers to himself as "Cardinal sin. Monks of the screw." Then, in an evolutionary regression that blends the biological and priestly fathers who still loom large within him, Simon and Stephen merge: "*His Eminence Simon Stephen Cardinal Dedalus, Primate of all Ireland, appears in the doorway, dressed in red soutane, sandals and socks. . . . Round his neck hangs a rosary of corks ending on his breast in a corkscrew cross.*" Sardonically reprising his role at the Christmas dinner in *Portrait,* Stephen "invokes grace from on high with large wave gestures and proclaims with bloated pomp." Attacked by a swarm of midges, he says now what he could not say then: "I'm suffering the agony of the damned" (491–92).

When Zoe, another prostitute, hears that Stephen is back from Paris, she demands that he "Give us some parleyvoo." Obliging for once, Stephen falls into the role of stage French guide to the delights of Parisian night life that he had rehearsed in "Proteus," playing shill or pimp in broken English for tourists of the sex trade: "Thousand places of entertainment to expenses your evenings with lovely ladies . . . perfect fashionable house very eccentric where lots cocottes beautiful dressed much about princesses like are dancing cancan and walking there parisian clowneries extra foolish for bachelors foreigns the same if talking a poor english how much smart they are on things love and sensations voluptuous"—a performance that provokes much laughter and encouraging cheers from Bella and the whores (530).

Stephen's thoughts of his flight to Paris, like numerous others, evoke Simon Dedalus, "grandoldgrossfather" (530), a debased reincarnation of *Portrait*'s heraldic "fabulous artificer, . . . a quaint device opening a page of some medieval book of prophecies and symbols, a hawklike man flying sunward above the sea" (*PA,* 196). In "Proteus," Stephen recalls Simon's Daedalian imagery that derides him both as would-be artist and in his relationship with his mother's family: "Did you see anything of your artist brother Stephen lately? No? Sure he's not down in Strasburg terrace with his aunt Sally? Couldn't he fly a bit higher than that, eh?" (*U,* 38–39). Stephen remembers Kevin Egan in Paris telling him, mainly on the basis of oral similarity, "You're your father's son. I know the voice" (43). The recollection serves to emphasize that Stephen remains Icarus to his father's Daedalus, a thought that recurs explicitly in "Scylla and Charybdis": "Fabulous artificer, the hawklike man. You flew. Whereto? Newhaven-Dieppe, steerage passenger. Paris and back. Lapwing. Icarus. *Pater, ait.* Seabedabbled, fallen, weltering. Lapwing you are. Lapwing be" (202). His journey out was a deflated version of what he had imagined at the end of *Portrait;* his journey back, like the last moments of Icarus and Jesus, seems to have culminated in a vain cry for help from an indifferent father.

Simon, who contemptuously performs the authoritative paternal role with Dilly (228–29), is equally dismissive of Stephen's needs and fate even as he threatens to write a letter complaining about Buck Mulligan's bad influence on his son (85–86). In "Sirens," Simon rejects the implicit appeal that Lenehan, still "in his role of professional jester and entertainer for drinks"[28] but misreading his audience, makes in his flattering reference to "Stephen, the youthful bard" who had enthralled Dublin's intellectual elite with his interpretive performance of *Hamlet* (*U,* 252). The Simon who appears in "Circe," drunkenly reprising the role of "Old father, old artificer" from *Portrait* (*PA,* 299), "swoops uncertainly through the air, wheeling, uttering cries of heartening, on strong ponderous buzzard wings," urging Icarus/Stephen onward and upward to his destruction with cries derived from the Joyce family coat of arms: "Head up! Keep our flag flying! An eagle gules volant in a field argent displayed" (*U,* 532).[29] Toward the end of "Circe," the paternally protective Bloom assures the Watch, who threaten to arrest Stephen: "Father is a wellknown, highly respected citizen" (561), though this is one role that Simon (who is "all too Irish," according to Stephen [579]), never plays.

In the dance that follows his vision of Simon, Stephen waltzes with the three whores in turn, but then, as all the others "wheel, whirl, waltz, twirl" in couples, he becomes isolated, dancing with his ashplant, soaring on his own: he "*frogsplits in middle highkicks with skykicking*" in what he calls a "dance of death" (538). As if summoned to participate, the ghost of Stephen's mother appears, deformed by leprosy and putrefaction (539), and bodying forth his guilt and oppressive past that, like the fox in his riddle, he thought he had safely buried. Recoiling in fear and rage from her command to repent, Stephen once again proclaims "*Non serviam!*" (541) before smashing the light fixture in a temporal and historical climax: "*Time's livid final flame leaps and, in the following darkness, ruin of all space, shattered glass and toppling masonry*" (542). Subsequently accosted by Privates Carr and Compton, drunken English soldiers, Stephen dismisses threats of violence as if he were defining himself in his guise of minor poet (as MacCann calls him [*PA*, 231]): "Noble art of selfpretence. Personally, I detest action" (*U*, 547). Reenacting losses at the hands of the British that recur throughout *Dubliners* and Irish history, Stephen's fall and defeat are assured by Private Carr, who punches him in the face and nearly knocks him out (558).

A sympathetic and perhaps prescient Bloom offers Stephen a last chance for success as a performer: "With a touch of fear for the young man beside him . . . he brought to mind instances of cultured fellows that promised so brilliantly, nipped in the bud of premature decay, and nobody to blame but themselves" (600). Recalling Simon's superb singing in the Ormond bar (615), Bloom recognizes in the talents of the son those of the father as Stephen sings to him on their way to Eccles Street: "A phenomenally beautiful tenor voice like that, the rarest of boons, which Bloom appreciated at the very first note he got out, could easily, if properly handled . . . command its own price where baritones were ten a penny" (617). But like father, like son: the continuing strong presence of Simon Dedalus, Joyce's most fully developed exemplar of such a noncareer, saps Stephen's energy and blights his life. "The youthful bard," in the fawning phrase Lenehan speaks to Simon, remains "the famous son of a famous father" (251–52), and Bloom's suggestion and offer, like all the others Stephen has received that would advance a career, are ignored. Instead, he keeps on singing, "boldly, but not loudly" (618), as they traverse the empty streets.

References to Bloom as an artist, albeit mainly ironic ones, recur throughout the text. In "Aeolus," MacHugh suggests that Bloom embodies "the gentle art of advertisement" (130); in "Wandering Rocks" Lenehan says "seriously": "He's a cultured allroundman, Bloom is. . . . There's a touch of the artist about old Bloom" (225).[30] In "Circe," when Bloom and Stephen gaze in a mirror together, only the "face of William Shakespeare, beardless, appears there" (528), reflecting each and both. Advising Stephen to take up a musical career, Bloom hints at a thwarted career of his own: Stephen would, thereby, be "made a lot of by ladies out for sensation, cases of which, as he happened to know, were on record, in fact, without giving the show away, he himself once upon a time, if he cared to, could easily have . . ." (617), a thought endorsed by the "Ithaca" narrator who claims that Bloom's possible "future careers" had once been "in the church, . . . at the bar, . . . [and] on the stage" (642). Although this narrator subsequently calls Bloom's temperament scientific as opposed to Stephen's artistic, the pronouncement occurs in a context that conflates them as consubstantial—"Bloom Stoom" and "Stephen Blephen" (635)—and shortly before Bloom is again said to personify "the modern art of advertisement" (636).

Throughout the day, Bloom displays far more interest in and knowledge of theater, music, literature, photography,[31] and art than Stephen does; and "nearly every aspect of Bloom's personality," even more than Stephen's, "is reinforced or described somewhere in the book in musical terms."[32] He contemplates going to see the minstrel performer Eugene Stratton or a play (though distracted by concern for others—Mrs. Dignan, Mina Purefoy, Stephen—he does not do so): "Could I go to see *Leah* tonight, I wonder. . . . Or the *Lily of Killarney*? Elster Grimes Opera company. . . . *Fun on the Bristol.* Martin Cunningham could work a pass for the Gaiety" (*U,* 89). Bloom, who is supportive of Molly's singing career and even considers arranging tours for her (582), regrets the absence of music when he visits All Hallows Church: "Not going to be any music. Pity. Who has the organ here I wonder? Old Glynn he knew how to make that instrument talk, the *vibrato*. . . . Molly was in fine voice that day, the *Stabat Mater* of Rossini. . . . I told her to pitch her voice against that corner. I could feel the thrill in the air, the full, the people looking up" (79).

Familiar with Ireland's oral tradition, Bloom, alluding to one of Moore's melodies, thinks of the appropriateness of the location as he passes Tommy Moore's statue: "They did right to put him up over a urinal: meeting of the waters" (155). Despite some typical misattributions, Bloom displays a nuanced appreciation of music, while valuing a variety of aesthetic achievements: "Some of that old sacred music is splendid. Mercadante: seven last words. Mozart's twelfth mass: the *Gloria* in that. Those old popes keen on music, on art and statues and pictures of all kinds. . . . Still, having eunuchs in their choir that was coming it a bit thick. What kind of voice is it? Must be curious to hear after their own strong basses" (79). He also knows and appreciates various literary texts, including *Hamlet* and *Robinson Crusoe* (105), and operas (Donizetti's *Lucia di Lammermoor* and Mozart's *Don Giovanni,* for example

[106, 171]). He displays an interest in ancient Greek statuary and Irish architecture (174–75), even if his interests are primarily prurient and strategic: hiding from Boylan.

Yet temperament and situation conspire to cast Bloom in passive more than active roles, as audience—for Catholic ceremony, Molly, Blazes Boylan, and Simon Dedalus—rather than as creator or performer. The pattern is firmly established in "Calypso," when he serves Molly breakfast in bed, and "Lotus Eaters," the chapter of indolence and inertia. He observes, listens, remembers. Sitting on the "cuckstool" at the end of "Calypso," for example, Bloom recalls "The Dance of the Hours," a song central to the novel's structure, that played the night that he and Molly first met Boylan: "Morning after the bazaar dance when May's band played Ponchielli's dance of the hours. Explain that morning hours, noon, then evening coming on, then night hours" (66–67).[33] Already he accepts, passively and with equanimity, "the passage of time and the cyclical nature of things, including Molly's passions."[34]

Barbara Hardy persuasively argues that "Bloom does not excel at public story-telling, being frequently ill at ease in society, subdued by other men's talents, embarrassed, preoccupied and solitary. He is a great story-teller nonetheless, though the stories he tells are not in the least Homeric. . . . But Bloom also gets through his day, and his life, by telling stories, chiefly to the excellent audience of himself."[35] Except at certain key moments and more generally in "Circe," "Eumaeus," and "Ithaca," Bloom's rejoinders, usually arising in response to someone else's performance, seem constrained by circumstance and his instinctive deferral to others. En route to Dignam's funeral his voiced narrative about the near-drowning of Reuben J. Dodd's son is interrupted and preempted by Simon Dedalus and Martin Cunningham, although he tells silent stories about each of them, and then about Dlugacz the butcher, the girl in his shop, O'Connell the cemetery keeper, the chemist in "Lotus Eaters," the blind man he helps across the street, Gerty MacDowell, and numerous others he encounters during the day.

He conjures up the image of the confession as all coded masque, a kind of dance of mutual desire, with the recounting of sin turned into a drama of seduction, if properly interpreted: "More interesting if you understood what it was all about. . . . Confession. Everyone wants to. Then I will tell you all. Penance. Punish me, please. Great weapon in their hands. More than doctor or solicitor.

Woman dying to. And I schschschschschsch. And did you chachachachacha? . . . Then out she comes. Repentance skindeep. Lovely shame" (*U,* 79). Bloom's reaction to the mass is one in a series of variously motivated Joycean parodies: for self-aggrandizement (Stephen's mock mass that begins chapter V of *Portrait*); for the expression of salacious wit (Mulligan's intoning of the *Introibo* at the beginning of *Ulysses*); and for the expression of amused respect for the church as an organization and opiate: Bloom's "*Corpus.* Body. Corpse. Good idea the Latin. Stupefies them first. . . . Rum idea: eating bits of a corpse why the cannibals cotton to it" (77). As Ophelia says of Hamlet, Bloom is "as good as a chorus" (*Hamlet* 3.2.224).

Twice during the ride to the cemetery, and again after his arrival there, Bloom listens intently and reacts silently to others holding forth as his own most insightful and entertaining lines remain unspoken. In response to Simon's going on about Stephen, Bloom thinks: "Noisy selfwilled man. Full of his son. He is right. Something to hand on. If little Rudy had lived" (*U,* 86). After Power's denunciation of suicide, "Mr Bloom, about to speak, closed his lips again." He then silently recalls the self-inflicted death of his father, ill with a fatal disease, and the coroner's kindly summation: "Verdict: overdose. Death by misadventure" (93). And at the cemetery, Bloom's internal running commentary on the Catholic service that he understands only minimally echoes his thoughts in All Hallows Church in the previous chapter (77): "Makes them feel more important to be prayed over in Latin. . . . Said he was going to paradise or is in paradise. Says that over everybody. Tiresome kind of a job. But he has to say something" (100). Keeping his thoughts to himself, Bloom, like Molly, performs primarily for his own inner audience. Yet it is in this section that, for the first time in the book, he is physically described ("a face with dark thinking eyes" [98]), as if, in his silent performance, he were being carefully observed by his fellow-mourners.

In "Lestrygonians," Bloom's pattern of passivity contrasts with the shared passion he recalls in his first lovemaking with Molly on Howth Head: "Wildly I lay on her, kissed her. . . . Hot I tongued her. She kissed me. I was kissed. All yielding she tossed my hair. Kissed, she kissed me" (168). The memory is, however, framed and mocked by an image of copulating flies: "Stuck on the pane two flies buzzed, stuck" and "Stuck, the flies buzzed" (167, 168). The stuck flies, suggesting both a debased carnal embrace and Bloom's deflated sense of his own sexual worth—"Me. And me now" (168)—anticipate chapter 11, "Sirens," which occurs at the 4 P.M. trysting hour and displays Bloom at his most passive, anticipating not love but cuckoldry in a chapter that, by my count, uses variations on the word "wait" fifty-two times, verbs of aurality ("listen," "hear") seventy-two times, verbs of viewing (primarily "look" and "see") seventy-one times, and "lost" about twenty times.

Bloom considers rushing after Boylan—"Follow. Risk it. Go quick. At four. Near now. Out" (253)—but restraint is the Odyssean note of "Sirens," and Bloom remains in the Ormond bar, listening and waiting, an audience not a performer: "Want to listen sharp. Hard. Begin all right: then hear chords a bit off: feel lost a bit" (267). Interwoven with the entrance and exit of Blazes Boylan on his way to the expectant Molly (254, 257) and conversations Bloom overhears that seem to be about Molly's extramarital affairs, various party pieces are performed as if for his delectation and distraction. The songs he hears mostly concern lost love: Simon plays "Goodbye, Sweetheart, Goodbye" on the piano, which seems to sing of "the strain of dewy morn, of youth, of love's leavetaking, life's, love's morn" (253); Richie whistles "All Is Lost Now" (from Bellini's opera *La Sonnambula*): "—A beautiful air, said Bloom lost Leopold. I know it well" (261–62); and Simon sings "M'appari" from Flotow's opera *Martha:* "*When first I saw that form endearing*" (262). Bloom then recalls the night he met Molly: they were the last two contestants in a game of musical chairs, which she won, and then she turned siren, "Singing. *Waiting* she sang. I turned her music. . . . Bosom I saw, both full, throat warbling. . . . Fate. Spanishy eyes. . . . At me. Luring. Ah, alluring" (264).[36]

Contrasting with Bloom's passivity and sense of fatefulness, Boylan is in nearly constant motion in this chapter. He stops briefly to listen to Simon playing "Goodbye, Sweetheart, Goodbye," but immediately departs as it ends: "—I'm off, said Boylan with impatience" (256).[37] Bloom, immersed in musical performance and nostalgia, "sang dumb," stuck, waiting passively: "Wish they'd sing more. Keep my mind off" (265, 269). His only overt contribution to the performative mode of "Sirens" is his "musical" passing of gas—"Ppffff" (279)—that echoes the transformation of Simon's pipe into a fife through which he blew "two husky fifenotes" (250).

Bloom's musical performance, such as it is, has both sexual and political implications. Envisioning female anatomy, he thinks of women's bodies as wind instruments: "Play on her. Lip blow. Body of white woman, a flute alive. Blow gentle. Loud. Three holes all women" (273). But Boylan rather than Bloom gets to play Molly—"Blazes doing the tootle on the flute" (306)—while Bloom recalls his failure even to learn whether Greek statues have anuses (273). The political implications are equally ambiguous, for Bloom's gaseous "music" accompanies his reading of the last words of Robert Emmet (an Irish rebel executed by the British in 1803 for treason):

> *When my country takes her place among.*
> Prrprr.
> Must be the bur.
> Fff! Oo. Rrpr.
> *Nations of the earth.* No-one behind. She's passed. *Then and not till then.* Tram, Kran, kran, kran. Good oppor. Coming. Krandlkrankran. I'm sure it's the burgund. Yes. One, two. *Let my epitaph be.* Kraaaaaa. *Written. I have.*
> Pprrpffrrppffff.
> *Done.* (279)

Bloom's "performance" here, which serves as commentary on both Boylan's sexual prowess and Emmet's grandiose nationalistic rhetoric, harmonizes sense and sound in a way that provides a fitting overture to the next chapter, "Cyclops," in which an aroused Bloom, in the novel's boldest action, fearlessly confronts the Citizen's hyperbolical and phallic performance of Irish patriotism.

Like Odysseus, Bloom is a man of many parts and many roles. As Lenehan says, "He's a cultured allroundman, Bloom is. . . . He's not one of your common or garden . . . you know . . ." (225). Bloom is, in fact, what Mr. Best quotes Coleridge as calling Shakespeare, "myriadminded" (197), or, in the crude neologism of the priestly vision, Father Farley, in "Circe," an "anythingarian" (463). Dr. Dixon sums him up as "a finished example of the new womanly man" (465), and he has, according to the narrator of "Ithaca," a "firm full masculine feminine passive active hand" (627). "Sirens" depicts Bloom as a composite of cuckolded husband, despairing lover from Flotow's opera *Martha*, pseudonymous flirtatious correspondent, and virile lover from Molly's raunchy novel-reading: "Lionelleopold, naughty Henry with letter for Mady, with sweets of sin with frillies for Raoul with met him pike hoses" (276).

In "Cyclops," Bloom bravely opposes the Citizen's violent xenophobia and anti-Semitism, proclaiming justice and love, and attaining an apotheosis of sorts as a contemporary Elijah. Given both his character and the novel's paucity of overt action, Bloom's audacious self-assertion here stands out as uniquely and unexpectedly heroic and transformative, as he later acknowledges: "People could put up with being bitten by a wolf but what properly riled them was a bite from a sheep" (612). The confrontation gains resonance from its context: Bloom's metaphoric defeat of Boylan that, though it initially makes his situation more difficult, inflects the book's final chapter in a perhaps unexpected way. For in "Cyclops" Joyce reveals that the phallic Sceptre, on whom Boylan had bet two pounds for himself and Molly, has lost the Gold Cup race despite being the overwhelming favorite. Instead, the race is won by Throwaway, "a bloody dark horse," a "rank outsider" (321, 312)—epithets that are attached to Bloom throughout the day. We have, consequently, reason to anticipate a sexual triumph for Bloom by the book's end.

In "Circe," the chapter constructed as dramatic performance, Bloom, though he is in quest of Stephen, largely reverts to passivity and acquiescence, being assaulted in most of his visions. As if completing the suspended phrase Bloom writes in the sand ("I. AM. . . . A.") and verbalizing the image at the end of "Nausicaa" ("The stick fell in silted sand, stuck" [364]), Molly appears to mock his passivity: "O Poldy, Poldy, you are a poor old stick in the mud!" (418). Visions of both his father and Mrs. Breen chide him for being in nighttown, with Mrs. Breen then waxing nostalgic about his success as a performer of party pieces: "You were the lion of the night with your seriocomic recitation and you looked the part. You were always a favorite with the ladies" (422). Gerty MacDowell of "Nausikaa" accuses him of looking at "all the secrets of my bottom drawer" (420). The Watch call him a public nuisance (430), triggering a review of his day's events through the prism of his sense of guilt and isolation. Challenging Bloom's "*false badge of the Legion of Honour,*" Martha Clifford accuses him of being a "heartless flirt," and Mary Driscoll of sexual "carryings on" (432, 433, 436). Called upon to "make a bogus statement," Bloom pleads not guilty and "begins a long unintelligible speech" that unintentionally provokes laughter (437). Several women then appear to accuse him of writing obscene letters with masochistic fantasies (like those Joyce wrote to Nora): "He implored me to soil his letter in an unspeakable manner, to chastise him as he richly deserves, to bestride and ride him, to give him a most vicious horse-whipping" (442). Bloom, whose intensest desires are for self-abasement, claims that "I meant only the spanking idea. A warm tingling glow without effusion. Refined birching to stimulate the circulation" (443). But Alexander J. Dowie attacks him as both a libertine and a hypocrite (464).

In his greatest masochistic vision, Bloom acts out "with desire, with reluctance" (496), kneeling in submission before "Bella Cohen, a massive whore-mistress" (494). As "anythingarian" he becomes female, a pig, a footstool; he is attacked savagely, ridden by Bello, dressed as a woman, treated as a dirty animal; his repressed sins rise up to denounce him; he is enslaved, sold at auction, mocked as a cuckold. His latent feminine inclinations coalesce with his sense of failure as a husband: Bello accuses him of following women while other men romp with Molly. She tells him, "Die and be damned to you" (508), and his funeral follows. In his subsequent vision of Boylan and Molly's tryst, Bloom plays facilitating flunky, willing cuckold, voyeur, cheerleader. When Boylan tells him, "You can apply your eye to the keyhole and play with yourself while I just go through her a few times" (527), Bloom fawningly asks if he might bring along two friends to watch and take photographs (527), and then cheers on Boylan's performance.

Yet as if reprising and playing out on a far grander scale Stephen's enumeration of Simon's career in *Portrait,* Bloom in "Circe" becomes a man of many parts: not only passive voyeur, "well-known cuckold," and "adorer of the adulterous rump," but a performer extraordinaire—dancer, singer, impresario, author-journalist, as well as good Samaritan, Lord Mayor of Dublin, president, king, and czar, among others. Contrasting with his masochistic visions are Bloom's delusions of grandeur, triggered by Zoe's saying: "Go on. Make a stump speech out of it" (452). An agitator against tobacco as an alderman, he is hailed as "our future chief magistrate!" "the world's greatest reformer," "emperor-president and king-chairman . . . Leopold the First," and, according to John Howard Parnell, "successor to my famous brother!" (452–56). As a street is renamed Boulevard Bloom, he makes an impassioned political speech against undefined evils, repudiates his morganatic wife and marries a princess, and is granted freedom of the city. Commanding the building of "the new Bloomusalem," he is hailed as czar, dispenses Jewish law (as Moses) and justice (as Daniel), and, while rejecting bribes, solves the myriad problems presented to him.

Woven into both Bloom's masochistic and supremacist fantasies is his vision of himself first as artist and then as performer. He makes grandiose artistic claims that implicitly mock Stephen's: "I follow a literary occupation. Author-journalist. In fact we are just bringing out a collection of prize stories of which I am the inventor, something that is an entirely new departure" (434). Relieving himself in the outhouse in "Calypso," Bloom contemplated writing a "prize titbit" in the manner of Philip Beaufoy for the newspaper *Titbits:* "Might manage a sketch. By Mr and Mrs L.M. Bloom. Invent a story for some proverb" (66–67). But Beaufoy, with whose story Bloom had then wiped himself, now rises up to denounce him as "a plagiarist. A soapy sneak masquerading as a littérateur" (435). Yet the thought recurs in "Eumaeus" when Bloom, "a bit of an artist in his spare time" (607), again thinks of writing for publication and profit: "*My Experiences,* let us say, *in a Cabman's Shelter*" (601). The venture seems unlikely to come to fruition, but Bloom's thought does anticipate Molly's; for, like Haines with Stephen, Molly affirms such a project: "If I only could remember the one half of the things [he says] and write a book out of it the works of Master Poldy yes" (705). It's one of many things she affirms about him in her soliloquy.

Unlike its treatment of Stephen, Strick's film expands Bloom's performative role, especially in "Nighttown." It adds a soft-shoe routine that he performs with Josie Breen, while preserving "the myriad scenes that show Bloom to be a man of infinite variety—a spiritual human circus troped by the theatricality of a central circus ring and patent burlesques."[38] Amid the "pantomimic merriment" of "Circe," Bloom turns entertainer, a career that he, like Joyce, had once contemplated (*U,* 617, 642). As if to vouch for his pedigree, his mother appears as Alladin's stage mother, "*In pantomime dame's stringed mobcap, crinoline and bustle, widow Twankey's blouse with muttonleg sleeves buttoned behind*" (417). Bloom performs juggler's tricks and draws rainbow-colored handkerchiefs from his mouth (459). Nosey Flynn, echoing Florry's fruitless appeal to Stephen, urges him on: "Give us a tune, Bloom. One of the old sweet songs" (463). More outgoing and responsive than Stephen, Bloom performs for an appreciative audience, singing a song of cuckoldry "with rollicking humour" that leads Paddy Leonard to acclaim him a "Stage Irishman!" and the Veiled Sibyl to hail him enthusiastically: "I'm a Bloomite and I glory in it. I believe in him in spite of all. I'd give my life for him, the funniest man on earth" (463–64).

Though Lenehan, repeating Beaufoy's charge, denounces Bloom as a plagiarist for stealing his riddle (463), numerous women commit suicide for love of him even as the fickle mob turns antagonistic as it did toward Parnell (464). Bloom pleads his innocence, calling on Dr. Mulligan to explain his medical problem—he's a "virgo intacta" (465)—but he then gives birth to eight sons. Performing miracles to prove he's the Messiah (467), Bloom achieves a theatrical martyrdom, being pelted with "soft pantomime stones" and defiled by "bonafide travellers and ownerless dogs" (469). But he shortly reappears as a stage Irish peasant out of Synge, bidding farewell to the woman of the house (470). In a final self-assertive gesture, Bloom, preparing to depart the brothel, rouses himself in defense of Stephen's money. Impressed and bested, the sarcastic Bella offers him a grudging accolade: "(*admiringly*) You're such a slyboots, old cocky. I could kiss you." Zoe expands the compliment: "Deep as a drawwell" (520–21). Bloom does not bow and depart the stage triumphantly at this point, but he might well have done.

Between "Circe" and "Ithaca," Joyce's itinerants stop at the cab-man's shelter where, in Irish parlance, they "shorten the road"[39] by listening to the tales of D. B. Murphy, a false Odysseus who has no intention of returning to his Penelope. Murphy's guise is that of the Gaelic storyteller who "excelled in the interpretation of wonder-tales, the voyage-tales (*immrama*), and the intricate overseas-adventure type of narrative."[40] Murphy embodies a culture and chapter of fabrication in which tales, unfolding with a logic of their own, accord with circumstances of time, place, occasion, audience, and so on. Their meaning and shape, as Zimmermann maintains, largely depend on the active and creative responses of listeners, who are their "final arbiters."[41] Bloom responds with skepticism and wariness to Murphy and his stories: trying to prevent Stephen from revealing his name, asking probing questions, doubting his veracity. Bloom's thoughts employ such phrases as "sailing under false colours," "discrepancy," "fictitious," "wily old customer," "not much inherent probability," "spurious." "Sherlockholmsing him" (*U*, 582–90). Bloom asks Stephen, "Do you think they are genuine? He could spin those yarns for hours on end all night long and lie like old boots" (590). But successful storytelling stimulates narrative responses from its audience, and Bloom reacts by contemplating husbands returning home to faithless wives, adventuring at sea, arranging a concert tour for Molly, opening up new tourist routes between Ireland and

England, Ireland's mythic past, the life of sailors—all stories that, in part, narrate his life and day. Murphy's storytelling also reminds Bloom of the value of selective narration, especially for returning adventurers, which will serve him well when he later recounts to Molly his expurgated version of his experiences out in the world.

After all his wanderings, Joyce's peripatetic Greek/Jew Dubliner makes his way home where, instead of slaughtering suitors, he accepts them (or rather him[42]) with equanimity, and plays host to his homeless guest with "supererogatory marks of special hospitality" (629; the words "host," "guest," and "hospitality" recur frequently throughout "Ithaca").[43] Leo, the zodiacal sign of Bloom, Gifford suggests, belongs to those who "are creative, authoritative and kind, those who are . . . intent on seeking the welfare of others as well as of themselves. They like to be good hosts and are profoundly loving and scrupulous in their homes."[44] An expansive host who has tacitly welcomed (or at least accepted) the impresario Blazes Boylan into his house, Bloom now opens a welcoming door for Stephen, kindles a hearth fire, prepares "a collation for a gentile . . . and served extraordinarily to his guest and, in reduced measure, to himself, the viscous cream ordinarily reserved for the breakfast of his wife" (*U*, 629). Though said to be of scientific temperament, Bloom had "written a really beautiful letter, a poem in itself" (466); and he now recalls the concluding lines of "his first piece of original verse written by him, potential poet" (630), anagrams he had once made on his name (631), and an "acrostic upon the abbreviation of his first name [that] he (kinetic poet) [had] sent to Miss Marion (Molly) Tweedy" (631)—a set of achievements not notably inferior to those of the "artistic" Stephen.

As gestures of reciprocity, Bloom and Stephen perform for each other: first, on Bloom's turf (ads), so to speak, then on Stephen's (song). Bloom's ad to sell stationary—one that he had proposed to Wisdom Hely who rejected it "because he didn't think of it himself first" (147)—is slightly titillating: he would have "an illuminated showcart . . . in which two smartly dressed girls were to be seated engaged in writing" (637), although such a live performance seems likely to misfire. Stephen counters by describing a scene in a hotel parlor of a restless young woman writing "Queen's Hotel, Queen's Hotel, Queen's Hotel, Queen's Ho . . ." (637), which proves unsettling to Bloom as he recalls that the Queen's Hotel—the same one or another—was where his father had died. Stephen seems not to know this, so the pain he causes Bloom is presumably unintentional; in fact, his description with its use of the word "solitary" five times in six lines, seems self-referential. Bloom, in any event, assumes a benign interpretation: "Coincidence" (637). The contrasting ironies of the songs they sing for each other are, however, far more striking. First, Stephen offers his fragments from *Shule Aroon,* a Gaelic lament for young Irishmen who have gone abroad to fight for others; Bloom counters with a description of the bride's beauty from *The Song of Solomon* (640).[45] Bloom then chants for Stephen what he can remember of *Hatikvah,* "The Hope," the song of Jewish freedom and independence that became the Israeli national anthem. Recalling only the "first distich," Bloom completes the performance with "a periphrastic version of the general text" (641). Stephen reciprocates, insensitively and all too fully, with the nasty ballad of *Little Harry Hughes,* in which "the jew's daughter" entices Harry Hughes, a Christian boy, into her house and then ritually murders him, a performance that, understandably, makes Bloom extremely uncomfortable (643–45).[46]

Despite Stephen's violation of guestly propriety, the hospitable Bloom offers him lodging for the night, an offer that Stephen, perhaps fearing he would share Harry Hughes's fate now that Bloom has musically proclaimed his ethnicity, "Promptly, inexplicably, with amicability, gratefully" declines (648), as Bloom had once declined a dinner invitation given by Stephen, aged five, and seconded by Simon (632). The narrative responder of "Ithaca," who enumerates the advantages that would accrue to guest, host, and hostess should Stephen stay, is at a loss to explain his departure. But having rejected Simon's drunken posturing as an inadequate embodiment of Irish authority and performance, Stephen has turned completely inward and become incapable of accepting a substitute paternal figure, regardless of how good-hearted.

Having urinated alone, if poetically, on the beach early in the day, Stephen now urinates companionably alongside Bloom (655), before, unlike Joyce, heading off alone (though he has no place to sleep [573]), as cut off from the future as from the past. If Molly is Nora on this most important day in Joyce's life, then this fictionalized version of himself at twenty-two, bereft of partner and having progressed little in the direction of discovering "the mode of life or of art whereby [his] spirit could express itself in unfettered freedom" (*PA,* 290), is heading off in another direction entirely. Having in fact regressed from where he was at the end of *Portrait,* with its imagery of flight that augured achievement that has remained unfulfilled, Stephen lacks even such a good omen as that as he departs 7 Eccles Street with nowhere to go and no one to go with him. No Stephen's-day book lies in his creative future.

The focus at the end returns to Bloom, and then turns to Molly—and hence to their relationship. In "Ithaca," the catechism's questioner notes that new stars have marked not only Shakespeare's birth, but also "(presumably)" those of Bloom, his son Rudy, Stephen, and myriad others; and Bloom himself is skeptical of astrological explanations of earthly phenomena (654). His homecoming is, nonetheless, marked by two omens of good fortune: both what the narrative questioner calls a macroscopic "celestial sign" and a successful manipulation of a difficult lock that results in the opening of "an obsolescent unhinged door" that enables Stephen to depart (656). As Harry Blamires puts it: "A star (Molly) shoots across from Vega in the Lyre (Boylan) towards the sign of Leo as Bloom unlocks the garden gate. . . . The insertion of male key in 'unstable' lock also prefigures sexual reunion."[47]

Bloom then reclaims his household and restores order: "downturning the upturned rugfringe" (*U*, 659), presumably the result of Boylan's moving the furniture at Molly's behest;[48] fumigating with "aromatic oriental incense" (659), as Odysseus did after slaying the suitors;[49] reverting "the inverted volumes" on his book shelf (662); and brushing from the bed the remains of Plumtree's Potted Meat that Boylan and Molly had shared there (683). He then executes what may be his finest performance of the day: a sanitized version of his adventures for his most intimate and skeptical audience, who considers his recounting "a pack of lies" (691), but nonetheless welcomes him home. The prudent Bloom, like Odysseus, carefully expurgates his narrative, omitting "the clandestine correspondence between Martha Clifford and Henry Flower, the public altercation at, in and in the vicinity of the licensed premises of Bernard Kiernan and Co, Limited, 8, 9 and 10 Little Britain street, the erotic provocation and response thereto caused by the exhibitionism of Gertrude (Gerty), surname unknown" (687). He thus safely completes his journey back to "Warm beds: warm fullblooded life" (110) that had saved him from death in "Hades" and to his wife's acceptance and affirmation that includes even a possible future son (273) with moly/Molly, his charm against Circean wiles and nonprocreative sex. He and Molly come to "rest relatively to themselves and to each other, . . . the childman weary, the manchild in the womb" (688).

Between Bloom's losing consciousness in sleep and Molly's stream-of-conscious recapitulating of *her* day and life (also a censored performance), an implicit interchange occurs that seems to augur well for their future. Drifting off, Bloom becomes a figure from *Sinbad the Sailor,* a pantomime, loosely based on *The Odyssey,*[50] for which he was once commissioned to write verses for "a topical song" (631; his failure to do so provokes an extended, roundabout explanation [631–32]). Bloom recalls one episode from the pantomime in particular: "There was a square round Sinbad the Sailor's roc's auk's egg" (689). Molly's first words as Penelope—"Yes because he never did a thing like that before as ask to get his breakfast in bed with a couple of eggs" (690)—suggest that she has mistaken the mythical allusion for a mundane request, or else that Bloom actually made the request between the last words Joyce affords him and Molly's "Yes" that begins (and ends) "Penelope." Either way, her affirmative response is at first somewhat grudging: she resents his "giving us his orders for eggs and tea and Findon haddy and hot buttered toast" (714). But confident of her own sexual prowess ("I could quite easily get him to make it up any time" [695]), she then acquiesces in her fashion: "Ill just give him one more chance Ill get up early in the morning . . . then Ill throw him up his eggs and tea in the moustachecup" (729),[51] implying that Bloom has successfully sung in advance for his breakfast, and that this implicit rapprochement may bode well for their future together.

Although Molly reenacts Penelope's caution at accepting the returned Odysseus, is undeceived by his bowdlerized narrative, and enumerates his many faults at length, Bloom emerges from her interior monologue as central to her life and superior to Boylan, whom she finally views in wholly negative terms: "*no* thats *no* way for him has he *no* manners *nor no* refinement *nor no nothing* in his nature slapping us behind like that on my bottom because I *didnt* call him Hugh the ignoramus" (726; my emphasis). Having displayed an all too expansive hospitality toward Boylan earlier in the day, Molly as Penelope offers a disapproving assessment of Boylan that contrasts strikingly with the nearly one hundred occurrences of "yes" with which, from first to last word in "Penelope," she affirms Bloom.

At his lowest moment, at 4:30 P.M., the trysting hour when time (or at least his instrument for measuring it) had stopped for him, Bloom had heroically accepted responsibility both for what has happened to his marriage and for a future that even now still seems possible:

> Last of my race. . . . Well, my fault perhaps. No son. Rudy. Too late now. Or if not? If not? If still?
>
> He bore no hate. (273)

Though she blames Bloom for her affair with Boylan, is as yet unready to give up her new lover who "anyhow . . . didn't make me pregnant" (719),[52] and even fantasizes an affair with Stephen, Molly comes round to the same thought as Bloom in her soliloquy: "Supposing I risked having another not off him [Boylan] though . . . Poldy has more spunk in him yes thatd be awfully jolly" (694). Having left Calypso and returned to Penelope, Bloom manages, through equanimity and attenuation, to overcome all suitors save one. And even that one, especially since his star may be on the wane with Molly, might now be dispatched by "ben Bloom Elijah" (330), who, having stood up for justice and love and his reclaimed Jewish heritage against the Citizen's violent anti-Semitism, and having out-performed all competitors throughout the day, has achieved an apotheosis of sorts, albeit a highly imaginary and theatrical one.

The "Penelope" chapter of *Ulysses* reprises the ending of "The Dead" by depicting, as their names rhythmically suggest, an analogously semi-estranged couple: the dactylic Gabriel and trochaic Gretta have metamorphosed into the euphoniously reincarnated Leopold and Molly. Further, the women's doubly trochaic and overheated lovers, Michael Furey and Blazes Boylan, are doused by death-dealing rain, in the case of the former, and by Molly's less fatal but perhaps equally dampening vision of "that awful deepdown torrent[53] O and the sea the sea" (732) that links Gibraltar and Howth, first love and married love. In her final affirmation Molly conflates Mulvey, the husband that might have been, with Bloom, the returned hero, while Boylan fades from the picture—a process enacted, in part, through the changing representation of certain recurring songs ("All Is Lost Now," "Those Lovely Seaside Girls," "M'appari," "Là ci darem") throughout *Ulysses,* none more crucially than "Love's Old Sweet Song."

In "Calypso" (61) and "Lotus Eaters" (72) both Molly and Bloom recall this song in a way that implies that it has a shared significance for them; subsequently, it becomes part of a motif of musical allusions to Molly's sexual liaison with Boylan that, beginning with "Calypso," appear in every chapter except "Wandering Rocks."[54] Among the detritus of Boylan's visit, Bloom discovers "the music in the key of G natural for voice and piano of *Love's Old Sweet Song*" (*U*, 659), suggesting that the adulterers at least spent *some* of their time together preparing for the upcoming concert tour. In "Penelope," however, the song reprises its original modality, recurring as Molly's thoughts, like Bloom's earlier, turn back to the "dear dead days beyond recall" of their first lovemaking on Howth Head, which they nonetheless summon up with similar vividness and nostalgia: "Loves old sweet sonnnng. . . comes loves sweet ssooooooong. . . comes looooves old. . . piano quietly sweeeee pianissimo eeeee one more song," completing the song as she "let[s] a fart" (706, 713, 714) that echoes Bloom's "performance" at the end of "Sirens."[55] In bed together and perhaps on the verge of procreative sex (Bloom's "proximate erection" and Molly's "incipient excitation" suggest a first stage in that process [686]), Bloom and Molly are already considerably closer to consanguinity than the Conroys at the end of "The Dead." It is not in the failed artisthood of Stephen Dedalus, but in this loving meeting of minds and bodies, skewed though they are, that Joyce offers his greatest hope for an artistic and domestic future.

5 Vying for Center Stage in Beckett's Early Plays

Beckett's career, it may be said, began both where Joyce's began and also where it ended. Their initial parallel flights from Dublin and Ireland, from what Kevin Whelan calls "the vacuity of post-Famine Irish culture,"[1] took both of them to the expatriate life in Paris, which proved congenial to iconoclastic writings that remained focused on Ireland. Gluck demonstrates that Beckett's writings from 1929 to 1934 are "filled with puns, witty analogies, multilingual allusions, and occasional but unmistakable references to Joyce's own works. Not so readily apparent, but perhaps more significant with regard to the future novels and plays, is the presence in these early writings of peculiarly Joycean themes and motifs."[2] For example, just as the old milkwoman who represents Ireland for Stephen Dedalus not only cannot speak Irish but thinks it's French when she hears it (*U,* 14), so Molloy is also ignorant of his native tongue: "Tears and laughter, they are so much Gaelic to me" (*Molloy, SB2,* 32).[3] Like Joyce's fiction, Beckett's early writings are saturated—though less overtly and directly, and as echoes and traces rather than full-scale representation—with both the places and atmosphere of Dublin, especially its performative nature, as well as with the twin Odyssean themes of exile and oral narration.

Joyce's writings also often resound, as parody or reductio ad absurdum, in Beckett's work after World War II. In both "Sirens" and *Godot,* for example, watches cease functioning to mark the sense that "Time has stopped" (*Godot, SB3,* 30),[4] but Beckett elaborately dramatizes the theme of waiting, and in *Godot,* despite Didi's pronouncement that "Time flows again already" (70), it never does, while Hamm proclaims, "time is over, reckoning closed and story ended" (*Endgame, SB3,* 153). Didi, like Bloom, is a fund of useless information and speculation, but Bloom's is part of a rich imaginative life, one that helps him to negotiate, more or less successfully, his way through his day and city.

Lucky's speech, which Lionel Abel considers a parody of Joyce's style,[5] derives in part from *Finnegans Wake:*

> He lifts the lifewand and the dumb speak.
>
> —Quoiquoiquoiquoiquoiquoiquoiq! (*FW,* 195.5–6)

Stephen's self-directed exhortation ("Folly. Persist." [*U,* 177]) anticipates Beckett's wearily, feebly, insistent voices: "Come on, Gogo, return the ball, can't you, once in a way?" (*Godot, SB3,* 7); "You must go on, I can't go on, I'll go on" (*Unnamable, SB2,* 407); and "Try again. Fail again. Fail better" (*Worstward Ho, SB4,* 471). Beckett's failing better, in contrast to Joyce's, ultimately seems to mean failing finally.

In *Endgame,* which Abel reductively asserts "is directly and undeviatingly about Joyce and Beckett's relationship to him,"[6] Mother Pegg, like Molly Bloom, is referred to as "a flower of the field," but "she's extinguished" (*SB3,* 121). Krapp, like Joyce's Eveline, experiences his life-determining moment at Dublin's waterfront: Eveline stands rooted at the North Wall, resisting Frank's call to sail away with him; Krapp has his vision on Dún Laoghaire's pier (where Stephen awaits a different sort of transport at the end of *Portrait*) and then bids "farewell to love" in a punt on the stream. Despite the stagnation of his life in *Ulysses,* it's still possible to view Stephen at its end as heading toward artistic achievement, love, or both; Krapp's future is already behind him. *Embers* reprises the meditative mode and littoral setting of the "Proteus" chapter of *Ulysses* (the isolated self confronting strand, sea, sky, and memory), though the world that Stephen, opening his eyes, determines is "there all the time without you: and ever shall be, world without end" (*U,* 38) is reduced to fading voices in Henry's head that he pleads with to sustain the dialogue and his existence: "Keep it going, Ada, every syllable is a second gained" (*SB3,* 208). *Embers* has no world outside of Henry's head, and he exists only, and only so long, as he speaks his monologue, as a voice inside our own.

The trimming of fingernails by the man in *Act Without Words I* (*SB3,* 192), like the filing of them by Winnie in *Happy Days* (*SB3,* 293–94) and the mistress in *Play* (*SB3,* 358), mimes Stephen's vision of the artist as "like the God of the creation . . . indifferent, paring his fingernails" (*PA,* 252); in *Embers,* Henry evokes, and repeats, an Irish version of Bloom's night sky vision of Boylan's constellation: "Vega in the Lyre very green" (*SB3*, 199). But Beckett's paring and night sky lack cosmic resonance. *Words and Music* meshes language and rhythm in an abstracted, enfeebled version of the full-scale performance of "Sirens," while the Music Masters in both *Embers* and *Words and Music* are bodiless, radio-play reincarnations of Beatrice, the semi-ethereal piano teacher in Joyce's play *Exiles.* All three characters in *Play* begin their monologues with "yes," Molly Bloom's first and last word in "Penelope," but they affirm nothing except that they are constrained to speak their invariant script. Joyce seems to have sought to embed *Finnegans Wake* in Beckett (by encouraging Beckett's *Exagmination* essay and his work on translating "Anna Livia Plurabelle" into French) and Beckett ("Bethicket," *FW,* 112.5) in *Finnegans Wake,* perhaps so that Beckett would stick there or at least have to begin where Joyce ended.[7] Or to suggest that Beckett had already done so, as with the apparent reference to his first single-authored publication, *Whoroscope: "a Good Horuscoup"* (*FW,* 105.28–29).

In his late plays, too, Beckett returns to Joycean beginnings. *Ohio Impromptu* is a Beckettean homage to his predecessor and their mutual storytelling, with its "old world Latin Quarter hat" of the sort Joyce often flamboyantly wore (as did Stephen Dedalus in Paris [*U,* 41]); its setting on Paris's Isle of Swans, where Joyce and Beckett would walk together, two of a kind yet mirror opposites; and its depiction of the Seine, "in joyous eddies its two arms conflowed and flowed united on" (*SB3,* 474), recalling Joyce's Anna Livia Plurabelle coursing to the sea. *What Where* echoes Joyce through being inspired in part by Thomas Moore's "Oft in the Stilly Night," the song sung by the Dedalus children in *Portrait* (*PA,* 177), and Rimbaud's "Voyelles," which Joyce would recite by heart. As in *Footfalls, Ghost Trio, . . . but the clouds . . . ,* and *Nacht und Träume, What Where* occurs in a ghostly playing area where, as Moore has it, "*Sad Memory brings the light/Of other days around me.*" Rimbaud's poem dresses the vowels in different colors ("A noir, E blanc, I rouge, U vert, O bleu"), which Beckett considered for *What Where*'s Bam, Bem, Bim, and Bom (as he had the players in *Quad*), before reclothing them, "in the stage version at least, in identical long gray gowns."[8]

Both Joyce and Beckett had vexed relationships with their ostensibly completed texts, not unlike their characters—Gabriel Conroy and Stephen Dedalus; Pozzo, Hamm, and Winnie—who endlessly rehearse or neurotically command the staging and audiences for their performative pieces. Both writers had enormous difficulty publishing in Ireland and then with French printers who introduced numerous errors when typesetting *Ulysses* and *Watt.* Joyce was conflicted by process and product—desperate to have *Ulysses* published, yet so reluctant to let it finally go that it "grew by one third in proof" (*JJ2,* 513). Beckett, after having published his plays, became increasingly engaged with their productions, and so, as his working notebooks demonstrate, revised them (often substantially) during rehearsals, and then republished them, often, though not always, in transformed versions.

What was supposed to be product for Joyce (page proofs) became integral to the creative process; at all stages, Joyce fleshed out his art "with a multitude of particulars. . . . His manuscripts, at least the later ones, are revised by accretion" (*ED,* 55). For Beckett what had at first seemed secondary process (performances of published works) often led to substantially revised, usually significantly reduced, products. Such categorical subversion of process and product has led to the copyright wars over *Ulysses* and the publication of variant versions of such plays as *Waiting for Godot, Endgame, Krapp's Last Tape,* and *Rockaby.* As Knowlson writes of the resulting textual instability of Beckett's plays, "Beckett stated that, when he came to direct his own work in the theatre, he studied the text as if it had been written by someone else, adding that perhaps it did come from someone else, since it had been written so long ago."[9] Beckett initially determined that he would direct in order to ensure the accurate translation of text into production,[10] but changes invariably occurred, and usually at Beckett's instigation. As Gloria MacGowran, the wife of the Beckett actor Jack MacGowran put it, "The only way Sam can find out how things work theatrically is to be there, to direct."[11] Each new production, even (or perhaps especially) with Beckett as director, differed from previous ones; hence, all his dramatic writings became work that was always still in process, performance scripts rather than completed texts.

The arcs of the two writers' careers, however, took antithetical shape. When Beckett, a few years after Joyce's death, determined that he had to make a second break—a break that took him into writing in French, into the theater, and toward minimalism and the depiction of bleakness—it was in part a reaction against Joyce's continuing strong influence. Ever more expansive and inclusive, Joyce's published writings began with the *Dubliners* miniatures and culminated in *Finnegans Wake*'s "endless Dublin night, the centuries of it, an encyclopaedia of world history to rival *The Book of Kells* in its intricate and ornate detail. . . . an example of the human condition in all times and all places."[12] Beckett, who saw Joyce as a synthesizer and himself as an analyzer,[13] formulated the break with Joyce in these terms: "The more Joyce knew the more he could. He's tending toward omniscience and omnipotence as an artist. I'm working with impotence, ignorance."[14] Or again, "I realised that Joyce had gone as far as one could in the direction of knowing more, [being] in control of one's material. He was always adding to it; you only have to look at his proofs to see that. I realised that my own way was in impoverishment, in lack of knowledge and in taking away, in subtracting rather than adding."[15] Beckett's work became ever more constrained and constricted as he sought refinement into silence, moving ever closer toward his implicit ideal: not a Joycean compendium of human experience, but the blank script or empty theater that he told Alan Schneider, his American director, would be achieved if *Godot* were performed "my way."[16]

Beckett parallels Joyce in seeming to have launched many of his early characters from Wilde's epigrammatic comment that I quote in the preface: "We Irishmen have done nothing, but we are the greatest talkers since the time of the Greeks." But the contrary trajectory of Beckett's dramatic career suggests, rather, the transformation that Neil Jordan implies in *Michael Collins* when he has the brutal British Secret Serviceman Soames reinflect the stereotype. After his torturing of Broy, who has betrayed his British employers by aiding Collins, proves unsuccessful because he still refuses to speak, Soames comments, "The trouble with the Irish is they'll sing at the drop of a hat; ask them to talk and they won't."[17] Soames's vaudevillian image, which is straight out of Beckett, replicates the latter's performative extremes: at one end, the compulsive "singers" of party pieces like Lucky in monologue, Mrs. Rooney in *All That Fall,* Henry in *Embers,* Winnie in *Happy Days,* the figures in *Play,* Mouth in *Not I;* at the other, the mute characters who are poked and prodded like Broy and put through their paces in *Act Without Words I* and *II, Rough for Theatre II, Film, Eh Joe, Ghost Trio, . . . but the clouds . . . , Catastrophe,* and *What Where.* For all they endure, these latter will not, or cannot, simply perform as required.

In addition to the salon, *Godot*'s characters emerge from the cross-talk tradition of the vaudeville stage, the burlesque, the music hall, and the movies of Charlie Chaplin, Buster Keaton, Laurel and Hardy, and the Marx brothers to present their party pieces: songs, stories, riffs, games, practical jokes, and interactive routines, often using the audience as foil or target rather than trying to serve or please them. (For the play's first production, Roger Blin wanted to cast Chaplin as Didi and Keaton as Gogo.[18] For the first American production Keaton was considered for Didi and Marlon Brando for Gogo; its failure to come off was a bitter disappointment to Beckett.)[19] There is a kind of appropriate irony that *Godot*'s American premiere in 1956 was staged at the Coconut Grove Playhouse in Miami, that it cast Bert Lahr as Gogo reprising his Cowardly Lion riffs, and that its "advertising bill[ed] the play as 'the laugh sensation of two continents.'"[20]

The resulting turmoil caused by the production was not on the scale of the Abbey Theatre uproar over Synge's *Playboy of the Western World* in 1907 (although Jonathan Croall mentions "a near riot" during one of Blin's productions and blows between supporters and protestors on another occasion[21]), but the cultural dissonance was surely as great. Those who viewed the play as about the human condition predicated upon doubt and incertitude, ignorance, impotence and stasis, defeat, and the desperate assertion of hope in the face of despair tended to view the characters' performances as gutsy, if ineffectual, attempts to assert meaning of a kind against the void, to perform a life they are precluded from living, to kill time as it kills them. Many others felt cheated, victimized by a hoax. When "The Best New Play" award for 1956 was being considered, *Godot* was impossible to ignore, but nor were the contradictory responses to the play easily reconciled. It was, consequently, awarded a prize that has never been given before or since but that seems appropriate under the circumstances: "The Most Controversial Play of the Year." And, as Knowlson notes, "its success was assured when it became controversial."[22]

Joyce sought to fictionalize Dublin with such accuracy that, were it to be destroyed, it could be reconstructed from his writings. Hence, his characters inhabit a socially interactive world that affords the full panoply of ritual performance as defined by Rappaport (see preface) and that judges them largely by their ability or failure to perform party pieces. In contrast, Beckett created a theatrical existence beyond such a prospect: his settings exhibit increasingly fewer traces of a social past, and it seems impossible to imagine an offstage existence to which his dramatic figures might have recourse or occupy. Instead, they become script- or score-bound, like musical notes, as Beckett becomes less an author and director and more a composer and conductor. Whatever world his characters might once have inhabited has run down and out, its traces remaining only in brief recollections and allusions. When Didi tries to conjure up a different reality, "a million years ago, in the nineties," Gogo tells him to "stop blathering" and help him off with his boots (*Godot, SB3,* 4); he later recalls that they spent the entire evening—which was worse than the pantomime,[23] the circus, the music-hall (28)—"blathering about nothing in particular" (58).

Written in the aftermath of World War II, *Godot* is set in countryside suggestive of "the defoliated landscape of post-Holocaust Europe."[24] Like *Endgame,* in which there "is no more nature," *Godot* dramatizes a depleted world whose inhabitants are at the end of their tethers (literally in Lucky's case), barely managing to hang on with receding, or no, hope of release from either desperate privation or their lives. The loss of food for Didi and Gogo (the last carrot, denuded chicken bones) also recalls the Irish Famine, a catastrophe that, according to William Wilde, broke "up the very foundations of social intercourse."[25] Rather than foreground the Irish catastrophe, however, Beckett's "tragicomedy in two acts" anticipates his later stage narrators by telling a deflected story, one that encapsulates the broader view of history that Karl Marx derives from roughly contemporary events in France.[26] For Marx too history became a farce where "'nothing happens' not just twice but indefinitely, 'wearying with constant repetition of the same tensions, the same relaxations.' The ancient plot takes over,"[27] and historic personages, like scripted characters, seem to have no option but to play out predetermined roles.

Like Marx's Napoleon III, Pozzo, a wealthy landowner, enters *Godot* bearing a strong sense of entitlement, marked by genteel manners and decorous performance—or, rather, an unintentional parody of them. In Act 1 he can scarcely bring himself to acknowledge that he belongs to the same species as Didi and Gogo. In Act 2, however, Pozzo's savage denunciation of time seems to target not only Didi's persistent questions but also those, like *Ulysses*'s supercilious Haines, who blame some abstract notion of history rather than England for Ireland's plight (*U,* 20), and thereby imply that the past represents a meaningful process or story: "Have you not done tormenting me with your accursed time! It's abominable! When! When!" (*SB3,* 82). Pozzo finds even less meaning in history's narrative sequence than Marx does.

Beckett originally conceived of Estragon and Vladimir (as he later did Krapp) as clowns in the line of Chaplin, Keaton, and Laurel and Hardy, but with his approval they quickly assumed the tramp personae that their clothes and circumstances imply, the outcast figure that Yeats found in Irish tradition: the wandering beggar, vagrant, fool (often blind, like Pozzo and Hamm) who is also a master storyteller. *Godot,* like *Endgame* and *Happy Days,* recalls more expansive times, social worlds and occasions once conducive to party pieces, but though these plays are saturated with performative imagery and their characters are always "on," always performing, never allowed any privacy, their performances are maimed rituals, vestiges of a social environment and occasions—"pre-cataclysmic . . . more festive, colourful"[28]—that are only dimly remembered or imagined by Act 2 of *Godot.* As Eric Bentley noted as early as 1956, *Waiting for Godot* "is undramatic but highly theatrical,"[29] which the characters emphasize by displaying a self-conscious awareness of being on a stage.

Though barely able to recall old skits and routines, Didi and Gogo nonetheless vie for center stage, compete for performative priority, even dominance, and insist on imposing themselves on their indifferent or hostile and begrudging audiences. As if taking its cue from Stephen's horrific experience as retreat audience in *Portrait, Godot* repeatedly assails the fundamental notion of a willing audience, without which performance is meaningless. Didi maintains that bearing witness has become excruciating, dangerous to one's health: "One daren't even laugh any more" (*Godot, SB3,* 5); "You'd make me laugh if it wasn't prohibited" (13). Lacking a social context, both Didi and Gogo contemptuously comment on their theater audience, assailing it metaphorically as part of a degraded landscape: "Inspiring prospects," says Gogo sarcastically (8); "that bog," according to Didi (9). When Gogo, feeling besieged, "*recoils in horror*" from a possible exit through the auditorium, Didi comments, "Well I can understand that" (66). The only audiences that enjoy themselves within this play are those who watch Didi—who, directed to "end of the corridor, on the left," seems to be leaving the auditorium when he asks Gogo to "keep my seat" (28)—unwittingly perform what is received as a party piece while he urinates offstage. First Gogo, who makes gestures "*like those of a spectator encouraging a pugilist*" (10), and then Gogo and Pozzo together (29) find pleasure in what, for Didi, is a painful act.

Didi and Gogo themselves determinedly avoid being relegated to the role of audience for each other—a resistance that adumbrates the declining vitality of party pieces. Didi wants to narrate the story of the two thieves crucified with Christ ("Shall I tell it to you?"); and although Gogo tries to prevent it ("No."), Didi persists: "This is not boring you I hope." When Didi demands an engaged response, a bored Gogo mockingly feigns interested audience: "(*with exaggerated enthusiasm*). I find this really most extraordinarily interesting" (6–7). Didi, in turn, rebuffs Gogo's attempt to tell him "the story of the Englishman in the brothel" (10), and three times he violently refuses to allow Gogo to narrate his dreams, "Don't tell me! . . . DON'T TELL ME!" (10; also 63 and 82)—even though doing so would please Gogo ("It's not nice of you, Didi. Who am I to tell my private nightmares to if I can't tell them to you?") and perhaps also afford access to another, more appealing realm or stage: "This one is enough for you?" Gogo sarcastically asks while gesturing "*towards the universe*" (10).

Alone at the beginning of Act 2, Didi sings, falteringly, a round that replicates the play's senseless circularity, and that suggests he once sang socially. But Gogo, revealing that he heard the singing from offstage, protests becoming an accidental auditor: "I heard you singing. . . . That finished me. I said to myself, He's all alone, he thinks I'm gone for ever, and he sings" (51). Each needs the other as audience, but neither finds pleasure in, or offers encouragement for, the other's performance. This dichotomy prepares the scene for the more rehearsed and stagy, and even more grandly inappropriate, performances of Pozzo and Lucky.

As the evening's main diversion, master and slave portray caricatures of the performer and audience roles. Lionel Abel suggests that, "Pozzo's only possible action is to exhibit Lucky's tricks as a theatre manager might put on those of an acrobat or a freak."[30] He does at first seem little more than a bully or director: harshly ordering Lucky about, controlling the scene and those in it, browbeating Didi and Gogo, and putting them on the defensive for having mistaken him for Godot and for waiting on his land (*SB3*, 16–17). But he then presents himself as a self-conscious social performer (he has recently left his "manor"[31] [39]), a reincarnated *seanchai* (or storyteller) of a particular type, as in this description from 1841:

> He was a very stout well-built man, about fifty years of age, with a round head somewhat bald, and an expansive forehead that argued a considerable reach of natural intellect. . . . His voice was loud, his enunciation rapid, but distinct; and such was the force and buoyancy of his spirits, added to the vehemence of his manner, that altogether it was impossible to resist him.[32]

As one used to commanding attention, Pozzo demands of his stage audience: "Is everybody ready? Is everybody looking at me? . . . Is everybody listening? Is everybody ready? . . . I don't like talking in a vacuum" (*SB3,* 24). He becomes histrionic, "(*groaning, clutching his head),*" over Lucky's treatment of *him:* "I can't bear it . . . any longer. . . . you've no idea . . . it's terrible" (27). But he then insists it was all an act: "Gentlemen, I don't know what came over me. Forgive me. Forget all I said. . . . you may be sure there wasn't a word of truth in it. . . . Do I look like a man that can be made to suffer?" (28). And then, as if responding to his audience's appeal, Pozzo declares, "I can't refuse you. (*Vaporizer.*) A little attention, if you please. . . . be a little more attentive, for pity's sake, otherwise we'll never get anywhere" (30).

After performing his party piece on "what our twilights can do" and life's brevity "on this bitch of an earth," Pozzo eagerly seeks approval: "How did you find me? . . . Good? Fair? Middling? Poor? Positively bad? . . . I have such need of encouragement!" (30–31). Pozzo's reviews, like Beckett's during his early dramatic career, are decidedly mixed: at first mildly positive, they become more qualified as he persists:

> POZZO You find it tedious?
> ESTRAGON Somewhat.
> POZZO (*to Vladimir*) And you, Sir?
> VLADIMIR I've been better entertained.

Yet Pozzo seems satisfied with their tepid response, calling them "civil . . . correct . . . honest." And in recompense for their having served him as audience, he offers to have Lucky entertain them with a presentation from his repertoire: "Shall we have him dance, or sing, or recite, or think, or—" (32).

They agree that Lucky, who has no say in the matter, should perform a double feature, dancing first and thinking afterward: "It's the natural order"

(33). Lucky, according to Pozzo, was once a multitalented performer: "He used to dance the farandole, the fling, the brawl,[33] the jig, the fandango and even the hornpipe.[34] He capered. For joy" (33). But now he stands immobile, puffing "like a grampus," his every move dictated by Pozzo's imperious stage directions: "Up pig! . . . Up hog! . . . Back! . . . Stop! . . . Turn! . . . Closer! . . . Stop! . . . Coat! . . . Hold that! . . . Coat! . . . Whip! . . . Stool! . . . Closer! . . . Back! . . . Further! . . . Stop! . . . Basket! . . . Basket! . . . Further!" (18–19). The incessant imposing of such control (harsher versions of the imperatives Stephen hears throughout *Portrait*) may help to explain Pozzo's exhaustion. According to Pozzo, Lucky's other performative talent is also debased: "He even used to think very prettily once, I could listen to him for hours" (32).

Pozzo commands the presentation: "Do you hear, hog? . . . Dance, misery!" and "Think, pig!" (33, 35). The nomenclature may be especially apposite since, as Zimmermann indicates, "that a person who is unable to tell stories is not an estimable member of the community can be expressed crudely . . . (a man without a story is of no more account than a pig)."[35] Yet pigs once played an important role in the economy of the household and its inverse: folk carnival and, as Joyce emphasizes in *Ulysses,* in popular representation of the Irish.[36] Eagerly anticipated by those, momentarily and only for him, willing to configure themselves as audience, Lucky's dance quickly degenerates into spastic movements of pain and despair, a dumb show of Didi and Gogo's situation. His few halting movements seem to parody "the unofficial Cross-roads dancing which had been part of the life of rural Ireland."[37] They suggest "The Scapegoat's Agony" (to Gogo) and "The Hard Stool" (to Didi), while Pozzo, in a verbal echo of Stephen's attempt to escape entrapment in *Portrait,* calls Lucky's performance "The Net. He thinks he's entangled in a net" (33).

Lucky seems mute as well as immobile, unable to speak until commanded by Pozzo, his monologue a verbal and emotional outpouring that, rather than entertaining or edifying his listeners, assails them. Delargy comments that "Good story-tellers, proud of their art, were intolerant of badly told tales, and sometimes stopped the unskilful narrator in the middle of his story, saying such nonsense should not be allowed to represent the real traditional narrative!"[38] Lucky's stage audience contains no skillful storytellers, but even more than Dawson's speech in chapter 7 of *Ulysses* (as I discuss in chapter 4) his monologue nonetheless makes them restless, despondent, and then provokes an assault: "*protest[ing] violently, . . . All three throw themselves on Lucky who struggles and shouts his text*" (*SB3,* 33). Once Lucky has broken into speech, he seems bound to continue, "like a phonograph record getting faster and faster and faster until it is out of control,"[39] and his listeners rebel forcibly. The melee finally terminates in the "*Silence of Lucky,*" as Lucky, and his performance, collapses into permanent muteness.

Verbal performative failures followed by communication breakdowns and silence recur throughout *Godot.* "Let's stop talking for a minute, do you mind?" an exhausted Gogo pleads at one point (*SB3,* 9). When Didi and Gogo first contemplate suicide, they have difficulty analyzing and expressing the dimensions of the problem, though Gogo makes a valiant attempt through an improvised mime: "Gogo light—bough not break—Gogo dead. Didi heavy—bough break—Didi alone" (12). When Gogo talks incomprehensibly with his mouth full of carrot, Didi responds with, "I don't hear a word you're saying" (15). Twice they confuse Pozzo with Godot (16–17, 69–70), and then have difficulty making themselves understood by him. After asking three times why Lucky fails to put his bags down, Gogo truncates and pantomimes the question: "(*forcibly*) Bags. (*He points at Lucky.*) Why? Always hold. (*He sags, panting.*) Never put down. (*He opens his hands, straightens up with relief.*) Why?" (23–24). Didi similarly repeats, with variation, "You want to get rid of him?" when he receives no response: "You waagerrim? . . . You want to get rid of him?" (25).

But despite all the failures of communication and performance, *Godot* alone of Beckett's plays also depicts pleasing interchanges that produce moments of shared enjoyment, when Didi and Gogo perform in tandem, one for the other, as a duo rather than solo. They have moments of unadulterated tenderness, also rare in Beckett: Didi offers Gogo food (14, 60), a lullaby and comfort after a nightmare (62–63), gestures that Gogo appreciatively acknowledges at times: "We don't manage too badly, eh Didi, between the two of us?" (61). Most affecting, perhaps, are the performative interchanges during which, as if simultaneously recalling old routines, the two are rhythmically in synch with each other, displaying genuine rapport that momentarily deflects or overrides everything that disunites and dispirits them.

Gogo, usually the initiator, urges them on—"Let's make a little conversation," he says (41); "In the meantime let us try and converse calmly, since we are incapable of keeping silent" (54); "Let's contradict each other" (56)—and

Didi falls readily into the responsive role. Their music-hall cross-talk riffs cover a wide spectrum, not only their waiting (12–13) but also the quality of carrots, and life (14–15); Lucky's sufferings (19–20); the evening they're having (28); on being happy (52); their "dead voices" (54–55); abusing each other and killing time (65–68). The exchanges are not intended to help them think (Didi: "We're in no danger of ever thinking any more" [56]) or communicate; virtuosity to no end becomes its own end, a static ritual devoid of meaning beyond itself, a way of keeping the show going and sustaining "the impression we exist" (61).

These quick, almost breathless exchanges suggest that Didi and Gogo have performed them often, reenacting the traditional contest of wits played out by Irish poets:

> When two of them met, one repeated the first half of a verse or very short poem, which was a challenge to the other to complete it. Sometimes it was a quotation from some obscure, half-forgotten old poem, sometimes an effusion composed on the spot, in which case the second poet was expected to give, extemporaneously, a second half of the same length, prosody, and rhyme, and making continuous sense.... In Ireland, it was believed that a true poet never failed to respond correctly, so that this was a test often applied to expose a poetical pretender.[40]

After the collapse of the patronage system in eighteenth-century Ireland, the mendicant poet became a commonplace figure, one that both Joyce and Beckett represent: a decrepit version of Stephen Dedalus unsuccessfully soliciting payment for his performances, Gogo, who says that his rags should make it obvious that he used to be a poet, begs for Pozzo's chicken bones (*SB3*, 6, 21).

Perhaps because of his bardic stature, Gogo usually has not only the first lines of these exchanges but also the last—has them twice, in fact, because he repeats them identically, savoring, like Stephen, their sounds and rhythms rather than their meanings:

> ESTRAGON It's so we won't think.
> VLADIMIR We have that excuse.
> ESTRAGON It's so we won't hear.
> VLADIMIR We have our reasons.

ESTRAGON All the dead voices.
VLADIMIR They make a noise like wings.
ESTRAGON *Like leaves.*
VLADIMIR Like sand.
ESTRAGON *Like leaves.* . . . (54–55; my emphasis)

These shared, balanced routines seem often to have been performed or rehearsed, party pieces trotted out on numerous occasions for no audience but themselves.

Implying a need to expand their repertoire, Didi suggests that they "play at Pozzo and Lucky" (65), while Gogo, stepping back from his role as performing artist, offers encouraging metacommentary on their interchanges: "That's the idea, let's contradict each other" and "That's the idea, let's ask each other questions" (56). He praises one of their performances, "That wasn't such a bad little canter" (57); at the end of another he hurls the ultimate insult—"Crritic!" (68)—at Didi. Both kinds of routine are, nonetheless, shared and balanced, participated in by a performing duo who, knowing each other's every move after long experience, play off them effectively, even affectionately.

But Beckett also deploys rhetorical strategies that juxtapose contrarieties and set them harshly against each other, rather than harmonize them or valorize one over the other. He does this, for example, with imagery of light and dark, stasis and mobility, sound and silence, but perhaps most crucially with regard to the continuity and cessation of life, as starkly summarized by Pozzo's "They give birth astride of a grave, the light gleams an instant, then it's night once more" (82), and at the end of *The Unnamable:* "You must go on, I can't go on, I'll go on" (*SB2,* 407). No synthesis results from such juxtaposing of thesis and antithesis—and finally the mutuality of interchange, like "this long day[,] . . . is very near the end of its repertory" (*SB3,* 78). A very different repertory is performed in Beckett's subsequent plays.

In *All That Fall,* Beckett's first radio play, Maddy Rooney, a dying performer manqué, makes a Pozzo-like journey out from her home and back, dragging herself along the road to the train station to meet her returning husband. Beckett's most overtly Irish play (based on characterization, setting, diction, speech rhythms, and so on) and one of his "most visually suggestive"[41] despite its being a radio play, *All That Fall* occurs in a death-saturated countryside, with its dung, "vile dust" and "viler worms," dead dog, and rotting leaves. "It is suicide to be abroad," Maddy says. "But what is it to be at home . . .? A lingering dissolution" (*SB3,* 160). Schubert's *Death and the Maiden* plays at the beginning and near the end (157, 186). Maddy mourns her long-dead child. Mr. Slocum's car, which he declares "is dead," runs over a hen: "What a death!" Maddy exclaims. "One minute picking happy at the dung, . . . and then—bang!—all her troubles over" (165). Dan Rooney asks his wife, "Did you ever wish to kill a child? [*Pause.*] Nip some young doom in the bud" (179), perhaps implying that that's what he just did on the train. The landscape is desiccated, barren: "All is still. No living soul in sight" (180). Even the stage directions evoke mortality: the music, and then Maddy's murmuring response, "*dies*" (157); when the music later recurs Dan instantly recognizes it ("[*Indistinctly.*] Death and the Maiden") before it "*dies*" again (186); at the end Jerry's "*steps die away*" (188).

Like many Beckett characters, Maddy sarcastically thinks of herself as posthumous: "I do not exist. The fact is well known" (166), but she goes on. What sustains Maddy, who seems a trial run for Winnie in *Happy Days,* is bravura performance: her journey is achieved against the odds; it is epic, a tour de force. She holds forth in various ways as she goes: murmuring the music she hears; commenting on and critiquing all she encounters ("Christ what a planet!" [170]); receiving and declaiming to a series of visitors along the road as if she were hosting and entertaining them; and singing Newman's hymn, "Lead, Kindly Light," which discomposes Miss Fitt (although Maddy suggests that it offered comfort to the dying "on the *Lusitania.* . . . Or was it the *Titanic?*") and for which she attracts a startled audience (171). Maddy is fully self-conscious of herself as something of an archaic, anachronistic verbal performer with a peculiar way of speaking: "I use none but the simplest words, I hope, and yet I sometimes find my way of speaking very . . . bizarre" (158). But Maddy is most striking as a conductor or sound technician, the first of Beckett's radio characters who comment on noises as yet unheard—the mail, a horse (which we never hear), the cooing of doves, and then the wind, birds, cows, sheep, dogs, hens (158, 180)—as though she were summoning up all of nature for an orchestral finale before it ceases to exist.

One major reason why *Endgame* is so much harsher than *Godot,* with, as Beckett puts it, a greater "power of the text to claw, more inhuman than *Godot*" (*No Author,* 11), is that Hamm and Clov lack the pleasurable rhythmic interactions performed in *Godot.* Unlike Didi and Gogo the later pair inhabits a largely recognizable interior world in which social events might recently have occurred, and traces of which remain; but their relationship is hierarchical, a harsher version of the Rooneys' old married couple routine: "The old folks at home!" (*Endgame, SB3,* 98). Like Beckett's other blind characters (Pozzo; Dan Rooney; A, the blind beggar in *Rough for Theatre I*), Hamm is a bully, akin to the dictatorial Pozzo commanding a subservient, resentful Lucky (a relationship reprised by D and P in *Catastrophe*), who is bound to perform only when and how ordered to do so. Yet all three subordinate figures—Lucky, Clov, and P—violate the prescribed limits of their parts in theatrically striking ways.

Clov and Hamm posit contradictory but structurally similar opening performative ploys. Clov begins, "Finished, it's finished, nearly finished, it must be nearly finished"; Hamm proclaims, "Me . . . to play" (92; he twice repeats this self-reflexive performative assertion [140, 151])—and these contrarieties abut and clash but remain unreconciled. Both Hamm and Clov initiate their roles with pronouncements about temporal continuity, philosophical speculation, and then assertions about their absurd personal circumstances. The result, as Stanley Gontarski puts it in his discussion of Beckett's directorial insistence on the separation of voice and motion (specifically in *Endgame,* but also in *Krapp's Last Tape,*[42] *Eh Joe,* and *Footfalls*), is to reaffirm "a nearly Cartesian duality in Beckett's theatre; it is Beckett's almost Manichaean reluctance to mingle opposites."[43] Like *Godot, Endgame* offers several solo pieces, but the later play lacks harmonious duets.

Hamm, whose name suggests, among other things, histrionic actor, tries to personify the continuity and performance expressed in his opening line: "we breathe, we change! . . . We do what we can. . . . We're getting on" (*SB3,* 99–101). He expounds an impossible vision not only of change but also of renewal, of revitalization within nature: "If I could sleep I might make love. I'd go into the woods. My eyes would see . . . the sky, the earth. I'd run, run, they wouldn't catch me" (104). Despite nature's demise and his inability to stand or see, Hamm, like Stephen at the end of *Portrait,* proclaims his determination to set off heroically to new worlds: "Alone, I'll embark alone! Get working on that raft immediately. Tomorrow I'll be gone for ever" (116). As ham actor he insists on occupying absolute center stage ("more or less. . . . Bang in the center!"

[110–11]), and, his father's son, on controlling the performative interchange. As master of ceremonies, Hamm announces "It's time for my story" (125), asserting himself through his oral narrative of "a madman who thought the end of the world had come" (122) and then of the crawling man with the son who may or may not be Clov (127–30), which he calls an "audition," perhaps for "the life to come" (126).

Like Didi and Gogo, Clov turns his mocking gaze, enhanced by his telescope, on the auditorium: "I see . . . a multitude . . . in transports . . . of joy. (*Pause.*) That's what I call a magnifier" (122). But Hamm, a self-conscious performer in the Pozzo mold, is unamused because he is keen to have an audience. After Nell, like Gretta hearing Gabriel's story of Johnny in Houston's film of *The Dead*, "has remained impassive" to Nagg's extended "story of the tailor" (106–7) and then immediately dies (108), Hamm determines to take preemptive action, and so bribes Nagg to serve as audience when Clov refuses.

A poor but complacent storyteller, Hamm offers metacommentary on his story's progress: "I'll soon have finished with this story. (*Pause.*) Unless I bring in other characters" (130). Then, echoing both Prospero's terminating of the masque in *The Tempest* and Clov's opening pronouncement, he proclaims the end of performance: "Our revels now are ended" (133). Yet like Didi with Gogo, Hamm demands that Clov show some interest in his story, and Clov, like Gogo, is constrained to respond with faux enthusiasm:

> HAMM (*Irritably.*)
> Ask me where I've got to.
> CLOV Oh, by the way, your story? . . .
> HAMM (*angrily*): Keep going, can't you, keep going!
> CLOV You've got on with it, I hope.
> HAMM (*modestly*): Oh not very far, not very far. . . . I've got on with it a little all the same.
> (*Pause.*)
> Technique, you know.
> (*Pause. Irritably.*)
> I say I've got on with it a little all the same.
> CLOV (*admiringly*): Well I never! In spite of everything you were able to get on with it! (134)

Beckett said that this interchange "should be played as *farcical parody of polite drawing-room* conversation" (*No Author,* 23). It also parodies the situation noted by one student of Irish storytellers:

> The most successful conversations with old men are . . . with some modest and apparently dull old person who is successfully probed by intelligent and sympathetic questions, till he is actually reminded of long-forgotten scenes which have perhaps not been suggested to him for years, and then he draws from his memory, with the help of further questions, some passage of life and adventure of the highest interest.[44]

Hamm makes overtly stagy, self-reflexive pronouncements as the play moves toward its end: his way of speaking is an aside, he is "warming up for my last soliloquy" (*Endgame, SB3,* 148), and his final monologue is proceeding well, as a sympathetic audience might note: "Nicely put, that" (153).

In contrast to Hamm, Clov asserts a teleology throughout. Beginning by stagily pronouncing the end in Christ's last words—"Finished, it's finished, nearly finished, it must be nearly finished" (92)—Clov tells Hamm not only that he has had enough, but that "I always had," and that "It may end" (95). Trying and failing to terminate "this . . . this . . . thing" by leaving (95–96), Clov announces a series of depleted categories: there are no more bicycles, pap, nature, gulls, tide, rugs, painkillers, coffins (97, 98, 99, 113, 136, 140, 143, 148). His seeds will never sprout (100); outside, he says, is "Zero . . . zero . . . and zero" (112, 114); and all is "Corpsed" (113), the whole universe "stinks of corpses" (124). He proclaims that Nell "has no pulse" (108); that the doctor is dead (109); and that Mother Pegg, though Hamm says she "was bonny once, like a flower of the field," is "extinguished" (121). Near the end of the play he envisions the whole earth being "extinguished, though I never saw it lit" (151).

Death is Clov's arena of action, such as it is, as well as pronouncement: he says that he would "die happy" if he could kill Hamm (111), though when Hamm proposes it Clov says he cannot (118). He kills a flea (115–16), tries to exterminate a rat because "If I don't kill that rat he'll die" (140), and moves to kill the boy he sees outside, though Hamm stops him (149). Clov dreams of an ultimate order, an end of performance that is synonymous with the end of life: "A world where all would be silent and still and each thing in its place, under the last dust" (133). Late in the play he tells Hamm he will look out the window, "since it's an order. But it's the last time" (148).

Crossovers occasionally occur, moments when Hamm and Clov assume each other's defining stance, speak each other's language because, as Clov says, they have only one between them: "I use the words you taught me. If they don't mean anything any more, teach me others. Or let me be silent" (122). But even then they remain out of synch, dissonant. Having been forced to play audience, Clov demands that Hamm continue his story even as he flags:

> CLOV Keep going, can't you, keep going!
> HAMM That's all. I stopped there.
> (*Pause.*)
> CLOV Do you see how it goes on?
> HAMM More or less.
> CLOV Will it not soon be the end?
> HAMM I'm afraid it will.
> CLOV Pah! You'll make up another.
> HAMM I don't know.
> (*Pause.*)
> I feel rather drained.
> (*Pause.*)
> The prolonged creative effort. (136)

Later Clov says that he wants to sing (144), and Hamm declares there are no more sugar-plums (132) or navigators (138). And it is Hamm who pronounces, "Outside of here it's death" (97), and then, "It's the end, Clov, we've come to the end. I don't need you any more" (149).

Beckett said that Hamm and Clov are Didi and Gogo at a later date, at the end of their lives, beyond waiting.[45] "Hamm," he told an actor in the 1967 Berlin production, "is a king in this chess game lost from the start. . . . Now at the last he makes a few senseless moves as only a bad player would. A good one would have given up long ago. He is only trying to delay the inevitable end."[46] The sheets covering him and the ashbins at the beginning suggest shrouds; the setting is a skull inhabited by characters even more bitterly aware of themselves as characters than Didi, temporary survivors of some unknown catastrophe, occupants of civilization's dustbin or Purgatory. If Didi and Gogo's interchanges are a way of going on while waiting, those between Hamm and Clov are a way of getting from Clov's opening "Finished, it's finished, nearly finished" to his final "This is what we call making an exit" (*SB3,* 151). But habit being "a great deadener" (as Joyce's Stephen acknowledges in *Portrait* and as Didi says [83]), Clov merely stands, "dressed for the road . . . impassive and motionless, his eyes fixed on Hamm, till the end," a resentful yet immobile and mute audience, as Hamm performs the play's concluding monologue, one he seems to have rehearsed or performed before: "Me to play. . . . Old endgame lost of old, play and lose and have done with losing." He then disappears beneath his "Old stancher" (151–54) before the larger curtain falls.

Only traces of traditional performance remain in the transitional *Krapp's Last Tape* (1958),[47] which can be read as satirizing attempts to record and preserve a dying oral culture, as described by this mid-twentieth-century storyteller: people "no longer care for stories, and the stories would have died out altogether, for the young people weren't ready to pick them up. But now, thank God, there's a gadget for taking them down, if there were any story-tellers left."[48] Initially a clown like Didi and Gogo, Krapp was given a white face, purple nose, ill-fitting clothes, and "*Surprising pair of dirty white boots, size ten at least, very narrow and pointed,*" and performed an elaborate opening mime, with keys, desk drawers, and bananas, conceived to last for several minutes (221–22).[49] Krapp, again with Beckett's approval, also became a derelict figure on stage, something closer to the stereotypical wandering performer of Irish tradition.

Krapp is the work in which Beckett most overtly represents himself, though he does so less than he did in the draft of the play. It retains allusions to his mother's long widowhood and death (1933–50); an early love (disguised as Theodor Fontane's character, Effi Briest); the humiliation of the French *Murphy,* which sold only seventeen copies; walks on the heath with his dog; and, most important, the epiphanic revelation he had in 1946 of his creative path: to accept his bleakness of vision, and to write out of personal experience and largely in first-person monologist form. Reacting to the experience, Beckett saw himself as "doomed to spend the rest of my days digging up the detritus of my life and vomiting it out over and over again," and he realized that "optimism is not my way. I shall always be depressed, but what comforts me is the realization that I can now accept this dark side as the commanding side of my personality. In accepting it, I will make it work for me."[50] The vision induced a new sense of purpose and resolve that, despite writing blocks, depression, and near breakdowns, remained with him the rest of his life—and that he could self-mockingly dramatize in *Krapp's Last Tape.*[51]

The play is pivotal not only in its self-representation but in several other ways as well: it is Beckett's first major postwar work written in English; it inaugurates his increasingly economic theatrical style of writing as well as the kind of technical demands that impelled him to begin directing his own plays; and its protagonist is his first dramatic monologist, though Krapp's interplay with his tapes creates a technological dialogue of self and soul. Krapp portrays both performer and auditor in a metatheatrical play that, during rehearsal, Beckett nonetheless pared of its most explicitly performative moment: Krapp's "*brief burst of quavering song.*"

> Now the day is over,
> Night is drawing nigh-igh,
> Shadows— (*SB3,* 225; also 229)

Beckett's production omitted the Protestant hymn because he came to feel that it "is too self-conscious and artificial,"[52] but the deletion also strengthens an earlier passage in which Krapp asserts his nonperformative nature. Krapp is listening to the "Extraordinary silence this evening. I strain my ears and do not hear a sound. Old Miss McGlome always sings at this hour. But not tonight." He then reflects on himself as performer: "Shall I sing when I am her age, if I ever am? No. (*Pause.*) Did I sing as a boy? No. (*Pause.*) Did I ever sing? No" (224). In all productions directed by Beckett, and most subsequent ones, he no longer does—and therefore never did. A further consequence of this change is that present-day Krapp, for all his movement around the stage and machine manipulation, is essentially passive; breaking the pattern of recording a new tape on his birthday, he reduces his role as performer to the orality of past tapes, to which he listens with alternating anger and nostalgia.

Despite the play's loss of song in production, tone and rhythm remain vitally important, so much so that *Krapp's Last Tape* lent itself to being transformed into Marcel Mihalovici's opera, *Krapp; or, The Last Band.*[53] Beckett, who said that "Drama is following music,"[54] stressed *Krapp*'s musicality in his direction of the 1977 Rick Cluchy production: "The musical quality of the tape is important to him. Therefore, line by line, he explains intonations, pauses, tempi, voice level and voice volume. . . . We have to try to bring rhythm into every detail."[55] Character interplay for Krapp, who "has spoken monologues to himself throughout his entire life,"[56] is reduced to interchanges with previous versions of himself since, as Kalb notes, his self-obsession "ultimately leaves him bereft of any stable identity."[57] Since, as Barbara Hardy suggests, his present is "empty,"[58] Krapp is a performer curiously at odds with both himself and his role, whether he is playing clown or "*a wearish old man. . . . Disordered grey hair. Unshaven*" (the text has it both ways), and whether holding forth in a "*Cracked voice. Distinctive intonation*" (*SB3,* 221) as a shabby and desiccated sixty-nine-year-old or on the tape, proclaiming himself "sound as a bell" (223), that he made thirty years earlier.

Initially, contemporary Krapp is a man of few words, someone who has performed too much or too little, his "cracked voice" raw with abuse or non-use. He speaks falteringly at first, as if forming words is painful, a senseless expenditure of energy. Anticipating Henry's relationship to stories in *Embers*—"I never finished any of them, I never finished anything" (198)—Krapp can barely start a sentence, let alone finish one: "Nothing to say, not a squeak" (228). Similarly, the sample of his writing that he offers consists of headings and verbless clauses—"Box . . . thrree . . . spool . . . five. . . . The black ball. . . . The dark nurse. . . . memorable equinox" (222–23)—written in an old ledger. Like *Portrait*'s Stephen enjoying the rhythm of words, their "poise and balance" rather than their meaning, Krapp now takes pleasure only in the sound of words: "Revelled in the word spool. [*With relish.*] Spooool! Happiest moment of the past half million. [*Pause.*] Seventeen copies sold. . . . Getting known" (228). If, as seems likely, this book is "the opus . . . magnum" ("an explanation of the dark side of humanity")[59] whose "shadows" Krapp first glimpsed in his late twenties (*SB3,* 224), then it took more than forty years to complete. Not only his "best years" but also his writing days are behind him.

Pierre Chabert, who played Krapp in 1975 under Beckett's direction and came to view the text as a musical score, raises a fundamental question about the play and its protagonist's performance: "The basic problem of both production and acting lies in the listening. That is, how can a play which is based on the act of listening be made to work in the theatre? How can the act of listening be dramatized?"[60] Beckett's response was to emphasize the importance of the tape player as character and performer, while Krapp plays audience to himself: he suggested that Krapp should be hard of hearing (as Jack MacGowran brilliantly plays it), thus increasing the tension of his listening by making him strain to hear, and that, in his isolation and passivity, Krapp cling to the machine as if trying to reconnect his divided selves. Beckett's direction is for the actor to "Become as much as possible one with the machine," yet the Krapp we see on stage spends much of the play assailing and recoiling from this relationship.

Although the tape would seem to represent a kind of ultimate party piece because of its unvarying nature (as Schneider said of the making of *Rockaby*, "The good thing about tape is that it doesn't vary; the bad thing about tape is that it doesn't vary"),[61] Krapp takes control of the play's action not as taped performer, but as an increasingly demanding, rather than passive, audience in the present, manipulating (in a manner reminiscent of Pozzo with Lucky)

7. Jack MacGowran as Krapp embracing tape recorder in *Krapp's Last Tape* (directed by Alan Schneider). Courtesy of Pennebaker Hegedus Films.

both what the tape may not say and also what it is not only allowed to say but must repeatedly say.

Krapp assumes his most animated role as his tape's audience: laughing loudly and approvingly when his thirty-nine-year-old self mocks the aspirations and resolutions of twenty-something Krapp, stopping the tape to look up the meaning of "viduity," which he once knew. But he soon switches gears. Repudiating what he had once affirmed, he curses and fast-forwards through the epiphanic "vision at last," truncating it to, ". . . clear to me at last that the dark I have always struggled to keep under is in reality my most—" (*SB3,* 226). He critiques what he now considers the pretentious self-aggrandizing of his younger self ("Just been listening to that stupid bastard I took myself for thirty years ago, hard to believe I was ever as bad as that" [228]), and repeatedly plays the description of what the ledger, interrupted by its mockingly placed stage direction, calls the "Farewell to—[*he turns page*]—love" (223) scene that set him on the lonely, asocial course of his life. As audience-become-director, sixty-nine-year-old Krapp retaliates against thirty-nine-year-old Krapp—"his dying self [controlling] his dead one," as Beckett put it (*No Author,* 59). He now silences what he had once valorized (creative energy and artistic commitment) and has the tape repeat (three times) the scene of romantic intimacy in the boat, presumably the last such moment in Krapp's empty life.

Though no longer a clown, Krapp remained, in Beckett's jaundiced view, "an old fool, who is rather less of a fool as a very old man than he was, as he listens to the recording of his stupidity of thirty years earlier."[62] Yet Beckett also implies that Krapp has been metaphorically blind all along, and that what had seemed the great decision of his life (rejecting intimacy, like Joyce's Eveline, Mr. Duffy, and Stephen Dedalus) was a choice without a distinction: had he opted for passion over ascetic renunciation, Krapp would have become enmeshed in familial entanglements, like those Joyce depicts in "A Little Cloud" and that Beckett satirizes in *Endgame* and *Play,* and with equally dismal consequences. Beckett laughingly told the actor Pierre Chabert, "I thought of writing a play about the situation in reverse: Mrs Krapp, the girl in the boat, would be prowling around behind him, and his failure, and his solitude would be just the same."[63] Beckett suggested that the actor Rick Cluchy imagine "an old Krapp who had made the opposite decision: surrounded by an aged wife and many, many children . . . 'good God!'"[64] At each stage (sixty-nine, thirty-nine, mid-twenties), Krapp can see only the fool he was, not the fool he is; all his versions misperceive and misnarrate themselves.

Krapp indulges in one last fantasy before the play ends: "Could have been happy with her, up there on the Baltic." Like Bloom contemplating having another child with Molly ("Too late now. Or if not? If not? If still?" [*U,* 273]), Krapp briefly conjectures that he might yet act: "Sometimes wondered in the night if a last effort mightn't. . . ." But he abruptly terminates the Bloomian reverie, "Leave it at that. . . . Be again, be again. [*Pause.*] All that old misery. [*Pause.*] Once wasn't enough for you. [*Pause.*]" (*SB3,* 229). Second chances at life are no more viable for Beckett's characters than first ones.

The play represents the end for Krapp: his *last* tape, which originally contained the ambiguous possibility of meaning "most recent," increasingly came to imply a deathwatch, a final performance.[65] Of Krapp's verbal and physical play with "spool. . . . [*With relish.*] Spool! [*Pause.*] Spooool! [*Happy smile. Pause.*] . . . [*With relish.*] Spooool! [*Happy smile.*]" (*SB3,* 222), Beckett comments, "that's his whole life," and now it's finished. In production, Beckett had Krapp turn around anxiously once or twice (MacGowran on film does it three times), staring at the dark, as if, according to Beckett, "Death is standing behind him . . . and unconsciously he's looking for it because it's the end . . . he's through with his work, with love, and with religion."[66] Jean Martin recounts that Beckett told him that "it is death who is waiting for him there," and Beckett added, "Next day, when the play is over, he is found dead at his table."[67] At some level Krapp seems aware that what he starts to record in the play's present is not just his latest but also his "*last* tape," his last performance, the title expressing his death wish, which he helps to fulfill by ripping out the new tape he was making, breaking the pattern of annual birthday recordings, refusing to perform any more for an audience of some future Krapp. The play ends with the third reprise of the thirty-year-old tape (which consequently becomes the play's titular *last* tape), and then its silent running, down and out, as the sixty-nine-year-old Krapp stares blankly at the darkness that is about to claim him.

Happy Days, which Knowlson and Pilling called "Beckett's boldest piece of dramatic writing to date,"[68] combines the performative monologue of *Krapp* with the duologue of *Godot* and *Endgame,* creating a hybrid of the two forms. The published stage directions call for "*Maximum of simplicity and symmetry. . . . Imbedded up to above her waist in exact centre of mound, Winnie*" (*SB3,*

276), repeating the emphasis on theatrical centrality and dominance of *Endgame,* though in a stage direction rather than the protagonist's commands. But unlike Krapp, Winnie, desperate not to be talking to herself, chose a companion whom she requires to confirm her existence (the reverse of *Film*'s O who, seeking to deny his, desperately and unsuccessfully flees E) by hearing her perform.

She says for Willie's ears, "If only I could bear to be alone, I mean prattle away with not a soul to hear. . . . even when you do not answer and perhaps hear nothing, Something of this is being heard, I am not merely talking to myself, that is in the wilderness, a thing I could never bear to do. . . . That is what enables me to go on, go on talking that is" (282; she repeats this thought twice: 285–86, 299–300). Without Willie, she insists, she would be mute: "Simply gaze before me with compressed lips. . . . Not another word as long as I drew breath, nothing to break the silence of this place" (282). So Beckett "gave Winnie and Willie their balancing names"[69] and final long look at each other, and, directing the play for the first time in Berlin in 1971, dramatized Winnie's dependence on Willie as auditor by decentering her mound, thus creating a more equivalent space for Willie and a less hierarchical relationship between them.

The visual impact of *Happy Days* contrasts strikingly with that of *Krapp's Last Tape.* Winnie's Dantean "blaze of hellish light" (*SB3,* 277) holds at bay the "everlasting perishing cold" and "black night without end" that she only imagines, and that claims Krapp. Imbedded in her mound, a realization of Clov's "impossible heap" (*Endgame, SB3,* 92), Winnie rummages in her "*capacious black bag*" (*SB3,* 275), seeking something of herself amid the props that represent history's detritus in *Finnegans Wake:* "All spoiled goods go into her nabsack: curtrages and rattlin buttins, nappy spattees and flasks of all nations, clavicures and scampulars, maps, keys and woodpiles of haypennies and moonled brooches with bloodstaned breeks in em, boaston nightgarters and masses of shoesets and nickelly nacks and foder allmicheal and a lugly parson of cates and howitzer muchears and midgers and maggets, ills and ells with loffs of toffs and pleures of bells and the last sigh that come fro the hart . . . and the fairest sin the sunsaw" (11.18–26). Carey Perloff suggests that "*Happy Days* is all about props, for in a metatheatrical sense *Happy Days* is a play about making theater, a play about creating a theatrical world from as few physical givens as possible,"[70] with Winnie as her own archivist and impresario.

As in *Krapp,* the dominant mode of expression and perception in *Happy Days* is verbal: Winnie, who equates "going on" with talking, says she could not bear "merely talking to myself," at least not "for any length of time" (282). Addressing herself to the mostly silent Willie, Winnie the monologist, with her stereotypical Irish "gift for gab," narrativizes everything she does. The play's key question is whether Winnie is blithely unaware of her circumstances or is aware and stoically enduring, offering comic performance as a deflection and distraction, a way of *not* confronting her situation. Beckett offered the former explanation when he told Billie Whitelaw: "I don't think she knows herself what kind of woman she is. She's a mess. An organized mess. Her strength is through unawareness. She has a kind of profound frivolity, she's scatterbrained, she babbles." He added that "The first act establishes a kind of quality—the interruption, the strangeness, the gracefulness—she's not stoic, she's unaware. A child woman with a short span of concentration—sure one minute, unsure the next."[71]

Yet Winnie comments several times on her physical and performative circumstances: the "earth is very tight today" (*SB3,* 286); takes note of "changing conditions" (290), including her own decay; recalls a time "when I was not yet caught—in this way—and had my legs and had the use of my legs, and could seek out a shady place" (291); and knows that she is "stuck up to her diddies in the bleeding ground" and needs digging out (294). In Act 1 she both imagines that "perhaps some day the earth will yield and let me go, the pull is so great, yes, crack all round me and let me out" (289) and also anticipates that "one day the earth [will likely] cover my breasts" (291–92). In Act 2 she speaks of her suffering: "The bell. (*Pause.*) It hurts like a knife. (*Pause.*) A gouge. (*Pause.*) One cannot ignore it" (302). Though she contemplates using the revolver to "put myself out of my misery" (289), her compelling performance demonstrates stoical courage rather than blindness or indifference.

Winnie's performative medium is words, which supersede action, and which she produces at a rate that falls short only of Lucky's virtually nonstop flow in *Godot* and those of the talking heads in *Play* and *Not I*'s Mouth. Like them, she feels a compulsion to say words "as long as there are any." Words are immediate for Winnie, who speaks only in and of the present, as Beckett emphasized to Schneider: "'I used to think' too affirmative, hence 'I *say* I used to think.' Similarly later 'I *say* I used to say.' Nothing sure but immediate utterance" (*No Author,* 284). Like *Godot*'s and *Endgame*'s, her performance occurs in the theatrical, rather than the historic, moment. Winnie's fond allusions to "the old style" refer not only to the loss of assurance about the way time used to function, but also to a performance tradition, "a supposedly old manner of unaccompanied singing,"[72] that is irrevocably lost and unrepresentable in the present. Even when Beckett could easily have depicted a past that would help to explain the disastrous present—in filmed work like *Film* and *Eh Joe* and television versions of *Krapp's Last Tape* and *Not I,* for example—he never did.

Despite their immediacy, Winnie's words have largely lost, or are losing, their referential and functional purposes. Her opening line, "Another heavenly day" (*SB3,* 275), is radically at odds with her hellish (that is, all too earthly) situation; and her self-directed imperative—"Begin, Winnie. (*Pause.*) Begin your day, Winnie" (276)—implies an authority and control that she clearly lacks.[73] This grotesque disjunction between words and meaning recurs throughout the first act: "can't complain . . . so much to be thankful for . . . many mercies . . . great mercies . . . prayers perhaps not for naught" (277); "(*Head up, cheerfully.*) No better, no worse, no change" (278); "Oh this *is* a happy day! This will have been another happy day!" (296), and so on. And the dichotomy increases in the attenuated Act 2, as allusions to Dante's *Inferno* combine with Winnie's sinking deeper into the earth, furthering a descent from which no exit seems possible—except perhaps into *Not I,* which can be read as *Happy Days* Act 3.[74]

As a performer, Winnie echoes Didi, Clov, and Krapp in contemplating singing, and she too is economical in her musical efforts, emphasizing that timing is crucial. Although "the day is now well advanced," she determines that "it is perhaps a little soon for my song," and "To sing too soon is a great mistake, I find" (288), even "fatal." But one can also "leave it too late." Either way is problematic: "It bubbles up, for some unknown reason, the time is ill chosen, one chokes it back. (*Pause.*) One says, Now is the time, it is now or never, and one cannot. (*Pause.*) Simply cannot sing. (*Pause.*) Not a note. (*Pause.*)" (303). Winnie requires an audience as much as Pozzo and Hamm, but having one is insufficient to produce her party piece: "One cannot sing just to please someone, however much one loves them, no, song must come from the heart, that is what I always say, pour out from the inmost, like a thrush." Appropriate mood, occasion, audience—"with no thought of benefit, to oneself or anyone else" (292–93)—must all converge if a successful performance is to occur.

When not performing herself, Winnie produces from her bag a music box that plays the love waltz from Franz Lehár's operetta, *The Merry Widow*, evoking a "*happy expression*" from her and causing her to "*sway . . . to the rhythm.*" It also elicits "*Brief burst of hoarse song without words—musical-box tune—from* Willie," to which Winnie, a rare eager audience in Beckett's plays, responds with pleasure (292). Although she tells herself "Sing your song, Winnie" at the end of Act 1 (297), it is only when Willie finally presents himself in Act 2, for whatever reason "*dressed to kill*" (305), crawling toward her, staring hard at her, and calling out, "(*just audible*) Win," that she joyfully, if inappropriately, sings "I love you so" to her sole audience (307).

For all her expression of pleasure, Winnie, like Clov, spends much of the play enumerating the things that are running out: toothpaste, medicine, lipstick. Even words, as happened to Lucky and Hamm, and as Winnie acknowledges, fail her at times (284): "So little to say, so little to do, and the fear so great, certain days, of finding oneself . . . left, with hours still to run, before the bell for sleep, and nothing more to say, nothing more to do" (290). She determines to hoard her verbal resources: "Stop talking now, Winnie, for a minute, don't squander all your words for the day" (293). Doing so, she then finds, "Fortunately I am in tongue again" (290), but she foresees a time—perhaps in an implicit third act that is not *Not I*—"when words must fail" entirely (288, 301), be depleted, when she can no longer utter.

Yet though she is even more restricted in Act 2, being buried up to her neck and never allowed to rest by a bell that "hurts like a knife" (302) whenever she closes her eyes, she manages, before the end, both to tell her story (perhaps a deflected autobiographical one like those told by Henry in *Embers* and May in *Footfalls*) and to sing *The Merry Widow* waltz (307), "more poignant, less geographically specific" than Beckett's original choice, "When Irish Eyes Are Smiling."[75] Cued by the off-stage piercing bell, Winnie, who would perform as the *Titanic* is sinking or as the mound rises to cover her head, has gone a long way toward becoming one of Beckett's late dramatic figures: a performing automaton controlled by despotic force—whether human (*Catastrophe, What Where*), spotlight (*Play*), or percussive sound (*Quad*).

As in *Godot, Play,* and *Quad,* Beckett's other two-act plays, the second act of *Happy Days* is briefer and sparer, more melancholy and dream-like (*Quad*'s is literally washed-out and monochromatic). Nothing changes, yet everything becomes "more and more strange" and indefinite. Despite Winnie's buoyant optimism, she may know that her deferred performance will be her last; the action runs down and out, as she and Willie enact and embody a slow entropic decline. The ending of *Happy Days,* then, is like that of "The Dead": less an affirmation of performance than an inscrutable tableau. Is Willie "dressed to kill" because he has homicide in mind, or because he seeks an assignation (with a Winnie who became younger and sexier in production, though Beckett cut passages that endowed her with a sexual appetite), an assignation that Willie is constrained to acknowledge that Winnie, in her present condition, cannot manage? Does Willie sink down with his face to the ground out of frustration, or despair, or weakness, or relief? Is Willie's final call, "(*just audible*) Win," a last appeal, a feeble cry of exasperation in response to her relentless monologue, or some, perhaps ironic, expression of triumph?—as her reaction seems to imply: "*Happy expression appears, grows*" (*SB3,* 307). Does the look they exchange suggest that Winnie is terrified, perhaps because it both confirms her existence and threatens it by belonging to the Other, being alien and outside her control? Is Willie shocked that Winnie returns his gaze? Or is he overcome by her plight, and perhaps his own, which had not fully registered on him until this confrontation? The play ends by raising but not answering these questions, perhaps because of Beckett's own incertitude about Willie's motivation: "I know creatures are supposed to have no secrets for their authors, but I'm afraid mine for me have little else."[76]

Reinflecting the dramatic dynamics of *Happy Days, Film* (whose original title was *The Eye*) is a parable not only of nonperceivedness but also of antiperformance as O, like Joe in *Eh Joe,* enacts an elaborate but unsuccessful escape mime to avoid the camera's attention and then a series of vaudevillian skits and pratfalls when he thinks he has done so.[77] Winnie needs Willie to reassure herself that she continues to exist even as she disappears into the earth, and so she happily cedes center stage in production in order to provide him with a platform from which he can engage her. At the end she welcomes him as audience and finally sings her party piece for him. In *Film,* which is linked to the two *Acts without Words, Breath, Quad,* and *Nacht und Träume* as what Beckett called "literature of the un-word," O is Winnie's mute antithesis. Like a shy or unprepared party guest desperate not to be noticed, he flees the camera that is determined to put the performing spotlight on him. In both the text of

Film and the 1979 BBC version with Max Wall, "E's searching eye" picks out O amid a street scene of casual workers, a romantic couple on a bicycle, a horse cart driver, and others, all of them contentedly perceiving and being perceived. A dramatic change in mood occurs when, after O jostles a "shabby genteel" elderly couple holding a monkey, E momentarily halts in his pursuit of O in order to show the sort of observation he is fleeing: the couple's shocked reaction to his rudeness, an exchanged gaze between them, her shushing of him as if she were silencing an audience for a performance, and then their staring at O with "an expression only to be described as corresponding to an agony of perceivedness" (*SB3,* 373).

Working on *Film* with Schneider, Beckett, when he learned that the opening street sequence had misfired, suggested replacing it with "a simplified version in which only the indispensable couple is retained" (*CSPSB,* 162). The result fortuitously accorded with his growing interest in removing social context from his work, and his work from social context. The scene remains, however, in subsequent printings of *Film* (and appears in the Max Wall film), a discrepancy to which the introductory note in *Collected Shorter Plays* calls attention: "No attempt has been made to bring it [the text] in line with the finished work [the film]. The one considerable departure from what was imagined concerns the opening sequence" (162). One could argue, however, that "the finished" *Film* is not the 1964 movie that Beckett worked on or the version published in *The Grove Centenary Edition,* but the one in *The Collected Shorter Plays* that both includes the original text and acknowledges the film's deviation from it, and so represents an amalgamation of the two[78] as well as Beckett's increasing permissiveness in such matters, the result of his own directorial work.

Largely restricting its focus to E and O, determined audience and churlish performer, the Schneider/Keaton *Film* opens with a shot of a large, reptilian eye (presumably E's, or E), and then follows O's evasive, wall-hugging journey down the street, into a building, up the stairs, and into his mother's room. The determined E keeps O at the center of the camera's pursuing gaze as O covers the window and mirror, repeatedly puts out the dog and cat, "occlu[des] . . . parrot and goldfish," destroys "God's image," and evades objects with eye-like apertures (rocking chair, file folder [*SB3,* 375]). At last thinking he is safe from perception (and from his own perceiving of actual and potential perceivers),

O relaxes into the rocking chair at center stage where he tears up photographs, dead representations of a dead past, in a gesture of self-obliteration.

But despite his elaborate evasive and self-denying maneuvers, the reversed shot of E just before the end demonstrates that O remains inescapably self-observed—"It will not be clear until end of film that pursuing perceiver is not extraneous, but self" (371)—centered not only on stage but also in the camera's eye, still performing for an audience he has failed to elude. Thus, both *Happy Days* and *Film* end with their protagonists' disturbing confrontations with their alter egos: Winnie's with Willie, the audience she requires but perhaps fears to face, O's with his own observing E(ye) that reduces (or elevates) him to the object of its gaze. And just as sixty-nine-year-old Krapp is ultimately shaped and defeated by the choice made by the self he patronizes and mocks, so O, the silent monologist of his own attempt to deny both existence and observed performance, is horrified and overwhelmed by the audience of himself that he desperately, but unsuccessfully, sought to escape.

As allusively self-representational as *Krapp*,[79] *Play* (1963) triples the upper-torso monologist of *Happy Days* and combines it with the scrutinized object of *Film* who, to his horror, discovers at the end that his evasive action was the very performance that the camera demanded. In transition from characters to automatons and immobilized from the start, *Play*'s shadowy figures, called faces or heads by Beckett, have no such opportunity to delude themselves about resistance or escape. As Gontarski puts it: "They are rather voices, instruments, or things, part of the funeral urns which appear to have swallowed—like some leviathan—all but their protruding heads. . . . in the English première which Beckett oversaw (or, as Tynan claims, co-directed), the stage image became less a grouping of characters than a set of sculpted icons, a bas-relief triptych."[80] Two women and a man (or what is left of them) become, like desiccated, posthumous versions of Nagg and Nell and Winnie, "Faces so lost to age and aspect as to seem almost part of urns" (*SB3*, 355) and constrained recounters of a story they perform by rote.

Play depicts loss, Lost Ones: material being becomes flaky, attenuated, and truncated; names are reduced to labels, labels become letters and numbers (M, W1, W2 were originally called Syke, Conk, and Nickie);[81] characterization is a blazon of degraded body parts ("Pudding face, puffy, spots, blubber mouth, jowls, no neck, dugs you could—" [*SB3*, 359]); language is banal, stripped of nuance, "*faint, largely unintelligible*" in performance (355). *Play* inaugurates a pattern of diminution that, as Gontarski notes, plays out in Beckett's "dramaticules": "From *Play* onwards, Beckett's stage images would grow increasingly dehumanized, reified, and metonymic, featuring dismembered or incorporeal creatures as Beckett's became a theatre of body parts and spectres, a theatre striving for transparency rather than solidity, a theatre, finally, trying to undo itself."[82] Yet enforced performances simultaneously dramatize the very theatricality of Beckett's late plays.

The driving force in *Play,* like the piercing bell in *Happy Days* that "hurts like a knife," is a power from beyond the stage: the inquisitorial spotlight that isolates and prods, playing the three faces like musical instruments. The figures, who "face undeviatingly front throughout the play" (*SB3,* 355), respond always, only, and instantly, turn and turn about, to the sinister and punishing prompts of the spotlight. George Devine, *Play*'s first British director, compared it to "a dental drill"; Whitelaw called it "an instrument of torture" that, at least in the play's original version, demanded an endless identical reprise since, as Beckett explained, "the same text will go on *ad infinitum,* even faster and even softer without quite ceasing altogether."[83] The spotlight is also a demanding audience, bored or impatient with the monologues, and so constantly shifting from one figure to another, whom it prompts in turn and then cuts off, ever restless, ever seeking to hear, but not finding, a compelling narrative. During rehearsal, Whitelaw comments, the light became a directorial as well as a dictatorial force: "We used to rehearse it with the stage manager playing the light, pointing a finger at us, giving us a cue . . . , pointing his finger."[84] Under Schneider's direction the light was nicknamed "Sam."[85]

Obsessively linked when alive, the trio verbalize actions they can no longer perform, mouthing their invariant frenetic monologues from a straitjacketing script of their tawdry love triangle: "a Möbius strip of narrative," Gontarski calls it.[86] Seeing nothing, rigidly focused on the spotlight, and "impassive throughout," the three figures, whether indifferent, unaware, or resolutely determined to ignore each other and their extraordinary situation, seem oblivious to the parallel existence of the others.

In performance, the monologues become both relentless and largely incomprehensible (because of the speed of their speaking and their overlapping choruses, "rather like a fragmented musical round song, with each voice starting at a different point on the score,"[87] allowing the audience no opportunity for the laughter or reflection that their hackneyed tale might otherwise elicit. R. B. Kershner discusses Joyce's "delight . . . in invoking the material of cheap Victorian cliché . . . and then so embedding and enmeshing it in a complex text that its dramatic (or melodramatic) impact is lost."[88] Beckett similarly deploys sentimental plots in *Endgame, Happy Days, Krapp's Last Tape,* and, especially, *Play,* and the performances that depict them go even further than Joyce to shift focus from their stories.

Yet even as they perform their hackneyed story as automatons who seem unable to resist a cue or defy their script, the figures increasingly acknowledge their performative roles, and slippage begins to occur. Declaring his love for each of the women, M discovers that it's true (*SB3,* 357, 359), then thinks "God what vermin women" (359); W1 wonders if there's a way out through "Penitence . . . atonement" (365); W2 expresses her "doubt" in order to bolster it (364–65). Perhaps peace, they begin to hope, might follow a final telling. M: "Yes, peace, . . . not merely all over, but as if . . . never been—" (356); W1: "Some day somehow I may tell the truth at last and then no more light at last" (361). Perhaps out of frustration, they employ a defiant rhetoric that, while still recounting, increasingly challenges and subverts.

As Knowlson and Pilling demonstrate,[89] much of the text's commentary, which at first seems concerned only with the love triangle, takes on a second, theatrical and contemporary, significance in the "Meditation" section. Both W1 and W2, even as they address the spotlight retrospectively about M, seem also to be speaking *of* and *to* the light. W1 says, "You will weary of me. . . . Hellish half-light. . . . Get off me! Get off me! . . . Weary of playing with me. Get off me" (*SB3,* 360, 361, 365). W2 says, "Some day you will tire of me and go out . . . for good . . . Give me up, as a bad job. Go away and start poking and pecking at someone else" (361). M's stumbling rhetorical questions—"And all this? When will all this—. . . . All this, when will all this have been . . . just play?" and "Am I as much—. . . . Am I as much as . . . being seen?" (361, 366)—similarly suggest not only his self-reflexive awareness of himself as both actor and character, of being thus controlled and scripted, but also that the play's language and focus are sliding from enforced recollection to metaphors of theatrical entrapment and opposition, as their words become what George Devine called "dramatic ammunition."[90]

The rhetoric of resistance expressed by these figures again raises the question of whether Beckett's "stuck" characters—as in *Endgame* and *Happy Days*, and later in *Not I* and *Catastrophe*—are stoical about their condition or unaware. Beckett had implicitly answered this question in *Godot* when he has Didi assert, "At me too someone is looking, of me too someone is saying, He is sleeping, he knows nothing, let him sleep on" (83), and Winnie seems more self-aware than Beckett indicates. But the answer may well be different in the later dramatic works when the participants seem fully immersed in their roles. In this regard too *Play* is a transitional work: its speakers comment on their circumstances—stuck in their urns, stuck on the stage—but seem less than fully conscious of their situation or the implications of what they are saying.

The metaphoric theatricality and performative resistance embedded in *Play* (and propounded and commanded in its punning title) attained greater significance after Schneider's sole instance of failure of nerve. Directing *Play* in 1964, Schneider, under pressure from the producers to enhance intelligibility, sought and obtained Beckett's permission to have the actors say their lines, not twice rapidly, but only once and much more slowly. Schneider subsequently "despised myself for doing this," and never again asked Beckett to alter a text.[91]

Yet this experience may have turned back on Beckett, causing him to reconceive the light not as a fixed instrument of power, but as *Play*'s fourth character, perhaps created out of the figures' need or desire for an audience to validate their narratives. Directing a French production with Jean-Marie Serreau that same year, Beckett discovered "The inquirer (light) beginning to emerge as no less a victim of his inquiry than they and as needing to be free, within narrow limits, literally to act the part, i.e. to vary if only slightly his speeds and intensities."[92] Personifying the light, Beckett found that it ceased to be merely a mechanism and became more dynamic and alive than the inurned figures; and if it had a perspective, it would likely develop a growing weariness with the obsessive defensiveness and repetition of the monologues. Hence, although Beckett conceived *Play* to recur exactly, *da capo*, like the repeat in a musical piece, he had an experience analogous to Schneider's. He wrote to George Devine, who was preparing a London staging:

> According to the text it is rigorously identical with the first statement. We now think it would be dramatically more effective to have it express a slight

> weakening, both of question and of response, by means of less and perhaps slower light and correspondingly less volume and speed of voice. . . . The impression of falling off which this would give . . . would be reinforced if we obtained also, in the repeat, a quality of hesitancy, of both question and answer, perhaps not so much in a slowing down of actual débit as in a less confident movement of spot from one face to another and less immediate reaction of the voices.[93]

In Beckett's production, then, *Play* came to assume a structure something like that of *Godot, Happy Days,* and *Quad,* whose second acts are feebler, wearier versions of the first, enervated because the first round of performances have taken a toll. Instead of infinite repetition, *Play* could, therefore, eventually end like *Krapp:* in silence and darkness.

To an even greater extent than *Film,* the subsequent published version of *Play* was altered, so that it became permissive on the subject of the reprise:

> The repeat may be an exact replica of first statement [as in the 1976 Royal Court production directed by Donald McWhinnie] or it may present an element of variation.
>
> In other words, the light may operate the second time exactly as it did the first (exact replica) or it may try a different method (variation).(*SB3,* 368)

And Beckett refers acceptingly to "The London production (and in a lesser degree the Paris production) [as having] opted for the variation" (*SB3,* 368). Developing this ambiguity in the relationship of caught figures and mobile or offstage inquisitor, subsequent plays—*Film, Eh Joe, Not I, That Time, Footfalls, Catastrophe, Nacht und Träume, What Where*—dramatize talking (and silent) heads reduced and devitalized by an anthropomorphized theatrical spotlight or camera. As a consequence, performers displace characters in Beckett's later dramatic work even as party pieces virtually disappear from his stage.

6 Performers and Antiperformers in Beckett's Dramaticules

Waiting for Godot, Endgame, and *Happy Days* are radically different plays today than they were when they first appeared on the stage. Not only has controversial innovation become postmodernist classicism, but the view from the diminished scale and scope of Beckett's later plays, the dramaticules, has retrospectively transformed what once seemed cryptic, obscure, and self-contained into the vital, transparent, almost communal. All three plays end, or attempt to end, with a musical performance. In *Godot* Didi, who begins Act 2 by singing, asks Pozzo to have Lucky sing before they go; "But he is dumb," Pozzo responds (*SB3,* 81). When Hamm tells Clov not to sing, Clov asks, "Then how can it end?"; he adds, "I want to sing," but even when Hamm says "I can't prevent you," he fails to do so (144), though Beckett directed *Endgame* as if it were a musical comedy.[1] Winnie does finally sing her inappropriate love song to Willie, which produces her "*Happy expression . . . Smile*" (308) before their final shared gaze. After the dramaticules, suggested the Beckett actor Donald Davis, "*Godot* looks like an MGM musical"; Walter Asmus frequently described it as balletic. Gontarski's retrospective word for the early plays, one Beckett would likely have hated given his antipathy to the genre, is "operatic."[2]

Less hermetically self-contained than they had initially seemed, Beckett's early plays are still rooted in a recognizable communal and natural reality, and they enact something resembling mundane, personal, familial, and social dynamics. Dress them appropriately and give them something to eat and many of Beckett's early dramatic characters could pass in Joyce's social milieu. Yet Beckett's early plays inaugurate many of the performative themes, concerns, and devices that literally play themselves out in the dramatic works that follow, becoming traces of themselves, shadowy, attenuated—before disappearing altogether.

The contracting process that plays out in Beckett counters Joyce's growing expansiveness. In contrast to the earlier stories of *Dubliners*, "The Dead," though a moribund reality lurks just beneath its surface, portrays an enhanced world of social performance. Stephen Dedalus, like his father, auditions, if badly, for various roles in a quotidian world of recognizable possibilities. The protagonist of *Ulysses*, who goes in and out of performing the Odysseus role, possesses a plethora of stage names: his family name was changed from Virag by his father; he calls himself Leopold, L. Bloom, and Poldy (*U*, 631); uses the pseudonym Henry Flower in his epistolary affair with Martha Clifford; is variously called "O'Bloom, the son of Rory" (285), "Herr Professor Luitpold Blumenduft" (292), "Senhor Enrique Flor" (314), "S. Leopold" (324), "Nagyaságos uram Lipóti Virag" (328), among others; and merges consubstantially into Stephen as Stoom and Blephen (635). Recording names at Dignam's funeral, Hynes is uncertain of Bloom's christian name: "—L, Mr Bloom said. Leopold" (107), and he is transmogrified into "*L. Boom*" when his name appears in the newspaper account (602). Even when Bloom *is* given his own name, it is often with a sense of narrative surprise: "Leopold Bloom (for it is he)" (350); "Bloom (properly so dubbed)" (603). The slippage in Bloom's name, and its linkage with the revivalist preacher John Alexander Dowie at the beginning of "Lestrygonians," may also in part reflect Joyce's complicated attitude toward nationalist imagery of the Irish revival that "invoked withered rose-bushes brought to fresh bloom by the blood sacrifice of young men":[3]

> Bloo. . . . Me? No.
> Blood of the Lamb. (*U*, 144)

Yet the result is accretive, not disintegrative: rather than undermining who and what Bloom is such naming and renaming enhances a sense of his complexity and myriadness.

In contrast, Beckett's early plays depict the fading out, or ebbing, of identity and denomination—and the simultaneous assertion of a performative persona—which becomes increasingly central in the later plays. Walter Ong notes that names "give human beings power over what they name,"[4] and one's inability to name things and to retain one's own name signals the loss not only of authority but also of identity, stable relationships, and self-representation.

As if trying out possible stage appellations, Beckett's early plays problematize the names and identities of their characters, creating slippages of biography, history, and meaning, but with very un-Joycean results. Beckett's nominal displacements lack resonance; they confound and subvert rather than enhance identity. For no discernible reason, *Godot*'s stage directions call its main characters Vladimir and Estragon; in the dialogue they are invariably Didi and Gogo, except when Gogo tells Pozzo that his name is Adam (*SB3,* 30) and the Boy twice calls Didi "Mister Albert" (41, 83), to which Didi responds as if that is his name (or that it does not matter): "Yes" (42). Gogo takes Pozzo for Godot both times he appears (16–17, 69–70); and he and Didi wrestle with Pozzo's name—"Bozzo . . . Bozzo. . . . Pozzo . . . Pozzo. . . . I once knew a family called Cozzo" (16–17)—just as Pozzo struggles "with this . . . Godet . . . Godot . . . Godin . . . anyhow you see who I mean" (23). Stephen Dedalus says that "—Sounds are impostures, . . . like names" (*U,* 578), but he is proud of his name ("The great men in the history had names like that" [*PA,* 60]), and whatever else he lacks he has a secure, if often unhappy, sense of his personal and familial identity. David Hayman describes the difference this way: "Joyce tried to conquer the universe by naming its contrary but not necessarily contradictory components, elaborating its internal tensions. Beckett attempts to control it by canceling it out."[5]

In *Endgame,* Beckett raises but leaves unanswered the question of Clov's origins: Is he Hamm's son? is he the boy in Hamm's story? where does he come from and why is he there? Krapp echoes Joyce's Stephen, who fantasizes that he does not owe AE money because "Molecules all change. I am other I now. Other I got pound" (*U,* 182). But Stephen also acknowledges "I am another now and yet the same" (11), whereas Krapp vehemently insists on a discontinuity of identity, that he is not "that stupid bastard I took myself for thirty years ago, hard to believe I was ever as bad as that" (*SB3,* 228). And Winnie is, in Beckett's phrase, "an interrupted being" who, despite all she has lost, desperately asserts continuing identity by rerunning absurdly inappropriate old tapes: "Oh this *is* a happy day! This will have been another happy day!" (296). She is severed from her past, which is hard to visualize and about which nothing is certain, and she expresses a radical disconnect between her words (including the name Willie calls her: Win) and her situation. She performs her bravura party piece for an absent, no longer extant, and unimaginable salon audience.

Taking their cue from Winnie's prop obsession, virtuosity, and subsiding into the earth, Beckett's small-scale plays depict characters who are shrunk to performing remnants, or else displaced, in whole or part, by performing props, with devices like bells, lights, and tape recorders coming to "function more like dramatic principals than incidental side effects."[6] Remarkably, Beckett had at first thought that *Play* would be relatively unchallenging to stage, telling Alan Schneider that it would be "I think by far the easiest play of mine you have had" (*No Author,* 131). But less than three weeks later, responding to Schneider's recitation of difficulties with the staging, he radically altered his view: "I realize that no final script is possible till I have had work on rehearsals" (144), for even more than *Krapp, Play* had such extraordinary technical requirements that the text proved an inadequate guide to performance and Beckett felt compelled, if the production were to fulfill his exacting vision, to involve himself with rehearsal. As Gontarski writes of this defining moment, *Play* "drew Beckett further into the theatrical process, since it demanded a level of technical sophistication and precision unknown in his earlier work, and it was the writing of *Play* that may have, finally, forced Beckett—reluctant as he was—to assume full directorial responsibility for his own works. . . . the single inquisitorial spotlight—part torturer, part orchestra conductor, even part theatre director—situated amid the footlights, which instantaneously flashes from face to face, was not part of any technical director's repertoire of contraptions in 1963."[7]

From his earliest dramatic writings, Beckett maintained that his precise stage directions should be followed in production, so he prevented substantial changes when he could (the adaptation of *All That Fall* for the stage, all female productions of *Waiting for Godot* and *Endgame*) and suffered those he could not. In a famous episode, he was so unhappy with the American Repertory Theatre's staging of *Endgame* (1984) that he had this note inserted in the program: "Any production of *Endgame* which ignores my stage directions is completely unacceptable to me."[8] He might have said the same about all his plays—at least until he started staging, and revising, them himself.

Beckett, then, entered the theater, text in hand, seeking to realize the perfect and invariant performance through focusing intensely on the minutiae of its theatrical realization.[9] As virtual co-director, and then director, with, among others, Roger Blin in Paris, Alan Schneider, Rick Cluchy of the San

Quentin Drama Workshop, and television and radio producers of his work in Germany, in France, and at the BBC, Beckett found that his directing experience transformed work he had considered finished. Between 1966 and 1986, Beckett directed sixteen stage productions of his dramatic writings and seven productions for German television, "each time creating the final text in rehearsals. . . . By 1986 the textual variations of Beckett's productions suggested a repudiation of his originally published texts,"[10] the early plays being rewritten as he wrote new ones.

As a result of his theater work Beckett came to consider "the first run-through with actors as the 'realisation' of the play and when it has been performed publicly he will say that it has been 'created.'"[11] Advising Schneider on his productions of *Play* and *Film,* Beckett came to realize that even the text that emerged from this process remained a work in progress—a last script until the next one—since no production could be any more definitive than could a published text. The more Beckett sought to create the definitive work the more elusive that goal became, and yet the more that effort inflected both his earlier plays and the ones that followed.

Staging *Play* led Beckett both to rework all his previous stage writings and to write new dramatic work predicated on what his theatrical experience was teaching him. Beckett's participation in theatrical productions after the publication of *Play,* Gontarski argues, caused all of his work for the theater—including *Play*—to become "more overtly formalist and patterned as it became more visual . . . more static than active, more lyric than dramatic,"[12] hence the diminution of scale and vitality, the rhetoric of stasis and staging, and the ghostly presences that characterize the dramaticules. Gontarski adds that, "If what we tend to call Beckett's late style began with *Play,* then all of Beckett's theatre works are finally 'late plays', written in the 'late style', that is, all of Beckett's stage plays are 'written' (i.e. completed) after the publication of *Play*—even *Play* itself. . . . Beckett was re-creating his dramatic corpus, reinventing himself as a dramatist, rewriting history in effect during this mid-1960s period."[13] If *Waiting for Godot* changed the nature of the theater it had entered, *Play*'s entry into the theater changed Beckett.

Working in the theater led Beckett to new understandings of how productions occur and how performance could be incorporated, which meant, as Gontarski puts it, that "he was prepared to change and even at times substantially rewrite the published versions of his texts based on the practicalities, realities, and insights that working in stage space literally brought to light, and this at a time when he was rethinking the staging of all his work. . . . What Beckett could no longer 'escape' was full directorial responsibility or self-collaboration. . . . Directing became a crucial part of his creative process."[14] At times (though not always) Beckett would subsequently alter his published texts in conformity with script changes that he had worked out or sanctioned in production. And the process would be replicated if Beckett became involved in a subsequent production of a play, so that the work remained in flux—finished, then "created" in production, then susceptible to changes from that production, and so on, a process that played out in the repeats with variation within or of *Play, . . . but the clouds . . . , Rockaby, Ohio Impromptu, Quad,* and *What Where.*

As props and metonymic depictions displaced traditional characters in the plays Beckett wrote during this period, he sought self-effacing actors willing to surrender their own interpretive scope for the intensity and rhythm of his work. Beckett's ideal actor would do his bidding without regard to substance, would perform his meaning unmediatedly, with as little interference or even presence as possible, even as, under Beckett's direction, his scripts altered during rehearsal. For many playwrights, the script disappears into the actors; Beckett required actors who would disappear into his scripts, even when the scripts proved slippery and unfinished, works still in process and requiring performance to be fully realized. James Mays suggests that Beckett's "sense of the priority of the text and the director's authority is . . . teutonic; it allows no scope for free expression."[15] Bair cites Beckett as saying that "the perfect stage vehicle is one in which there are no actors or directors, only the play itself. When asked how such theater could be made viable, Beckett replied that the author had the duty to search for the perfect actor, that is, one who would comply fully with his instructions, having the ability to annihilate himself totally."[16] In Jack MacGowran, Patrick Magee, Donald Davis, David Warrilow, Barry McGovern, Billie Whitelaw, and a few others, Beckett found actors willing to accept such constraints.

Bair writes of Whitelaw, "Until now [1972], Beckett had only been able to convince actors and actresses in Germany to give up their own identities and interpretations and to do exactly what he wanted them to do, but he was fortunate in London that Whitelaw was able to bring an extraordinary intelligence and sensitivity to her part, . . . putting herself totally in Beckett's directorial hands, performing *Not I* exactly as he wanted."[17] Whitelaw seemed instinctively to understand this need for self-effacement: "You simply allow your own core to make contact with what comes off the page. Eventually everything then falls into place, the material takes off on its own. If you allow the words to breathe through your body, if you become a conduit, something magical *may* happen."[18] Whitelaw, whom Cronin calls "malleable material" for the "tyrannical" demands Beckett made of actors, "responded willingly and all the more so because they were gently and courteously couched."[19] MacGowran was equally malleable: "It's like emptying your own head completely. You let your self drift into his consciousness. . . . When I came to I was quite shattered."[20] Beckett perforce became author(ity) of stage as well as page, casting himself as, in effect, *Catastrophe*'s commanding Director nearly two decades before he wrote that part.

The great Beckett actors and directors readily accepted their instrumentality. Beckett told Billie Whitelaw, who viewed his scripts as musical scores, that *Happy Days* "was a sonata for voice and movement. By that he meant that everything was precisely timed—like notes of music."[21] Whitelaw cheerfully agreed, "When I work with Sam we don't analyze the plays at all. My first task is to find the music of it. At first you don't know if it goes fast or slow, or where to put the metronome."[22] For Warrilow, too, "What works is finding what musicians have called the 'right tone.' . . . if I sing it 'on key,' 'in tune,' it's going to vibrate properly for somebody else."[23] And according to his English director George Devine, "When working as a director on a Beckett play—one has to think of the text as something like a musical score, wherein the 'notes,' the sights, the sounds, the pauses, have their own special inter-related rhythms and out of their composition comes the dramatic impact."[24] Beckett himself sought to "score" *Play* when he directed it in Germany in 1978 by having a piano brought to rehearsal to provide a unique musical note for each of the three actors. The attempt was not a success and was abandoned.[25]

Despite such reiterated focus on Beckett's music, it is with his silent figures that he has gone furthest in reducing character to performer, since their lack of orality denies them the most expressive means of self-assertion and identity. Muted and deprived of language they usually lose all power of resistance, becoming utterly docile enactors of carefully prescribed movements like F in *Ghost Trio,* M in . . . *but the clouds* . . . , the players in *Quad,* A and B in *Nacht und Träume.* Beckett told the cameraman filming this last play "that it was difficult for him to keep writing words, without having the feeling that it was a lie."[26] External stimuli—whether physical violence (as in *Act Without Words I*), goads (*Act Without Words II*), peremptory bells or chimes (*Happy Days, Footfalls*), spotlights (*Play*), verbal commands ("More" in *Rockaby*), or table knocks (*Ohio Impromptu*)—demand and provoke performance. Chaffing against their constraints, handicapped or confined characters proffer narrative excess when they are able to speak, and then run down like worn-out machines. In *Godot,* Lucky's monologue is terminated by physical restraint; by Act 2 he has joined the ranks of Beckett's totally docile mutes. Nagg's trousers story provokes Hamm's demand for silence, and then that Nagg serve Hamm as audience. For even the verbal flows—of Winnie's voluble optimism; *Play*'s talking heads, like Krapp, endlessly rerunning old tapes; Mouth in *Not I* repeatedly overriding Auditor's objections—a time comes, or seems about to, when "words fail" (*SB3,* 284).

But Beckett's language-less characters, no less than his verbal ones, inhabit scripts created with words, whether the performances themselves are wordless—as in *Act Without Words I* and *II, Film, Breath, Quad, Nacht und Träume*—or its protagonists mute: Joe in *Eh Joe,* Auditor in *Not I,* F in *Ghost Trio,* M and M1 in . . . *but the clouds* . . . , Listeners in *That Time* and *Ohio Impromptu,* P in *Catastrophe.* The plays in the first group are comprised of nothing but silent stage directions; those in the second are little more than spoken stage directions. And such language is particularly exigent since stage directions are imperatives, commands that must be obeyed—except when changed under Beckett's direction.

As if struggling to recall an oral performative tradition that has died out, Beckett's stage world, increasingly devoid of even the veneer of human or social interchange, reduces its occupants from characters to constrained performing parts or automatons possessing little in the way of identities, relationships, lives actually being lived, or social milieus in which party pieces are willingly performed or enjoyed. Unlike the relentless focus on the present in *Godot* and *Happy Days,* the later plays, often harking back to more expansive lives, are largely retrospective, obsessive recreations of "that time" when something (or nothing) happened, and keeps on happening—whether from regret and nostalgia (*Krapp's Last Tape, That Time, Ghost Trio, . . . but the clouds . . .*, *Ohio Impromptu, Nacht und Träume*) or denial and despair (*Play, Eh Joe, Not I, Footfalls, Rockaby*). Life was once possible (or seems to have been); now only invariant (or nearly invariant) recalling or inventing of that life remains, like scraps and parodies of party pieces performed for attenuated or absent audiences. Speechmaking or oral narrative, whether demanded of or imposed upon the speaker, is the primary action in the dramaticules, with "the play on the verge of becoming something else," as Brater puts it, "something that looks suspiciously like a performance poem."[27]

Repeated recountings of former days in *Krapp, Play, Eh Joe, That Time, Rockaby,* and *Ohio Impromptu* imply that the past retains force, distract from the sentimentality or banality of the recalled stories and the vacuity of the present, and become a way (whether desired or not) of holding death at bay: "just one of those things you kept making up to keep the void out just another of those old tales to keep the void from pouring in on top of you the shroud" (*That Time, SB3,* 419). Charles Lyons suggests that "The division of voices within the same speaker manifests the antithesis that marks each of Beckett's heroes: the impulsion to continue speech and, thus, existence; the desire for silence, and, therefore, death."[28] Like *Eh Joe, That Time*—whose silent face is "simultaneously character, stage prop, and stage set"—is an antiperformance, a depiction of Listener's silent hearing of his own voice coming from three sources, each with its own narrative agenda. "The monologues of memory," as Brater puts it, offer "no release, no relief, no ritual purification, no denouement. What remains of the past is only the remnant of a threnody, the tattered shreds of what might once have been a coherent memory or a unified past."[29] Yet that remnant, that trace of performance, is all that sustains the present.

The process of diminution began early on for Beckett and gathered momentum throughout his writing career. *All That Fall* is his most overtly Irish work; and although "images of his childhood in Ireland . . . appear often in his work,"[30] Irish allusions and orientation were reduced during the writing and rewriting of subsequent plays. In *Happy Days* Winnie's music box was originally to play "When Irish Eyes Are Smiling";[31] Gontarski notes that the early drafts of *Happy Days* "tend to be more 'realistic' than the printed version. . . . The composition of *Happy Days* is almost a process of decomposition, a direction consistent with Beckett's professed aesthetic [in *Proust*]: 'The artistic tendency is not expansive, but a contraction."[32] *Not I,* which seemed to Schneider to call for certain Irish intonations, not only lost most of its references to Irish settings but led Beckett to insist, "No Irishness intended" (*No Author,* 283).

Similarly, autobiographical references were usually suppressed or else satirized, even in *Krapp's Last Tape,* the most self-referential of Beckett's dramatic work, though its theme of lost or betrayed love, based in part on Beckett's own life, continues to play out in subsequent plays like *Play, Eh Joe, Ghost Trio, . . . but the clouds . . . , Ohio Impromptu,* and *Nacht und Träume.* Krapp's Protestant hymn was eliminated; the opening mimes in both *Krapp* and *Film* were sharply curtailed—"quicker, simpler, more dramatic," as Beckett demanded of Clov's ladder-and-windows pantomime at the beginning of *Endgame* for the 1956 German production.[33] In addition, with rare exceptions like *Footfalls,* traditional elements of character, milieu, and social interaction disappear from Beckett's later plays, and even *Footfalls* is peopled by ghosts. Despite occasional "unexpected sumptuousness" (Ellmann's phrase, *4D,* 85) like the "lullaby" of *Rockaby* and the storytelling of *Footfalls* and *Ohio Impromptu,* language itself becomes stripped and bare, mainly utilitarian, imperatives like the voicing of stage directions in *Breath, Quad, Ghost Trio,* and *. . . but the clouds . . . , Catastrophe,* and *What Where.* The substance of performance yields to its details and techniques: meticulous staging, choreography, rhythm, music, and lighting.

Party pieces and the context for them also dissipate in the later plays. Little is left to tell, but that little, like Krapp's rerunning of old tapes, recurs again and again in the dramaticules, with their weakening repeats (*Play, Come and Go, Ghost Trio, Ohio Impromptu, What Where*), revolvings (*Footfalls, Quad*), and calls for "More" (*Rockaby*). Figures thus stuck because of their inability or failure to let go, to move forward, imaginatively return persistently as to the scene of a crime (or a life or a party piece), becoming shadows of shades, devitalized in the process of running down and out. The interactive couples of the early plays are at times displaced by sketchy and oddly paired figures set amid the merest traces of communal settings in *Embers, Film, Eh Joe, Footfalls, Rockaby, Ohio Impromptu,* managing to express only an illusion of interaction and social intercourse and, therefore, of life. The focus instead becomes artifice and theatricality, with alternative selves serving primarily as each other's audience or performing alter ego.[34] Or isolated figures (or parts of them) are enervated, posthumous, barely there. The voluble upper torso figures of *Endgame, Happy*

Days, and *Play* become either mute—head, torso, or full body, in, respectively, *. . . but the clouds . . .* (W), *Ohio Impromptu* (L), and *Catastrophe* (P)—or even more insubstantial, reduced, almost as in the radio plays, to little more than oral utterances: the recorded thirty-nine-year-old Krapp and W in *Rockaby;* Mouth in *Not I;* disembodied voices in *Eh Joe, That Time, Ghost Trio, . . . but the clouds . . .* , and *Breath;* the offstage Mother in *Footfalls.*[35]

Loss of names and identities increasingly became Beckett's norm. Viola, Poppy, and Rose in the first typescript of *Come and Go* are reduced to Vi, Flo, and Ru by the time of publication, and explicit allusions to their illnesses and adulterous affairs disappear.[36] In *Rough for Theatre I* and *II* characters are identified by initials rather than names, although A and B in *Theatre II* occasionally call each other by name within the text (Bertrand and Morvan), and B in *Theatre I* proffers a name—and a family connection—for A: "May I call you Billy, like my son?" (*SB3,* 233; B's posited relationship to A is one of this play's many echoes of *Endgame,* whose characters were initially designated A, B, P, and M). Such designation reverses what occurs in *Godot,* where Didi and Gogo nickname each other but are always referred to formally by the writer of the stage directions. Beginning with *Play* and *Film* numerous dramatic characters become merely initials or generic labels like M[an] and W[oman] 1 and 2 in *Play* (originally they were a woman and two men, named Syke and Conk;[37] E[ye] and O[bject] in *Film;* W[oman] and V[oice] in *Rockaby;* L[istener] and R[eader] in *Ohio Impromptu;* and P[rotagonist/Prisoner], D[irector/Dictator], and A[ssistant] in *Catastrophe.*[38]

Henry in the radio play *Embers* (1959) is a transitional figure. Like Pozzo, he inhabits a bourgeois environment and even, unusually, has a family: he inherits his father's money; his daughter takes piano and horseback riding lessons; he vacations in Switzerland; he sets his Bolton/Holloway story in a drawing room. But he is well on his way to becoming, like the figures in *Play* and *Film,* a creature of his performative medium. Exploring the paradoxical relationship of theatricality and self-reflexivity, *Embers* (whose original title "Ebb" suggests attenuation, fading) begins with Henry's triple set of double imperatives, which are uncertain in both their target of address and effect. He speaks after the opening sounds of the sea and his boots on the shingle: "On. [*Sea. Voice louder.*] On! [*He moves on. Boots on shingle. As he goes.*] Stop. [*Boots on shingle. As he goes, louder.*] Stop! [*He halts. Sea a little louder.*] Down. [*Sea.*

Voice louder.] Down! [*Slither of shingle as he sits. Sea, still faint, audible throughout what follows whenever pause indicated.*]" (*SB3,* 197). And he closes the play with "Not a sound" (211), which could be either a declarative or an imperative, and false or true (depending on whether it refers to what has preceded or to what follows). It is, in any event, followed by Henry's lapsing into wordlessness and silence, whether temporary or permanent, a condition toward which many of Beckett's protagonists aspire and which others dread.

In between, Henry's incessant telling of unfinished stories fictionalizes the pain of his existence and tells much about the fate of party pieces, and their performers, in Beckett's plays: "I usen't to need anyone, just to myself, stories, there was a great one about an old fellow called Bolton, I never finished it, I never finished any of them, I never finished anything, everything always went on for ever" (198). The reasonable, though ghostly, voice of Ada, his wife, says, "You should see a doctor about your talking, it's worse, what must it be like for Addie [their daughter]? . . . she said, Mummy, why does Daddy keep on talking all the time? . . . It's silly to say it keeps you from hearing it [the sea], it doesn't keep you from hearing it and even if it does you shouldn't be hearing it, there must be something wrong with your brain" (205–6), which suggests that the noise of the sea that we hear may be a product of Henry's imagination.

But it is silence and the lack of an audience, not noise, that Henry fears most. "Stories, stories, years and years of stories, till the need came on me, for someone, to be with me, anyone, a stranger, to talk to, imagine he hears me, years of that, and then, now, for someone who . . . knew me, in the old days, anyone, to be with me, imagine he hears me, what I am, now" (200). Like Didi demanding "Come on, Gogo, return the ball, can't you, once in a way?" (7), Henry, when Ada pauses in her comments, urges her, "Drive on, drive on! Why do people always stop in the middle of what they are saying? . . . Keep on, keep on! [*Imploringly.*] Keep it going, Ada, every syllable is a second gained" (208). Silence, narrative failure, signals death, especially in a radio play; and Henry prefers talk, keeping it going, to what he envisions of hell (which sounds very like his current situation): "small chat to the babbling of Lethe about the good old days when we wished we were dead" (201).

As with Maddy in *All That Fall,* Henry's monologue is part descriptive, part precise instructions for a sound technician, part commands directed at himself or the surrounding elements. Is he describing what he sees and hears?

Is he ordering the world to appear and sound as he wants it to? Are his commands aimed at keeping himself and his story going or at holding the attention of his listening audience, without whom he would cease to exist? At times he speaks (to himself? to the ghost of his father? to his other voices? to the stranger he is desperate to tell his "years and years of stories" [200]? to those hearing the broadcast?) as if he were aware of himself as a performer inside a radio play—asking, in the voice of Addie, "Will I play my piece now please?" (203), and trying to overcome the disadvantage of the medium: "That sound you hear is the sea. [*Pause. Louder.*] I say that sound you hear is the sea, we are sitting on the strand. [*Pause.*] I mention it because the sound is so strange, so unlike the sound of the sea, that if you didn't see what it was you wouldn't know what it was" (197). He repeats the process with the next sound, that of horses: "Hooves! [*Pause. Louder.*] Hooves! [*Sound of hooves walking on hard road. They die rapidly away. Pause.*] Again! [*Hooves as before. Pause. Excitedly.*] Train it to mark time! Shoe it with steel and tie it up in the yard, have it stamp all day!" (197–98). Henry blurs the line between descriptive and imperative, and thus between his role as character and that of radio technician, by naming the sound before he (or at least his audience) has heard it. And since the medium precludes the possibility that we *could* see what makes the sound, we cannot know whether to trust Henry when he insists that the noise we hear *is* external to him and natural, rather than internal—or just radio sound effects.

Obsessed with the aural as much as *Film*'s O is obsessed with the visual, Henry alludes repeatedly to sounds, especially those of the sea, which he hates, as if he were trying to obliterate them and the compelling memories they evoke, or trying himself to determine whether they, like the voices he hears, exist independently or only within his head. "In *Embers,*" Katherine Worth maintains, "the focus is always on the mysterious relationship between the willed and unwilled sounds, between those that stay in place and those that get out of hand, like Addie's uncontrollable paroxysms or the sucking sound of the sea." Desperate to come to terms with his father's life and death, Henry cannot get the Bolton/Holloway story "out of his mind; perhaps has to disguise it in fictional form before he can tolerate the tale of the two old men by the dying embers and somehow do what he feels he has to do, relate it to the other story of his father, whose spirit haunts the entire piece."[39] Henry is one of Beckett's first dramatic speakers to subvert his own identity by narrating a deflected or disguised story, and thereby call attention to himself primarily as performing storyteller rather than as character.

In the following radio plays, *Words and Music* (1962) and *Cascando* (1963), as Gontarski notes, the "nature of theatrical 'character' itself . . . was being redefined, dispersed. Words and music were personified, becoming protagonists—or antagonists—in the radio plays."[40] Summoned by their imperious master to perform, they decline into roles and categories, playing parts—in both senses of that phrase: "playing" as adjective as well as verb. In *Cascando,* Beckett explicitly evokes *The Arabian Nights,* the great work in which compelled storytelling forestalls the lapse into ultimate silence, although when Opener prompts Voice to tell a story, the narrative recounts the search for a story that will finally end storytelling. *Cascando*'s Voice begins *in medias* metanarrative: "—story . . . if you could finish it . . . you could rest . . . sleep . . . not before . . . oh I know . . . the ones I've finished . . . thousands and one" (*SB3,* 343). Just as Scheherazade's survival depends on repeated compelling storytelling, dramaticule performers narrate "as a strategy to sustain activity in the present":[41] they exist only so long as, and only while, they perform.

Voice seeks the story that will prove "the right one . . . then rest . . . sleep." So far each story has been "not the right one," and Voice "couldn't rest . . . straight away another" (*SB3,* 343). The final "dying away" may at last imply something of an achievement: Opener "[*fervently*]" pronounces "Good!" as Music and Voice conclude "[*Together.*] —this time . . . it's the right one . . . finish . . . no more stories . . . sleep . . . we're there . . . nearly . . . just a few more . . . don't let go . . . Woburn . . . he clings . . . on . . . come on . . . come on—" (351). But Beckett's oral narratives are rarely congruent with the plays that ostensibly contain them: in *Rough for Radio II, Play, Not I, That Time,* as well as *Cascando,* curtains rise on storytellers who are already well launched, and they fall on narratives that seem to continue to fade as the audience leaves the theater. Neither beginnings nor endings are quite what they used to be; they take on the rhythm and structure of Voice's final ". . . we're there . . . nearly. . . ." Wherever "there" is, whatever "nearly" means.

In *Words and Music* Joe and Bob, as Croak their maestro calls Words and Music, may be either the names of the characters who perform Words and Music, or they may represent human identities that are being lost as roles usurp the characters who once performed them. Croak, in fact, has already lost his since his name, if that's what it is, is never spoken: Words addresses him throughout as "My Lord." One sign of vestigial meaning may be Words's opening monologue on sloth as "the most powerful passion and indeed no passion is more powerful than the passion of sloth" (*SB3,* 333). The "theme" of sloth seems arbitrarily chosen and nonsensical, but it has historic resonance since sloth was, according to the common English view of the day, the defining Irish trait and thus the major cause of the Famine.

Words's initial effort, "*Rattled off, low,*" is a rehearsal, a limbering up exercise that occurs while Music, to Words's exasperation, is tuning. At Croak's command, Words, in his "*orotund*" second rendering, replaces "sloth" with "love," Croak's chosen theme, with the rest of his monologue remaining otherwise unchanged except when Words muddles up the two themes. Croak, a commanding taskmaster, responds at first with "*Rending sigh,*" then with "*Violent thump of club*" as the recital misfires. Demanding harmony, a unified performance—"Together. [*Pause. Thump.*] Together! [*Pause. Violent thump.*] Together, dogs!" (334–36)—Croak is a poor conductor who provokes dissonance, a clash between meaning and sound that Michel Poizat, in his history of sung words as a struggle for predominance between words and music, calls "a constantly negotiated tension between speech and music": "on the one hand, fusion or confusion of music and speech, and on the other hand, music's antagonism toward, challenge to, and even destruction of the spoken word" (44, 51), and of the "character" who embodies it.

For Beckett, Words is always culpable: perhaps envying Music's nonreferentiality and his own failure to create harmony, he vehemently protests Music's interruptions of his clumsy verbal performances. Trying to sing alone on Croak's next theme, age (which he, "*faltering,*" transposes: "Age is . . . age is when . . . old age I mean . . . if that is what my Lord means"), Words stumbles badly both rhythmically and substantively. Groping for appropriate imagery, he envisages "a man . . . huddled . . . nodding," an old hag with a bed pan, arrowroot and toddy, the face of lost or disappointed love amid old ashes. Music repeatedly tries to be helpful: offering an "*Improvement of above*" and "*Suggestion for following,*" and generously and supportively "*Plays air through alone, then invites* Words *with opening, pause, invites again and finally accompanies very softly*" (335–37).

Where Music is "*warmly sentimental*" Words is "*disregarding, cold,*" but the latter is finally sufficiently accepting, or humbled, to sing two lyrical, romantically evocative songs with Music. Croak, who groaned in anguish throughout Words's execrable solo performance, is silent during the two songs, perhaps satisfied. After the first song, which evokes the lost love "in the ashes," Croak repeatedly murmurs "The face." After the second, which penetrates "Through the trash . . . Through the scum" by a series of negations ("no begging / No giving no words / No sense no need") to "one glimpse / Of that wellhead," Croak lets fall his club and shuffles off. "*Shocked*" at this effect, Words, having performed a paean to wordlessness suggestive of the condition of music, then appeals directly to Music under the appellation "Bob." Music responds with "*Brief rude retort*" (337–40), perhaps because Words has previously abused him or because such denomination is anachronistic and insulting. But when Words appeals again, this time to "Music," the latter does perform for him. The play ends with "*Deep sigh*" from Words, perhaps a grudging acknowledgment of his dependence on and inferiority to Music.

Eh Joe (1966), which can be thought of as Beckett's first ballet, foregrounds technique that distracts attention from the story's soft center and directs it to the play's performative aspects. Its protagonist, who lacks Croak's "comforts . . . friends" (*SB3,* 334), seeks isolation and nonobservance like O in *Film,* taking the evasive actions of one desperate *not* to perform, *not* to be noticed. Unaware of the camera observing him during the opening (perhaps nightly) ritual, Joe performs the play's first "dance": he minutely searches his sealed room and "paranoiacally ascertains that he is alone."[42] Confident that he has successfully cloistered himself, Joe finally relaxes and begins to doze off. His elaborate mime of evasion proves fruitless, however, and seems to evoke precisely what he sought to preclude: the riveting camera and derisive Voice that serve first as his invisible audience and then as his inquisitors. Joe is startled awake not only when Voice first begins to speak, but on each succeeding occasion.[43]

After the opening sequence, the "action" of *Eh Joe* is a pas de deux of speaking Voice and camera movements toward Joe that is choreographed as precisely as the dances in *Footfalls, . . . but the clouds . . . ,* and *Quad*: "*nine slight moves in towards face, say four inches each time*" (*SB3,* 391). The camera unwaveringly—and in increasing close-up—focuses on Joe, who sits stationary after his opening activity (satisfied? exhausted? at a loss about what to do next?), suddenly reduced to constrained audience and struggling to display no reaction to the eerily persistent Voice: "*Low, distinct, remote, little colour, absolutely steady rhythm, slightly slower than normal*" (392). As in *Film,* Beckett uses the camera as an antagonistic pursuer, but the setting is entirely interior and sound has returned with a vengeance. And in contrast to *Not I,* for example, Joe is sound's target, not its source.

Joe's passion, which Beckett says is "to kill the voices which he cannot kill," plays out on the stage of his face (*Eh Joe* is, as Beckett called *Not I,* a "face play" [*No Author,* 139]), with its "*eyes unblinking during paragraphs, impassive except in so far as it reflects mounting tension of listening*" (*SB3,* 392). Despite all his precautions, Joe, like Krapp, is haunted by a talking ghost, though Krapp has confined his to recordings of himself that he can turn on and off and fast forward through. Joe's ghost, an avenging and vindictive woman's voice, also seems mechanical, like a tape recording, but Voice is represented as having an independent existence: she mocks Joe for thinking that he might escape observation ("Why don't you put out that light? . . . There might be a louse watching you") and that she is speaking from "that penny farthing hell you call your mind." She reminds him that he had once "admired my elocution! . . . You could have listened to it forever" (392–94). And now he does since, as Beckett wrote, "Voice should be whispered. A dead voice in his head" (*No Author,* 201), suggesting that Joe performs an internalized ventriloquist's trick, obsessively rehearsing his past as a way of filling the void because the alternative is worse ("Isn't it Joe?"): confronting the present, silence, death.

As in *Play* and many of the late plays, the separation of language and motion represents an assault on the oral tradition, with its performances that Ong describes as physical and cohesive: "The oral word . . . never exists in a simply verbal context as a written word does. Spoken words are always part of a total existential situation, which always engages the body. Bodily activity beyond mere vocalisation is not adventitious or contrived in oral communication, but is natural and even inevitable" (*SB3,* 67–68). Such separation is, of course, inevitable in radio plays—*All That Fall*'s Dan Rooney self-reflexively insists, "Do not ask me to speak and move at the same time" (176)—but beginning with *Happy Days* Beckett also increasingly staged this separation. As Katherine Hayles notes in her discussion of *Krapp's Last Tape,* "Body and voice no longer necessarily go together. Voice can persist through time outside the body, confronting the subject as an externalized other."[44] It is precisely what had long seemed "natural and even inevitable" that Beckett's plays are unwilling to countenance.

Although the triangular relationship of performer, performance, and observer is evoked in *Eh Joe,* bifurcation is central to its structure and meaning: Joe's actions in the past versus his present stasis; his muteness and the speaking Voice; his intense but unseeing gaze and the scrutiny of the camera; the alliance/antithesis of camera and Voice: are they complementary? co-conspirators? torturer and instrument? dual manifestations of a single entity? And the bifurcation subverts and deranges performance, leaving a final tableau: Joe's face in close up—perhaps relieved at Voice's cessation—and silence. In the German television production that Beckett directed, Joe's final reaction suggests a small triumph. As Zilliacus describes it: "A little sneer appeared on [his] face, and it remained there for the fadeout. In this way, perhaps, the author created an opportunity to repudiate the undeniable sentimentality of his drama by insisting on the incurability of the old lecher. . . . A more modest interpretation, and one more likely in the light of other Beckett works, would link Joe's grin to the fact that the voice seems to be relenting for the evening. He never hoped for more."[45] Yet Voice may well resume soon, and Joe may desire as much as fear it. Like *Film*'s O, Joe—both past and present—has anticipated none of what he experiences: *neither* self-knowledge, self-perception, and self-absorption to the point of masochism *nor* performance for and despite himself that seems likely to repeat, and repeat, despite the fade at the end. And yet such painful interaction as Beckett depicts here may be preferable to the utter isolation of Krapp and Joyce's Mr. Duffy.

Not I is, most overtly, about the speaker's desperate attempt to deny identity and, simultaneously, her failure to avoid recounting that attempt: evasion of selfhood manifesting itself as the necessity to perform obsessively and repeatedly. Yet the play began for Beckett not orally but visually, with the image of the cloaked Auditor who serves as what Knowlson calls Mouth's "silent witness" and the audience's "surrogate representative on stage,"[46] but who is more actively engaged than this implies since "he" silently insinuates himself inside Mouth's head (so to speak), becoming an internal voice, or prompter, to which she responds as if receiving unspoken cues. Beckett's account of the play's origin stresses the Auditor's centrality: "Sitting in a café in North Africa, . . . he observed a solitary figure, completely covered in a djellaba, leaning against a wall. It seemed to him that the figure was in a position of intense listening. . . . Only later did Beckett learn that this figure leaning against the wall was an Arab woman waiting there for her child who attended a nearby school."[47] *Not I* began, then, with the isolated listener who became the anonymous auditor: "The idea," Beckett added, "of someone watching the watcher." As a source for the Auditor Beckett also cites Caravaggio's *Beheading of St. John the Baptist,* a painting in which an old woman "observes the decapitation with horror, covering her ears rather than her eyes." In either of these cases, the main focus of *Not I* is the visual image, the staging of the response, rather than the titular action: the speaker's denial of selfhood.[48]

According to the text, Auditor, who is not the extrinsic driving force behind Mouth's monologue, performs only a single, weakening "gesture of helpless compassion" in response to Mouth's "vehement refusal to relinquish third person" (*SB3,* 405), her emphatic identical answers to four of Auditor's twenty-two questions that only she can hear: "what? . . . who? . . . no! . . . she! . . ." (406, 408, 411, 412). Auditor's movement "consists in simple sideways raising of arms from sides and their falling back. . . . It lessens with each recurrence till scarcely perceptible at third" (405). Although Beckett's *Note* to the play cites only three such movements it occurs four times in the text (406, 408, 411, 412), which is, nonetheless, one fewer than Mouth's denials. Mouth's response to Auditor's fifth and final questioning of her identity is doubly deflective and emphatic: "what? . . . who? . . . no! . . . she! . . . SHE! . . ." (413), and while it produces the same *Pause* as the first four, the hapless Auditor, presumably defeated by the verbal torrent and denial that overwhelms all objections, now fails to respond.

Early critical responses to *Not I* in performance remarked upon the centrality of the listening figure, Mouth's silent stage audience,[49] yet Beckett had, in "Kilcool," the draft of *Not I,* stressed the image of a speaking head: "Old woman's face, 4 ft. above stage level. Slightly off centre, lit by strong steady light. Body not visible. Stage in darkness. Nothing visible but face. Gray hair drawn slightly back from forehead. Shrill . . . voice, bad enunciation." Not yet reduced to just a mouth, this speaking figure had a personal origin for Beckett: "I knew that woman in Ireland . . . I knew who she was—not 'she' specifically, one single woman, but there were so many of those old crones, stumbling down the lanes, in the ditches, beside the hedgerows. Ireland is full of them. And I heard 'her' saying what I wrote in *Not I.* I actually heard it."[50]

Directing what turned out to be the world premiere of *Not I,* Schneider sought "to get maximum relationship, tension, dynamic" between the two figures because, he said, the play's energy derives primarily from "juxtaposition of MOUTH (emission) and AUDITOR" (*No Author,* 279–80). Yet Auditor caused him "Technical difficulties galore" (278): "Figure confuses almost everyone, not location but presence. I find the juxtaposition of two arresting but not really explainable" (285). Beckett's typically pragmatic response was, "try it without him," although he added, "The more he disturbs the better" (287). Deciding in the end to keep the Auditor, Schneider determined that "his presence contributes an ambient tension which is marvelous" (288), and that on opening night "the Auditor was completely part of the tension built, as even some of the critics noted. . . . The image of that mouth moving in space across from that mysterious shadowy figure will remain with anyone who has seen it forever" (290). What proved most memorable, however, was the irrepressible orifice itself, reduced from the initial full face: "The effect is super, just what I think you imagined it to be, alive, organic, a being all of its own . . . a live organism, not immediately clear what it is" (276, 279).

Although Beckett conceived *Not I* as a "face play" (139), he continued to attribute "considerable importance to the role" of Auditor (Animator?[51] Audience?), though in both the first French production (1975) and the television version with Whitelaw the figure was omitted. Beckett restored it for the Paris production he directed in April 1978, but altered his own written directions so that, instead of being effaced at the end, Auditor became even more of an active performer, more like Caravaggio's old woman, making a fifth, and different, response: "At the end of this production of the play, Auditor covered his head with his hands in a gesture of increased helplessness and despair, as if unable to bear any longer the torrent of sound."[52] This scenario, followed by curtain and "*Voice continu[ing] behind curtain, unintelligible*" (*SB3,* 413), emphasizes that the aural performance is not only unstoppable and undeflectable, but ultimately predominant, so that when difficulties arose in other productions the Auditor was eliminated, with Beckett's approval, and it has been absent from most subsequent productions (for example, the Dublin Theatre Festival, 1995, and the Beckett on Film project, 2000), although not from the published text. Once again, diminution won out in performance.

Whitelaw performed *Not I* with Beckett twice: first in the theater with Auditor (1973), then for the BBC without (1977). Although Beckett usually resisted having his work translated from its original medium into another,[53] he seemed to realize that more was gained than lost in the BBC filming of *Not I*. Instead of the Auditor/Mouth dramatic tension that he and Schneider initially stressed, the television camera, still and unwavering throughout, created an intense close-up of Mouth that is far more arrestingly physical, sensual, than could be achieved in the theater. The loss of Auditor also marked a significant cultural moment. In his historic account of traditional performers, Zimmermann indicates that the audiences for their work sometimes disappear before the performers do,[54] and the performance history of *Not I* enacts that loss by moving Mouth's manic monologue into a contextless void where the performing organ took on a life of its own as it filled the television screen. After seeing herself in *Not I,* Whitelaw noted that "my mouth filled the entire image. It looked strangely sexual and glutinous, slimy and weird, like a crazed, oversexed jellyfish." Beckett, who "displayed no trace of displeasure as . . . he realized that Mouth had the appearance of a large, gaping vagina," responded with only one word: "Miraculous."[55]

Whitelaw instinctively understood that rapidity and articulation were crucial to the performance: "It goes at this tremendous pace. I've been practising saying words at a tenth of a second, I could see myself spelling them out like

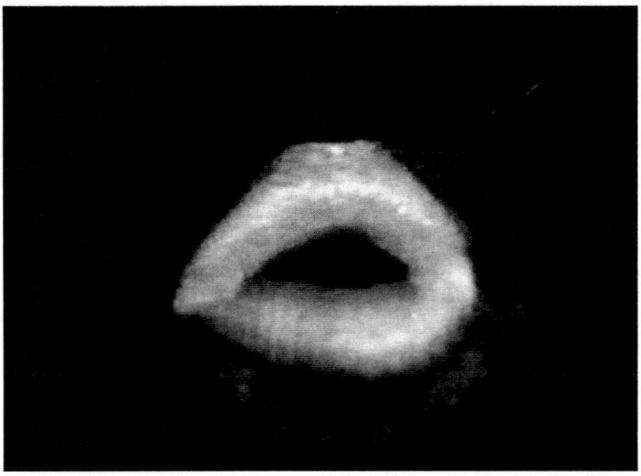

8. Billie Whitelaw as Mouth in *Not I* (directed by Beckett). Courtesy of BBC.

an Olympics clock. No one can possibly follow the text at that speed but Beckett insists that I speak it precisely. It's like music, a piece of Schoenberg in his head."[56] She knew that Beckett sought not meaning but sheer theatricality: "All I know is in the text," he wrote to Schneider. "'She' is purely a stage entity, part of a stage image and purveyor of a stage text. The rest is Ibsen" (*No Author,* 283), or Joyce's Ibsenish *Exiles.*[57] For Beckett as for Mouth, and therefore for Whitelaw: no story where none intended, and yet that is not the whole story.

The speed of Mouth's performance suggests that it is compelled and unstoppable, whether due to forces from without or from within; twice "she" compares her body to a machine, though a nonfunctional one: "Disconnected . . . never got the message . . . or powerless to respond" (*SB3,* 407, 409). Her monologue lacks both thought and control and, in contrast to Molly Bloom's, builds on a series of intensifying negatives: "*No* idea . . . what she's saying . . . imagine! . . . *no* idea what she's saying! . . . it was *not* hers at all . . . *not* her voice at all . . . *no* idea what she's saying! . . . and *can't* stop . . . *no* stopping it . . . now *can't* stop . . . imagine! . . . *can't* stop the stream" (409–10; my emphasis). Beckett insisted that Mouth's breakneck attempt to puzzle out the inner Voice she hears expresses exactly what her audience is meant to experience: "I hear it breathless, urgent, feverish, rhythmic, panting along, without undue concern with intelligibility. Addressed less to the understanding than to the nerves of the audience which should in a sense *share her bewilderment*" (*No Author,* 283). Further, she not only creates that shared bewilderment but, like the metatheatricality in *Play,* articulates it precisely: "Never got the message . . . or powerless to respond . . . not catching the half of it . . . not the quarter . . . no idea . . . what she was saying . . . straining to hear . . . straining to hear . . . piece it together . . . trying to make sense of it . . ." (*SB3,* 407–10). Technical virtuosity, not audience comprehension of her story, is the goal.[58]

Astounded by the "words [that] were coming . . . a voice she did not recognize . . . when suddenly she felt . . . gradually she felt . . . her lips moving" (408–9), she is constrained to perform a monologue of self-negation that keeps much of her story submerged, incoherent, voiced but uncommunicated, an insistent *saying* that becomes an end in itself, an effect achieved through speed of performance: "All I feel sure of is the text must go very fast, no pause except for breath and the two big silent holes after the screams" (*No Author,* 273). "The tempo, the repetitions, and the interruptions of the verbal onslaught are," as Ruby Cohn puts it, "designed for piecemeal understanding."[59] Beckett advised Jessica Tandy that she should "consider the mouth 'an organ of emission, without intellect.'"[60]

But more than meaningless noise emerges from Mouth's monologue. As Clov says, "Something is taking its course" (*SB3,* 100). Performing in panic, reenacting the unfortunate birth rather than coming to terms with it, Mouth nonetheless articulates one of Beckett's most haunting themes, "Someone in me trying to get out, saying let me out." She insists that she cannot really say how it had been, but yet there is "something she had to tell . . . something that would tell how it had been" (411). She cannot even get her age right, yet, accomplishing the opposite of what she intends, she performs a narrative of utter self-consciousness. Like the "rapid tempo" party pieces of the figures in *Play,* Mouth's monologue calls attention to what she denies: her long-suppressed history that, in the reading of it, verges on the sentimental given her premature birth (her first expulsion), abandonment, loveless childhood, loneliness, and so on. Desperate not to be identified as having experienced what she is thus doomed to repeat yet cannot simply communicate, she fails to emerge as a coherent character but remains a metonymic embodiment, and performer, of the heartbreaking story whose essence, despite herself, spews forth from her from ten seconds before curtain rises until ten seconds after it falls (405, 413).

The "well off centre" male Speaker of *A Piece of Monologue,* a companion work, similarly narrates a deflected life story, compressing Pozzo's "They give birth astride of a grave, the light gleams an instant, then it's night once more" (*SB3,* 82) into his opening line: "Birth was the death of him. Again" (454). The motionless monologist repeatedly, but in diminishing detail, describes frustrated or fruitless actions (trying to light his lamp, staring blankly out the window, destroying family photos), attending funerals until "Soon none left to die" (456), failing to live a life and so at the end "Unutterably faint. The globe alone. Alone gone" (458). Like Krapp and *Ohio Impromptu*'s Listener, he performs recollection to fill an emptiness, representing himself in the static present as merely a conveyor of what has been lost or never experienced.

Joyce has Bloom recall his first lovemaking with Molly in labial terms: "Ravished over her I lay, full lips full open, kissed her mouth. Yum. . . . Young life, her lips that gave me pouting. Soft, warm, sticky gumjelly lips" (*U,* 167). *Monologue*'s Speaker seems to echo Bloom, but his similarly suggestive language serves only to underscore his isolation and self-absorption: "Mouth agape. Closed with hiss of breath. Lips joined. Feel soft touch of lip on lip. Lip lipping lip. . . . Parts lips and thrusts tongue between them" (*SB3,* 457). He can lip only himself lipping his repeated refrain, "He all but said . . . loved ones" (454, 455, 457, 458), holding forth, like W in *Rockaby,* to himself alone, describing or prescribing, in and to a void where an audience should be: "Stands there facing the wall staring beyond. Nothing there either. . . . Nothing to be heard anywhere. Room once full of sounds. Faint sounds. Whence unknown. Fewer and fainter as time wore on. Nights wore on. None now." But then, correcting himself, not completely gone: "No. No such thing as none" (455), just as complete darkness is forestalled: "No such thing as no light. . . . Dies on to dawn and never dies" (456). But sound, words, oral performance seems to be different: "Stands there staring beyond waiting for first word. It gathers in his mouth. Birth. Parts lips and thrusts tongue between them. . . . Nothing stirring. Nothing faintly stirring" (457). The ghosts of those he has known or imagined—"Ghost light. Ghost nights. Ghost rooms. Ghost graves. Ghost . . . he all but said ghost loved ones" (458)—are summoned to accompany the fadeout and silence, the final tableau.

In 1976–77 Beckett worked on a television series that included *Not I, Ghost Trio,* and *. . . but the clouds . . .* to which he gave the collective title *Shades,* a Joycean word he might have remembered from its repeated use toward the end of "The Dead": "Poor Aunt Julia! She, too, would soon be a shade with the shade of Patrick Morkan and his horse. . . . One by one they were all becoming shades" (*D1,* 222–23).[61] Dramatizing what Gabriel Conroy envisages, Beckett could have used this title for any number of works beginning with *Play* (1963), whose ghostly figures are depleted, bloodless, and posthumous: "Three grey disks. . . . Voices grey and abstract as the faces, grey as cinders," in Beckett's phrase (*No Author,* 145), which again echoes the end of "The Dead": "His own identity was fading out into a grey impalpable world: the solid world itself, which these dead had one time reared and lived in, was dissolving and dwindling" (*D1,* 287). Attenuated and enfeebled, shades "gone . . . in the head" (*SB3,* 356, 367), the figures in *Play* both can and must speak when the inquisitorial light picks them out of the darkness. Maniacally or mechanically repetitive, they are bespoken rather than speak, caught up in an endless story that is at once their own and yet beyond their narrative control.

The embodied or partially embodied figures in *Shades,* like those in most of the late plays, are locked not only into their "negated subjectivity," asserting or embodying self-denial through their inability to escape the past or cease repeating its failures, but also into the artifice, rather than social context, of performance: stage sets, sound studio noises, theatrical lighting, meticulously contrived movements. Like *Eh Joe,* both . . . *but the clouds* . . . and *Ghost Trio* depict mute, ghostly figures busying themselves "with something . . . or with nothing, busied myself with nothing, that MINE" (448) in "The familiar chamber. . . . All grey. Shades of grey" (436). In both plays, V (Voice) predicts, describes, and perhaps commands (not always perfectly) the on-camera action that follows from the loss of the beloved. Unlike Joe, however, who goes rigid before his incessantly pursuing Voice demanding he recall "All your dead dead" (394), F(igure) in *Ghost Trio* and M(an) in . . . *but the clouds* . . . still long for or mourn their lost ones and ritually perform the gestures of reminder recounted and required by their haunting, if gentle, voices. The Voice in *Ghost Trio* instructs not only the camera and music (which gets louder as the camera moves closer to F), but also the television audience ("Mine is a faint voice. Kindly tune accordingly" [436]) and then F ("He will now think he hears her" and "Repeat" [438, 439]). Voice in . . . *but the clouds* . . . , which is M's, similarly declares, "Let us now run through it again" (448). Conflating memory and rehearsal, or enacting an audience "encore," they might be directing any number of late Beckett plays, endless reprises of what both endures and endlessly fades, in Yeats's words from "The Tower," "Among the deepening shades."[62]

Dramatizing shadowy versions of earlier pairs like Didi and Gogo, Hamm and Clov, and Winnie and Willie, *Footfalls* (1976), *Rockaby* (1981), and *Ohio Impromptu* (1981) are odd couples plays that obsessively, repeatedly, "revolve" but fail to resolve "it all." As in *Eh Joe, Ghost Trio,* and . . . *but the clouds* . . . , these later plays enact a different sort of bifurcation, a dichotomy of body and voice that subverts identity and social performance. *Footfalls*'s May creates an onstage/offstage dialogue by summoning a maternal voice out of a deep sleep to share her own; *Rockaby*'s onstage W(oman) demands "More" of V, "*Her recorded voice*" (*SB3,* 462), as her mechanically and memory driven rocker rocks her off; the mute Listener's knocks on the table in *Ohio Impromptu* (like Krapp manipulating his tapes) control the tempo and repeats of his alter ego's reading of his story, his life, perhaps for the last time. The structure in all of these plays is made explicit in *Ohio Impromptu:* the reiterated "Little is left to tell" becomes "The sad tale a last time told" and then the ambiguous, repeated, "Nothing is left to tell" (473–76) since, in Beckett, *nothing* is *always* left to tell, along with the "absolute necessity to tell"—and retell, to play and to repeat play, until time stops. All runs down or out and yet recurs, like social or theatrical performances: "A last time until the next time"—even as ultimate termination becomes increasingly insistent.

Footfalls represents a rare appearance, in the late plays, of a named, costumed, identifiable character in what seems almost a social situation—a struggling, isolated daughter caring for a dying mother—that again harkens back to the end of "The Dead" for the pacing figure: "a pale shade of grey" (430). But such certitude as this summary suggests is immediately threatened: though the characters call each other May and Mother, the directions use initials (M and V) for both the ghostly stage figure (dimly lit, lighting "*strongest at floor level, less on body, least on head*" [427]) and the ghostly voice "from dark upstage" (426); V hears M in her deepest sleep, while M is sleepless; each knows the other's age but not her own. V takes her place with many Beckettean narrators who hover between describing and prescribing—"let us watch her move, in silence. . . . Watch how feat she wheels. . . . Seven, eight, nine, wheel" (429)—while May's deliberate pacing, as precisely choreographed as a dance to a metronome,[63] takes on a senselessly repetitious, Sisyphean, symmetry and rhythm. Whitelaw sees the play as "a turning point in Beckett's work. All arts are contained in this one piece. It was like being painted with light. He used me as a piece of sculpture. I told him you could hang it on the wall."[64] May is, as Whitelaw remarks, "caged in by this one little strip. She's not even pacing around the room, she's confined to *one specific area* of the room, and there she has been pacing up and down, or so it seemed to me, for 999 years, unable to break out of her compulsive, narrow rut."[65] Beckett said that the pacing is primary: "If the play is full of repetitions, then it is because of these life-long stretches of walking. That is the centre of the play, everything else is secondary."[66] May's life, to the extent that she has one, is this endlessly repeated performance.

Yet *Footfalls* is also a deflection play, like *Endgame, Embers, Happy Days,* and, especially, *Not I,* one in which a shadow story (an attenuated party piece May trots out for the occasion) substitutes for the one ostensibly being dramatized. Beckettean storytellers offer narratives of others: Hamm's story of father and son; Henry's of Bolton and Holloway; Winnie's of "Shower—Shower ... or Cooker, perhaps I should say Cooker" (293); Mouth's insistence that her narrative concerns not herself but "She." In doing so, they foreground the performative present with what seems an oft-told story that denies history and identity. Also referring to herself in the third person and, curiously, addressing "the reader" (430, 431) rather than audience, *Footfalls*'s May improvises (Beckett's word) the mother/daughter story, displacing her shadowy mother and herself with a "semblance. Faint, though by no means invisible. . . . a pale shade of grey. [*Pause.*] A tangle of tatters. [*Pause.*] Watch it pass . . . ," that precisely describes what we see on stage and that anticipates the end of *Footfalls* by telling of Mrs. Winter and her daughter Amy disputing over whether or not the daughter *was there* (430–31). Responding to the only question Whitelaw ever asked him about any of his plays, "*Am I dead?*" Beckett said, "Well, let's just say *you're not quite there,*"[67] which may help to explain why this is the slowest paced of Beckett's plays (the opposite of *Play* and *Not I*), its approximately 1000 words taking thirty minutes to be spoken. Beckett's advice was yet another assault on his audience: "Bore them to death."

The performance may recall the kind of purgatorial and theatrical survival and continuity that Beckett also depicts in *Happy Days, Play,* and *Eh Joe,* but *Footfalls* has a coda: after the fade out into darkness, the fade up shows a bare stage with "No trace of May" (432). Knowlson and Pilling, echoing Beckett's direction that the mother's voice should be "like one ghost speaking to another," comment that "We realize, perhaps only *after* the play has ended, that we may have been watching a ghost telling a tale of a ghost (herself), who fails to be observed by someone else (her fictional *alter ego*) because she in turn was not really there. . . . For since . . . even the mother's voice may simply be a voice in the mind of a ghost, everything may be regarded as illusion in this little play."[68] Or a life stalled out, repeatedly running on its old tracks, a mobius strip to nowhere—until the empty stage at the end. Clov's penultimate line is, "This is what we call making an exit" (*SB3,* 151), but he remains; May is that rare Beckettean character who definitively disappears at the end of her performance.

"What is a ghost?" Stephen Dedalus asks as he begins his *Hamlet* lecture, and he answers, "One who has faded into impalpability through death, through absence, through change of manners" (*U,* 180). Beckett's ghosts also fade, but rarely into complete impalpability. *Rockaby,* which Whitelaw performed together with *Footfalls* in New York in 1984, is a sedentary version of the earlier play, depicting the same nebulous relationship: mother as voice only/onstage daughter stuck in rhythmical movement, or else one woman at two moments of her life. *Footfalls*'s erect position is replaced by seated one, pacing by rocking of chair, offstage maternal voice by recorded voice of the rocking woman. The ghostly May (M), who like Clov seems unable to sit, becomes the attenuated W, who like Hamm seems unable to stand. Whitelaw called these two women "a couple of old hags, one pacing up and down with a broken back, the other rocking herself to death in a chair."[69] Like many of the late plays, *Rockaby* is predicated on memory and nostalgia, with W's "More" (voiced four times, each time more softly) repeatedly setting in motion both the rocking and the recorded monologue that recalls or imagines a past for no audience but herself: "Whom else?" Kalb suggests that "the story heard about the past may or may not be a narration of events leading up to the action seen onstage."[70] It may, instead, be a way of organizing thought, or rhythm, in the present, positing an ersatz history and identity, another dramatized deflection, a way of repeatedly asserting "till in the end," "time she stopped," and "rock her off," and implying, but leaving uncertain, her own demise.

As usual, Whitelaw focused not on story but on tempo, "playing the right music," in this case on the rocker, which Schneider suggested should be played "like a harp." "Beckett blows the notes," Whitelaw said, "I want them to come out of me."[71] *Rockaby*'s music, appropriately, is that of a lullaby until the startling "Fuck life," which (startlingly?) is spoken in the same monotone as the lines before and after it, and therefore both does and does not disrupt the lullaby. *Rockaby*'s ending, Schneider implies, occurs just before that of *Footfalls.* He told Whitelaw: "I know what this play's about. . . . It's not about dying, not about coming to die. It's about accepting death. . . . It's coming to terms with m-o-t-h-e-r, 'mother rocker,' if you will. I'm not sure Sam would put it that way, but you're not dead by the end. You've accepted the inevitability of dying. You've accepted."[72] The final fade of light, as both Schneider and Beckett's text have it, offers a kind of penultimacy, something like Stephen's situation at the end of *Portrait,* only with death rather than life poised to follow, though it never quite occurs either:

stop her eyes
rock her off
rock her off
[*Together: echo of "rock her off," coming to rest of rock, slow fade out.*]
(*SB3,* 470)

W joins V in this final pronouncement, which both describes what is occurring and is prescriptive: a final wish and an imperative as peremptory and, it would seem, as unheeded as the one that ends *Godot:* "Yes, let's go. [*They do not move.*]" (87). Yet at the end of her filmed performance under Schneider's direction, Whitelaw's head slowly descended in what is unmistakably a dying fall.

Ohio Impromptu (1981) has the most deflected and misleading title of any Beckett work. It is, of course, neither about Ohio nor set there, but was written for and first performed at a conference at Ohio State University.[73] And it is

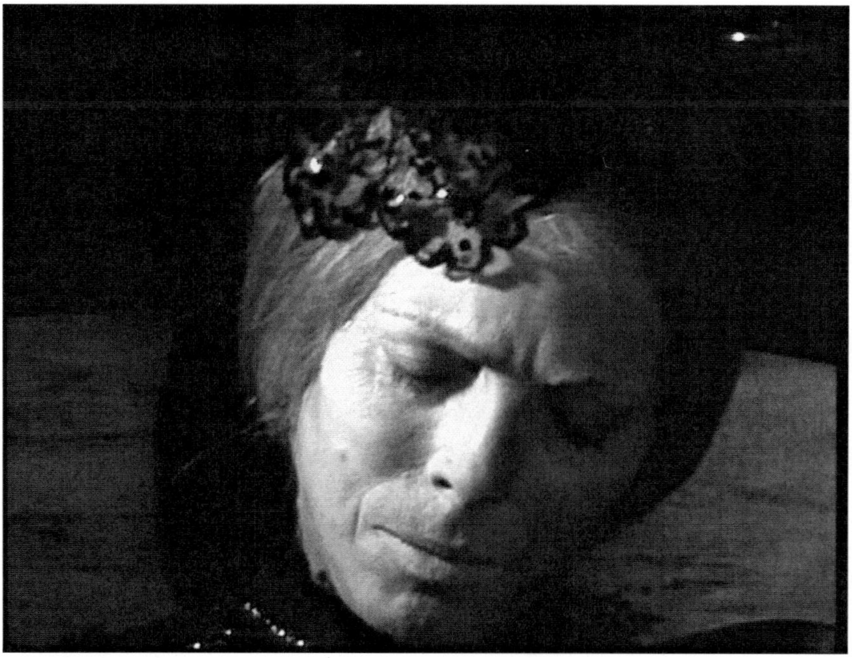

9. Billie Whitelaw dead at end of *Rockaby* (directed by Walter Asmus). Courtesy of Pennebaker Hegedus Films.

anything but an impromptu, which, by definition, is improvised, unrehearsed, makeshift.[74] Instead, it depicts the reading, not for the first time but perhaps for the last, of a carefully scripted text from the "*last pages*" of "a worn volume" (*SB3*, 473, 475), a repetition of a repetition of the same old "sad tale" (475) that had previously been read all the way through numerous times. R (Reader) reads to L (Listener) a story that represents L's sorrow and loneliness following the loss of a beloved ("the dear face")—the phrase "my shade will comfort you" implies that she is dead, though in Beckett one can rarely be sure—as well as the story of R's previous readings through which L and R "grew to be as one" (474–75). Although L faces audience while R is in profile, they are "*As alike in appearance as possible*" (473), suggesting that they are alter egos or two halves of a split self (whose single hat is on the table between them), an effect that can only be approximated on stage, but that is strikingly realized in the Beckett on Film version (2000), with Jeremy Irons playing both parts.

The power and performative relationship between the two figures is an unusual one. R performs by reading the story calmly and soothingly, treating it, as Beckett told David Warrilow, "like a bedtime story,"[75] another lullaby. L's

10. Jeremy Irons as both R and L in *Ohio Impromptu* (Gate Theatre production). Courtesy of Blue Angel Films.

deflected story thereby becomes R's party piece through expropriation or an act of creative empathy. R may therefore also be seen as author and L, presumably the subject and passive victim of the story of lost love and his inability to move past the grief of that loss (a reprise of *Krapp, Words and Music, Ghost Trio,* and . . . *but the clouds* . . .), as not only willing but exigent audience and prompter. His table knocks control R's reading as Krapp controls his tapes, variously interrupting and emphasizing as R instinctively understands them to mean either "repeat" or "continue." The knocks seem to allude as well to events within the narrative in the rhythm between "Then turn and his slow steps retrace" and the injunction to "Stay where we were so long alone together" (*SB3,* 474).

Like all of Beckett's couples plays, *Ohio Impromptu* raises questions about dominance and submission within the relationship of writer (or director) and performer.[76] In some productions the relationship is played with intense seriousness, with L controlling R; sometimes R is amusingly impatient at L's interruptions and insistence on repetition. Yet as happens in *Film* and *Happy Days, Ohio Impromptu* ends with R and L staring silently, enigmatically, at each other, a confrontation that destabilizes the performer/audience hierarchy by creating both doubt as to which is which and an uneasy equivalence between them as performance ends.

Quad, which is comprised entirely of unvoiced stage directions and could have been called *Act without Words III,* is particularly, obsessively, precise and stark. Beckett, who labeled its four characterless characters "players," referred to them as "mimes" rather than dancers, though "some ballet training desirable" (479, 481). Instead of names, or letters (as in *Rockaby, Ohio Impromptu,* and *Catastrophe*), or letters combined with numbers (as in *Play* and . . . *but the clouds* . . .), he assigns them numbers only. "As alike in build as possible" (481), they are burka-encased androids who exist solely to perform mathematically choreographed stage directions, energetically, colorfully, and endlessly, accompanied by percussive instruments and *Footfalls*-like sounds of footsteps. Each player was to have a different colored robe; a corresponding colored light "to be turned on when he enters, kept on while he paces, turned off when he exits"; a different percussion instrument; and a particular footstep sound (480–81).

But even more than *Play, Quad* exemplifies Beckett's radically changing a work as a result of production. Although the published text still calls for

"Four sources of differently coloured light clustered together" (480), Beckett determined in rehearsal that "the frequency of light going on and off with the entrance and exit of each player proved too distracting [and created a muddied rather than distinctive effect] and had to be abandoned."[77] The particularized sounds of instruments and footsteps worked no better than the piano notes for *Play* and were eliminated for similar reasons. Further, Beckett's text contains the direction: "Without interruption begin repeat and fade out on 1 pacing alone" (*SB3,* 480), which contradicts his final direction to complete "series 1 only" (482), since that series ends with 2 alone on stage. But the most radical change occurred when Beckett, working on *Quad* for German television in 1982, became intrigued by a replay on a black-and-white screen that he happened to see. It inspired him to produce a second act (washed out, enervated, without musical accompaniment) analogous to the second acts or repeats of *Godot, Happy Days,* and, in some versions, *Play:* "No colour, all four in identical white gowns, no percussion, footsteps only sound, slow tempo" (482). "Ten thousand years later,"[78] Beckett said, "ineffable weariness" follows "colorful frenzy,"[79] as if he has been flogging his players through rehearsal all that time.

Dramatic dominance is foregrounded in the two late works, *Catastrophe* (1984) and *What Where* (1984), Beckett's most overtly political plays, which are also among his stagiest and most self-reflexive. Their mute performers, in contrast to earlier ones who had little option, assert themselves as antiperformers who refuse to play their assigned parts. In reducing characters to stick or shadowy figures, automatons, body parts, and ghosts, and then treating actors similarly, Beckett surely recognized his own oppressive instincts and authority in the omnipotent offstage deities of *Act Without Words I* and *Happy Days,* the goad in *Act Without Words II,* the monomaniacal mathematician who devised *Quad,* and so on. When Whitelaw broke down while rehearsing *Not I,* which she thought of as "a form of torture," Beckett asked in anguish, "Oh Billie . . . what have I done to you?"[80] but the rehearsal soon resumed. Depicting that tyranny in the guise of D in *Catastrophe* and V/Bam in *What Where, Beckett,* as if divided against himself, licensed revolt in his two last plays in a way he denied his actors or refused to sanction in productions by others.

The metaphoric theatricality and performative opposition hinted at in *Godot* (Didi and Gogo's awareness of themselves as characters playing before a live audience), elaborated in *Play,* and momentarily breaking through in W's "Fuck life" in *Rockaby* climaxes in these late plays when constrained prisoners, lacking the exuberant complicity in defeat of Lucky, Nell and Nagg, Winnie, and the posthumous figures in *Play,* manage to perform not party pieces but the reverse: acts of silent opposition. Dedicated to Václav Havel, the dissident Czech playwright who later became his country's president, *Catastrophe* enacts the making of both art and political resistance. It is set in a theater during "Rehearsal. Final touches to the last scene" (*SB3,* 485), perhaps in anticipation of "the interrogation of a dissident" before a live audience or "to serve as a death's head warning to others who might dare to follow him into an act of rebellion," as Gussow variously suggests (75, 159). Clothed in "*Black dressing-gown to ankles. Barefoot. Head bowed*" (485), P (Protagonist/Prisoner) is the brutalized object of scrutiny and manipulation on the part of D (Director/Dictator), A (Assistant), and Luke (the offstage lighting director), who treat him not as an actor but as a stage set, aesthetic object, or exhibit of servitude. But this rehearsal of a carefully scripted one-character play becomes a very different sort of three-character drama.

A commissar or concentration camp commander in "*Fur coat. Fur toque to match*" (485), D has A modify P's stance to achieve the precise depiction of subjection and impotence that he desires. D gives A three kinds of orders—explain or describe something about P's appearance, alter it for the public presentation ("I make a note," she responds to these), and make a change immediately—and he speaks irritably to her when, as often happens, she mistakes one kind of command for another or when she ventures an idea of her own. When she "*timidly*" proposes "a little . . . a little . . . gag," for example, D denounces "This craze for explicitation!" (a Beckett neologism); her suggestion that P could "raise his head . . . an instant . . . show his face . . . just an instant," provokes D's outraged response, in a Joycean echo of exoticism from "Eveline," "Raise his head? Where do you think we are? In Patagonia?" (487–88).

But P himself picks up the cue. D, satisfied at last, prepares to leave for a political meeting, becoming, as he heads for the exit, another of Beckett's powerful offstage forces: "Terrific! He'll have them on their feet. I can hear it from here." As if summoned by this predictive/imperative assertion, the imagined audience suddenly responds enthusiastically: "*Distant storm of applause*" (489). The theatrical performance is stood on its head, however, when, challenging not only D but the in-play audience (and perhaps author) as well, "*P raises his head, fixes the audience*"—acting outside his scripted part not to deny hierarchy by creating equivalence between himself and D, as occurs between the gazers at the end of *Film, Happy Days,* and *Ohio Impromptu,* but to subvert both script and hierarchy: "It was a look of overcoming, of cowing his audience into submission, of causing the applause to die."[81] Utterly victimized and apparently devitalized, a reprise of Lucky but mute from start to finish, P nonetheless stages resistance with a look of defiance that appalls D, shatters P's assigned role as artifact/exemplum/slave, and enacts Beckett's ultimate assault on audiences both within the play and within the theater.

By quelling applause rather than provoking it ("*The applause falters, dies*"), P's extraordinary performance of silent rebellion reverses the theatrical experience, leaving the live audience perplexed about *its* expected role: should it show appreciation (or the opposite), and does it do so by applauding or remaining silent? Is it being assaulted as collaborators, goaded into uneasy contemplation of its political complacency, or urged to rebel—either as passive audience or actively in the world outside the theater? Should it feel that a theatrical breakthrough has occurred in which it is meant to share or is it being driven from the theater? And will its departure allow P to cease to exist, to disappear into an oblivion beyond enforced public performance and humiliation? Perhaps even more than other Beckettean endings, P's startling gesture raises a host of political, psychological, and theatrical questions that are not easily answered.

A similar subversion of power occurs in *What Where,* which, like *Not I,* was written for the stage and adapted for television by Beckett. Beckett describes V, the Voice of Bam, as merely a performing instrument "*in the shape of a small megaphone at head level*" (496); the text revised for German television (1985) represents V as "mirror reflection of Bam's face, slightly distorted, faintly lit," which in production became "an enlarged and distorted death mask" for what Beckett called this voice "from beyond the grave."[82] Again contemplating Rimbaud's "Voyelles" (and perhaps also recalling the multicolored dancing Rainbow Girls in *Finnegans Wake* who "toe by toe, to and fro they go round" [*FW,* 226.21]), Beckett considered dressing each of the figures in different colored clothes, but, he insisted, "No green"—no possible allusion to Ireland, perhaps.[83] But colored costumes, music, and other embellishments that Beckett had contemplated were all eliminated. With the same actor playing both Bam and Voice of Bam, *What Where* turned inward in this production, becoming another "face" and memory play in which "Torture becomes more explicitly self-inflicted, a function of memory, remorse and the relentless need to tell a story."[84] In the Beckett on Film production (2000), V was played by an actor, while Bam, Bem, Bim, Bom were not just "*Players as alike as possible*" (*SB3*, 496) but were all performed by a second actor.[85] Beckett's *dramatis personae* always omits "Bum," the stereotypical figure out of the Irish performative tradition he had often depicted early on and that disappears from the late plays.

However played, V/Bam, like the spotlight in *Play* and D in *Catastrophe*, is both stage manager and torturer, and perhaps ultimately victim. He directs a silent rehearsal or dumb show, "First without words"[86] (spoken three times [497–98]), and then the spoken play, "Now with words," while critiquing the performance he commands: "Not good. . . . Good" (499–504). Like *Play*'s demanding spotlight and Henry's commanding of sounds in *Embers*, Bam conjures up his victims, "figments" in Beckett's word, suggestive of ghosts of those departed, who appear after (because?) he says they appear. His "*head haught*" at the beginning and his authority unquestioned but futile throughout, Bam repeatedly, ritualistically, demands that his victims act their ascribed parts: "Give him the works until he confesses" (498, 501–4). But though, we are told, they weep, scream, and beg for mercy, the interchangeable and identically recalcitrant tortured, like the anti-Irish–stereotype Broy in *Michael Collins* and *Catastrophe*'s P, remain resistant to their torturers, who are themselves tortured in turn. V obtains no information, achieves nothing, and finally bows his head in failure. The torture's rhythm and repetition, its performance, become its only possible end, and thereby turns back on its persecutor, ultimately driving him into a silence that became Beckett's own.

Beginning in spring and in plural, communal inclusiveness ("We are the last five"), V ends in winter and solitude ("I am alone"), leaving him, and us, no wiser about his motivation, desires, or quest. Authors are supposed to know who what when where why about their characters, and, according to Hemingway, leave out nine-tenths of what they know. Cronin suggests that Beckett had long understood the advantages of this technique: "In his Trinity lectures decades before he had even defined modernism in terms of such eliminations with their resulting obscurities, knowing very well apparently . . . what a source of power they were."[87] Something of this process occurred with works like *Krapp's Last Tape* and *Not I,* as naturalistic detail dropped away during their creation. Yet Beckett usually disclaimed any special knowledge of what was omitted—whether, for example, Nell dies in *Endgame* ("So it seems, but no one knows"[88]) or what Willie is after at the end of *Happy Days.* In *What Where* he satirizes the commanding authority, a surrogate for himself, who futilely and for no apparent reason demands a confessional performance from the creatures under his control.

"Bam is 'Sam,'" writes Brater, "the B is 'Beckett'; and Bam's voice, like so many others we have heard on Beckett's stage, is speaking, as always, through metaphor."[89] V strives to emulate such potent deities as the offstage forces at work in *Act Without Words I* and *Happy Days,* but for all his power he experiences a series of false starts, perhaps suggesting writing blocks ("I switch off. . . . I start again"), and never learns what or where from those who, belying Wilde's truism about the Irish, refuse to perform on cue. Ultimately V admits defeat, lapsing into a despairing silence after his last words: "Make sense who may. I switch off" (*SB3,* 498, 504). Though not precluding the possibility that he could again "switch on," as he has done before, these final words read like what they effectively became: a last representation for Beckett of the oral tradition he inherited and helped to exhaust, and his own long implied and ultimate fading into silence and darkness, a final ending and appropriate Beckettean valedictory to the theater he had reluctantly entered into and seemed, during all the years he was writing and directing drama, always on the verge of leaving.

And yet there is another word beyond these final words, one that, like so many Beckett plays, implies a return to beginnings. In the run-up to a performative conference on his work at the University of Texas in 1984, Beckett was invited to produce a new work, as he had for a conference at Ohio State University in 1981. Beckett's reply—"All used up. Nothing left. What's your deadline?"—seemed an iron-clad guarantee that a new work would be forthcoming. But when it did not appear, he offered us the opportunity of staging *Human Wishes,* his never-before performed first dramatic attempt (1934), which we did in two very different versions. It was a chance for those present to perform a mental recorso, rethinking Beckett's theatrical achievement in the context of his beginnings. And that process was only intensified when we learned during the course of the conference that Alan Schneider, who had planned to attend and direct *Human Wishes* but who had had to change his plans when summoned to direct a new play in London, had been the victim of a terrible accident. Schneider's shocking and untimely death seemed an even more definitive end of a Beckett era than was Beckett's silence.[90]

Coda

Stage(d) Endings

If, as Roy Rappaport suggests about the term "ritual," party pieces are "performance[s] of more or less invariant sequences of formal acts and utterances not entirely encoded by the performers" (see the introduction), then Joyce's staging of the ordinary, which he considered the artist's proper domain, enacts slippages that cause representation to affirm what it sets out to parody. In *Ulysses* Odysseus becomes not only mock heroic, but also, if on a different scale, heroic again; so too does Bloom. Hence, in depicting the full panoply of human "mysteries"—the commonplace rituals of birth, maturation, first sex, death—Joyce valorizes the quotidian, including that rare event in modern literature: the funeral.[1]

The young boys at the beginning of *Dubliners* and *Portrait of the Artist* are, willy nilly, on track for adolescence; but one cannot imagine the boys in *Godot* or *Ghost Trio* undergoing alteration: rather, they seem stuck in their roles, destined only for identical, repeat (or diminishing) stage appearances. Beckett's characters may be as heroic as Joyce's—or even more so given their "going on" when that action seems utterly futile, counterintuitive, but they are never in transition. Despite their obsession with memory, they seem always to have been as they are, never as they portray themselves once to have been. Metempsychosis, a central Joycean theme, is largely absent from Beckett's writings: with rare exception (like Pozzo's going blind—and Nell's apparent death in *Endgame*), no one in Beckett is born, changes, or, with rare exception, even dies, although some of his declaimers (Pozzo, Mouth in *Not I*, Speaker in *A Piece of Monologue*) talk as if such transformations were once possible.

Joyce saw the macrocosm in the world of himself and his evolving family; Beckett came to see himself as a fixed exemplar of universal and unending misery. In Ellmann's iconic depiction, "Beckett was addicted to silences, and so was Joyce; they engaged in conversations which consisted often of silences directed towards each other, both suffused with sadness, Beckett mostly for the world, Joyce mostly for himself" (*JJ2*, 648). This lapse into brooding silence, which seems to anticipate R and L at the end of *Ohio Impromptu*, suggests more about Beckett than Joyce, since the older writer, believing that history was still possible, embraced the expansive Irish tradition of social occasion and communal interaction that he parodied and lamented.

Joycean texts end, therefore, in a state of penultimacy, allowing for, or even implying, the "More" that W demands throughout *Rockaby* or the "Sequel" that M pronounces in *Footfalls*—but which proves to be only a ghostly reprise of her own story: "I saw nothing, heard nothing, of any kind. I was not there" (*SB3*, 431). For Joyce there *are* more stories to tell, sequels to follow, the possibility that one might "seek well." Sometimes sequels are implicit, as when "The Dead" (and therefore *Dubliners*) concludes with an ending that looks both forward and back: to a possible new and revivified future for the Conroys (perhaps through Gabriel's "generous" concession to join his wife for a visit to her and Ireland's past); to Ireland's dead history that, for good or ill, refuses to stay buried; to the book's beginning with a story of a boy's first experience of death; to an optical illusional last paragraph that seems to read differently each time one encounters it. Yet however one views Gabriel's projected journey, he is ready for it to begin as the book ends.

Exiles ends with Bertha, physically close to Richard but psychologically distanced, pleading for his return: "O, my strange wild lover, come back to me again!" (*Ex*, 112), but with no certitude that he will—or will not. *Portrait* ends with its protagonist poised for a journey, and with what seems a much less ambiguous promise of a triumphant future; yet the seeds of Stephen's failure are planted throughout that text and they bear bitter fruit for him in *Ulysses*, where the explicit sequel—his failed journey to Paris and bathetic return to Dublin's entangling nets—proves confoundingly at odds with the implicit one anticipated by *Portrait*'s ending. Yet the end of *Ulysses* allows one to imagine an implicit sequel even for Stephen as he heads into the night to seek further "misadventures," leaving critics to argue that utter failure awaits or that he is going off to write *Ulysses* or any number of other possibilities.[2] Like "The Dead" and *Exiles*, *Ulysses* ends, rather, with a semi-estranged couple physically close but uncertainly, if very possibly, about to begin a process of (re)connection. And

Finnegans Wake becomes its own sequel, ending with an emphasis on ending—"I am passing out. O bitter ending! I'll slip away before they're up. . . . Coming, far! End here" (*FW,* 627.34–628.13)—that nonetheless becomes a recorso, an affirmation of renewal, of going through it all again.

Beckett's only explicit sequel is the bare stage he offers his "bored" audience as a coda to *Footfalls.* His posthistoric dramatic world records the death of performative tradition as well as of the social and natural worlds in which they occurred. Joyce took the dying oral culture in which he grew up seriously enough to satirize the attempt to preserve it: he has a student press a few Irish phrases from an old man in Connemara to document in his notebook (*PA,* 274) and the English collector Haines wants to make a book of Stephen's Irish "sayings" (*U,* 15). But satire is not Beckett's way: the dying oral tradition that he left behind in Ireland continually leaks into his performative and metaperformative writings, but its resuscitation is not possible. Beginning with *Godot,* he denigrated performance, assailed audiences, and minimized social occasions, although stories and songs were still sometimes offered as if party pieces remained doable, appropriate to the occasion, and even to willing listeners, while musical recordings—Schubert's *Death and the Maiden* in *All That Fall,* Lehár's *The Merry Widow* waltz in *Happy Days,* the Largo from Beethoven's *Fifth Piano Trio* in *Ghost Trio*—offer fairly conventional thematic commentary on present circumstances.

Increasingly, however, narrative within Beckett's drama becomes deflected and incomplete, then peters out, and performers become purgatorial creatures doomed to endless retellings and mistellings—to grudging or absent audiences—of stories that are fixed in the past, or to rerun old tapes of their lives repeatedly even after their lives have ended. Krapp, Listeners in *That Time* and *Ohio Impromptu,* W in *Rockaby,* Bam in *What Where* either record or recall, and play back, only themselves—and only for themselves—an utterly self-contained ritual that is static and sterile. As Kalb suggests of this practice, "The protagonist wants his imagined creations to exist as concretely and satisfyingly as corporeal companions, but then to go away, to switch off, at less than a moment's notice."[3] Further, verbal recordings render memory and oral performance rigid and invariant, and thus false as well as banal and apropos of nothing, an emptying out of meaning and color that Beckett masks to a great extent by obsessively detailing theatrical technique.

Often, especially in his early plays, Beckett stages tableau endings—in *Godot, Endgame, Rough for Theatre I, Happy Days, Ohio Impromptu*—with couples poised uncertainly between coming to a final end and going on in an increasingly weakened condition. This is especially true for double-act plays—*Godot, Happy Days,* and *Quad*—which may seem locked in either an endless process of attenuation, running down and out, or already engaged, like *Play* and *Not I,* in yet another (and feebler) "repeat." These plays conclude on a note of radical irresolution between these two possibilities, but either way the tone is vastly bleaker than that offered by the incertitude of Joycean endings since no possibility of renewal exists, no hope for amelioration.

A similar question mark hovers in the air at the end of works like *Film, Come and Go, Eh Joe,* and *Catastrophe.* One wonders if, as apparently occurs in *Rockaby,* the cycle will finally end, if it really is "time she stopped" (*SB3,* 462, 463, 465, 467). For termination that trumps unending decline seems increasingly to become Beckett's way of ending. The fade-outs that bring to a close such radio plays as *All That Fall, Embers, Words and Music,* and *Cascando* anticipate the deaths that seem to conclude *Act Without Words I, Krapp's Last Tape, Rockaby,* and *What Where,* or to lie just beyond. Where the Joycean desire is always to remain centerstage, to sustain the performance and begin again—and to posit the renewal of the world that will allow such continuity—Beckett seems finally ready to let go, to abandon the stage entirely, to switch off. Despite being as "hoarse as a crow," *The Dead*'s Bartell D'Arcy manages to sing for exactly the right audience and to inspire Gretta, in turn, to tell her husband the most important story of her life. In contrast, *Catastrophe*'s assault on its audience at last achieves that ideal condition Beckett had said his way of doing *Godot* would produce: an empty theater. The brilliant success of Beckett's depiction of failure adumbrates—even as it stages—the decline of a once vital Irish performative tradition.

NOTES

BIBLIOGRAPHY

INDEX

Notes

Introduction

1. C. Robert Elliott, *The Power of Satire: Magic, Ritual, Art* (Princeton: Princeton Univ. Press, 1970), 21.

2. Hugh Shields, *Narrative Singing in Ireland: Lays, Ballads, Come-All-Yes and Other Songs* (Dublin: Irish Academic, 1993), 164.

3. Walter J. Ong, *Orality and Literacy: The Technologizing of the Word* (London: Routledge, 2002), 1.

4. Roy A. Rappaport, *Ritual and Religion in the Making of Humanity* (Cambridge: Cambridge Univ. Press, 1999), 24, 117–18.

5. Richard Schechner, *Performance Theory* (New York: Routledge, 2003), 6–7. Schechner nicely summarizes the so-called Cambridge school thesis on the origins of ancient Greek drama, 2–6. O. B. Hardison's *Christian Rite and Christian Drama in the Middle Ages: Essays in the Origin and Early History of Modern Drama* (Baltimore: Johns Hopkins Univ. Press, 1969) is the foundational work that grounds English theater in Church ritual.

6. Rappaport, 24.

7. Ibid., 114.

8. Georges Denis Zimmermann, *The Irish Storyteller* (Dublin: Four Courts, 2001), 193, 472.

9. James H. Delargy, *The Gaelic Story-Teller. With Some Notes on Gaelic Folk-Tales* (London: Proceedings of the British Academy, 31 [1945]; Chicago: Univ. of Chicago Press, 1969), 20.

10. Erving Goffman, *The Presentation of Self in Everyday Life* (New York: Doubleday, 1990).

11. Delargy, *Gaelic Story-Teller,* 28.

12. Armin Woods and Stefan Köhl, *Famous Irish Songs: With the Lyrics, the Score and Guitar Support* (New York: Bergh Publishing, 1989), 9.

13. Delargy, *Gaelic Story-Teller,* 30.

14. Vivian Mercier, *The Irish Comic Tradition* (Oxford: Clarendon, 1962), ix.

15. The English had another reason for viewing Irish storytellers negatively: since they often extolled Ireland's "heroic" past or outlaw activity, they were considered fomenters of rebellion or sedition. Among many others, Edmund Spenser in the late sixteenth century and Sir John Davies, the attorney general for Ireland in the early seventeenth, urged the suppression or extermination

of all Irish poets and entertainers as dangerous. This viewpoint predominated for hundreds of years, and "'singing a ballad' (when it meant a political ditty) would remain a punishable offence throughout the nineteenth century." See Edmund Spenser, "A View of the Present State of Ireland," *The Works of Edmund Spenser,* vol. 10, edited by Edwin Greenlaw, Charles Grosvenor Osgood, Frederick Morgan Padelford, Ray Heffner (Baltimore: Johns Hopkins Univ. Press, 1949) and Zimmermann, 50–52, 68.

16. See, for example, Gene Feist, *James Joyce's Dublin* (New York: Samuel French, 1991); Hugh Kenner, *Dublin's Joyce* (London: Chatto, 1955); David Pierce, *James Joyce's Ireland* (New Haven: Yale Univ. Press, 1992); Maria Tymoczko, *The Irish Ulysses* (Berkeley: Univ. of California Press, 1994); John P. Harrington, *The Irish Beckett* (Syracuse: Syracuse Univ. Press, 1991); Thomas C. Hofheinz, *Joyce and the Invention of Irish History: Finnegans Wake in Context* (Cambridge: Cambridge Univ. Press, 1995); Mary Junker, *Beckett: The Irish Dimension* (Dublin: Wolfhound, 1995); Eoin O'Brien, *The Beckett Country: Samuel Beckett's Ireland* (Dublin: Black Cat, 1986); Noelle Ryan, *Samuel Beckett: Early Days in Foxrock* (Foxrock: Local History Club, 1982).

17. Luke Gibbons, *Transformations in Irish Culture* (Cork: Cork Univ. Press, 1996), 6.

18. Delargy, *Gaelic Story-Teller,* 31.

19. For a survey of such material, see, for example, Breandán Breathnach's chapter, "The Great Collectors," in his *Folk Music and Dances of Ireland* (Dublin: Mercier, 1980), 103–18.

20. Delargy, *Gaelic Story-Teller,* 4.

21. Mercier, viii.

22. Joseph Theodoor Leerssen, *Remembrance and Imagination: Patterns in the Historical and Literary Representation of Ireland in the Nineteenth Century* (Cork: Cork Univ. Press, 1997), 163.

23. Anthony Cronin, *Samuel Beckett: The Last Modernist* (New York: Da Capo, 1999), 265. Ernest Horry La Jeunesse, who was often there with him, describes Oscar Wilde, playing stage Irishman, wasting "himself entirely in words" in a Paris bar: "The chaos of hope of words and laughter, the mad sequence of half completed sentences with which this poet plunged, proving to himself his still unextinguished fancy. . . . He attempted his stories all over again. It is like nothing save the bitter, blinding brilliance of a superhuman firework" (*Recollections of Oscar Wilde,* edited by Percival Pollard [London: J. W. Luce, 1906]), 71, 83.

24. Gibbons, oral comment, James Joyce Symposium, Rome, June 1998.

25. Seán MacRéamoinn, "Words: Written, Spoken and Sung," in *Irish Life and Traditions,* edited by Sharon Gmelch (Syracuse: Syracuse Univ. Press, 1986), 209–10.

26. Paul Johnson, *The Birth of the Modern: World Society 1815–1830* (New York: HarperCollins, 1991), 917.

27. Michel Peillon, "Irish Festivities in Comparative Perspective," *Maynooth Review* 6, no. 2 (May 1982): 42–43.

28. E. Estyn Evans, *Irish Folk Ways* (New York: Routledge, 1989), 253; Sharon Gmelch also quotes this saying, 163.

29. Evans, *Irish Folk Ways,* 32.

30. Gmelch, 163, 168–69.

31. Maeve Binchy, "Festivals," in Gmelch, 224–25.

32. See Kevin Rockett's detailed discussion of Dublin cinema from 1896 through the failure of Joyce's Volta enterprise in 1909 ("Something Rich and Strange: James Joyce, Beatrice Cenci and the Volta," in *Film and Film Culture* 3 [2004]: 21–34).

33. Zimmerman, 246, 235, 237.

34. Neil Jordan, *Michael Collins: Screenplay and Film Diary* (New York: Penguin, 1996), 103. Kitty's call echoes Mrs. Madigan's reaction to a party piece in O'Casey's *Juno and the Paycock:* "A noble call, a noble call!" (Sean O'Casey, *Juno and the Paycock.* In *Modern Irish Drama,* edited by John P. Harrington [New York: Norton, 1991], 233).

35. Jordan, 103. Zimmermann cites this phrase as a typical storyteller's opening (189, 218, 258).

36. Sean McMahon, ed., *The Poolbeg Book of Irish Ballads* (Dublin: Poolbeg, 1991), 140.

37. Sean McMahon reproduces *Old Skibbereen* in a section of *Irish Ballads* called "Exiles' Laments" in *The Poolbeg Book of Irish Ballads,* 140–41. James N. Healy also includes it in his collection *Ballads from the Pubs of Ireland* (Cork: Mercier, 1966), 80–81.

38. Jordan, 43.

39. Ibid., 211–14.

40. Ibid., 46.

41. Patrick McCabe, *The Butcher Boy* (London: Picador, 1992), 32.

42. Elizabeth Cullingford, "Virgins and Mothers: Sinéad O'Connor, Neil Jordan, and *The Butcher Boy,*" in Andrew and Gibbons, 204.

43. McCabe, 84, 133, 180.

44. Ibid., 86.

45. Ibid., 181.

46. Ibid., 214, 215.

47. Joseph Conrad, *Great Short Works of Joseph Conrad* (New York: Harper, 1967), 58.

48. Walter Pater, *The Renaissance: Studies in Art and Poetry* (London: Macmillan, 1914), 135. See Brad Bucknell, *Literary Modernism and Musical Aesthetics: Pater, Pound, Joyce, and Stein* (Cambridge: Cambridge Univ. Press, 2001) for a full-scale treatment of music as central to the aesthetics of both the Symbolists, beginning with Pater, and the Modernists, with a focus on Joyce.

49. Oscar Wilde, preface to *The Picture of Dorian Gray,* ed. Donald L. Lawlor (New York: Norton, 1988), 3.

50. Declan Kiberd, introduction to *Ulysses* (London: Penguin, 2000), xxxvi.

51. See, for example, Ruth Bauerle, *The James Joyce Songbook* (New York: Garland, 1982); Zack R. Bowen, *Bloom's Old Sweet Song: Essays on Joyce and Music* (Gainesville: Univ. of Florida Press, 1995) and *Musical Allusions in the Works of James Joyce: Early Poetry Through Ulysses* (Albany: State Univ. of New York Press, 1974); Matthew J. C. Hodgart and Mabel P. Worthington, *Song in the Works of James Joyce* (New York: Columbia Univ. Press, 1959); Sebastian D. G. Knowles, ed., *Bronze by Gold: The Music of Joyce* (New York: Garland, 1999); Timothy Martin,

Joyce and Wagner: A Study of Influence (Cambridge: Cambridge Univ. Press, 1991); Jack W. Weaver, *Joyce's Music and Noise: Theme and Variation in His Writings* (Gainesville: Univ. Press of Florida, 1998). The musical note was acknowledged in one of the first reviews Joyce received (1907): Thomas Kettle, while observing the absence of Irish folklore and national feeling, praised *Chamber Music* for its "clear, delicate, distinguished playing, of the same kindred with harps, with wood birds, with Paul Verlaine" (quoted in *JJ2,* 261).

52. See, for example, Mary Bryden, *Samuel Beckett and Music* (New York: Oxford Univ. Press, 1998).

53. Virginia Woolf, "Modern Fiction," in *The Common Reader* (New York: Harvest, 1953), 151–56.

54. In Gmelch, 218.

55. Allan Hepburn, "Noise, Music, Voice, *Dubliners,*" in Knowles 197.

56. Ernest Hemingway, *Death in the Afternoon* (New York: Scribner's, 1960), 99.

57. Ong, 32.

58. I use the word "Holocaust" advisedly, with no intention of trivializing Nazi genocide or of taking sides in the ongoing controversy over whether England's laissez-faire policy and incompetence added up to genocide. My intention is to suggest something of the valence of the Famine in nineteenth-century Ireland and also that the events of the 1840s and 1940s may have had some analogous resonance for Beckett. Brecht, as Enoch Brater notes, was among the first to view Beckett's work as a metaphoric representation of post-Holocaust Europe (*Beyond Minimalism: Beckett's Late Style in the Theater* [New York: Oxford Univ. Press, 1987], 142–43).

59. Terry Eagleton, "Staging the Famine," *Irish Reporter* 19 (Third Quarter 1995), 12.

60. In Lawrence E. Harvey, *Samuel Beckett: Poet and Critic* (Princeton: Princeton Univ. Press, 1970), 249–50.

61. Conor Cruise O'Brien, "Irishness," in *Writers and Politics* (New York: Pantheon, 1965), 99.

62. See *JJ2,* 648–49; John Pilling, *Samuel Beckett* (London: Routledge, 1976), 127; and Linda Ben-Zvi, "Samuel Beckett, Fritz Mauthner, and the Limits of Language," *PMLA* 95, no. 2 (March 1980), 183–200. Beckett explicitly alludes to Mauthner's work in *Rough for Radio II* (*SB3,* 321).

63. See Lionel Abel, *Metatheatre: A New View of Dramatic Form* (New York: Hill and Wang, 1963), 134–40, and Junker, 17. Similar pairings occur in later Beckett plays, for example, *Happy Days* and *Ohio Impromptu.*

64. See, for example, Dudley Andrew and Luke Gibbons, "The Theater of Irish Cinema," *Yale Journal of Criticism* 15, no. 1 (Spring 2002): 23–58; Kevin Barry, *Ireland into Film: The Dead* (Cork: Cork Univ. Press, 2001); Ruby Cohn, *Just Play: Beckett's Theater* (Princeton: Princeton Univ. Press, 1980); Dougald McMillan and Martha Fehsenfeld, *Beckett in the Theatre: The Author as Practical Playwright and Director* (New York: Riverrun; London: Calder, 1988); John Fletcher and John Spurling, *Beckett, the Playwright* (London: Methuen, 1985); Stanley E. Gontarski, *The Theatrical Notebooks of Samuel Beckett, Volume II: Endgame* (London: Faber, 1993) and *The Theatrical Notebooks of Samuel Beckett, Volume IV: The Shorter Plays* (London: Faber;

New York: Grove, 1999); Jane Alison Hale, *Beckett's Dramatic Perspective* (West Lafayette, Ind.: Purdue Univ. Press, 1987); Clive Hart, *Joyce, Huston, and the Making of The Dead,* Princess Grace Irish Library, Lectures: 5 (Gerrards Cross: Colin Smythe, 1988); Sidney Homan, *Beckett's Theaters: Interpretations for Performance* (Lewisburg: Bucknell Univ. Press, 1984) and *Filming Beckett's Television Plays: A Director's Experience* (Lewisburg: Bucknell Univ. Press, 1992); Jonathan Kalb, *Beckett in Performance* (Cambridge: Cambridge Univ. Press, 1991); James Knowlson, *Happy Days: Samuel Beckett's Production Notebook* (London: Faber, 1985), *The Theatrical Notebooks of Samuel Beckett, Volume III: Krapp's Last Tape* (London: Faber, 1989), and *Theatre Workbook 1. Samuel Beckett: Krapp's Last Tape* (London: Faber, 1992); José Lanters, *Missed Understandings: A Study of Stage Adaptations of the Works of James Joyce* (Amsterdam: Rodopi, 1988); Anna McMullan, *Theatre on Trial: Samuel Beckett's Later Drama* (New York: Routledge, 1993); Lois Oppenheim, ed., *Directing Beckett* (Ann Arbor: Univ. of Michigan Press, 1994); Alan Schneider, *Entrances: An American Director's Journey* (New York: Viking Penguin, 1986); S. E. Wilmer, *Beckett in Dublin* (Dublin: Lilliput, 1992); Jordan R. Young, *The Beckett Actor: Jack MacGowran, Beginning to End* (Beverly Hills: Moonstone, 1987); Clas Zilliacus, *Beckett and Broadcasting: A Study of the Works of Samuel Beckett for and in Radio and Television* (Abo: Abo Akademi, 1976).

65. The most successful staging of *Exiles* that I know of was the London production with John Wood and Vivien Merchant that Harold Pinter directed at London's Mermaid Theatre in 1970. The Abbey Theatre version filmed for RTE in 1982 is static and uncompelling.

66. See James Knowlson, *Damned to Fame: The Life of Samuel Beckett* (New York: Simon and Schuster, 1996), 608. MacGowran's *Beginning to End* features not only his nephew and cousin providing musical accompaniment, but also Beckett himself "playing a simple pedestal dinner gong . . . to separate one extract from another." Knowlson notes that "this is Beckett's only recorded musical performance" (*Damned,* 478–79).

67. "Interview with Jack MacGowran" (20 Apr. 1971), in *Yeats, Joyce, and Beckett: New Light on Three Modern Irish Writers,* edited by Kathleen McGrory and John Unterecker (Lewisburg: Bucknell Univ. Press, 1976), 177.

68. One of the "Two Letters of Protest" included in *Our Exagmination* expresses an unsympathetic view of the same point: "Work in Progress" takes to an extreme the idea "of making words serve as music and letting their sound convey a meaning quite apart from the actual specific meaning of each word. . . . so far as reading words for sound is concerned we are but simple cave men with only the most elemental ideas of what might constitute rhythm, tone, and expression so it is extremely difficult for a reader in the folk tune stage of development to be faced with a literary Sacre du Printemps for full orchestra" (G. V. L. Slingsby, "Writes a Common Reader," in Samuel Beckett et al., *Our Exagmination Round His Factification for Incamination of Work in Progress* [New York: New Directions, 1962], 190).

69. In Deirdre Bair, "'No-man's-land, Hellespont or vacuum': Samuel Beckett's Irishness," *The Crane Bag* 1, no. 2 (1977): 14.

70. Alan Schneider, "Directing Beckett," *New York Times,* 18 Dec. 1977, sec. 2, 5.

71. See, for example, Phyllis Carey and Ed Jewinski, eds. *Re: Joyce'n Beckett* (New York: Fordham Univ. Press, 1992); Barbara Reich Gluck, *Beckett and Joyce: Friendship and Fiction* (Lewisburg: Bucknell Univ. Press, 1978); Hugh Kenner, *The Stoic Comedians: Flaubert, Joyce, Beckett* (Berkeley: Univ. of California Press, 1962); Friedhelm Rathjeu, *In Principle, Beckett Is Joyce* (13th International James Joyce Symposium, Dublin, June 1992, Edinburgh: Split Pea, 1994).

72. John Wyse Jackson and Peter Costello, *John Stanislaus Joyce: The Voluminous Life and Genius of James Joyce's Father* (London: Fourth Estate, 1997), xiii.

73. Though Ireland, unlike the United States and the Soviet Union, never banned *Ulysses*.

1. "Party Pieces": Oral Storytelling and Social Performance in Ireland

1. Joyce, "Oscar Wilde: The Poet of 'Salomé,'" in *OCPW*, 150.

2. Joyce, "Ireland: Island of Saints and Sages," in *OCPW*, 126. For Yeats's response to Wilde, see his review of Wilde's *A Woman of No Importance*, "An Excellent Talker" (*Uncollected Prose* 1: 1886–96, edited by John P. Frayne [New York: Columbia Univ. Press, 1970]), 354–55. Ellmann quotes Wilde on his nationality: "I am not English. I am Irish which is quite another thing" (*Oscar Wilde* [New York: Knopf, 1988]), 372). Beckett may have been echoing Wilde when, asked if he were an English writer, he replied "*au contraire*." For discussions of Joyce that emphasize textuality, literacy, and reading over orality, see Michael Boyd, "Joyce into Beckett: Prolegomena to Any Future Fictions," in *The Reflexive Novel: Fiction as Critique*, 118–45 (Lewisburg: Bucknell Univ. Press, 1983) and Patrick A. McCarthy, "Joyce's Silent Readers," in *New Alliances in Joyce Studies: "When It's Aped to Foul a Delfian,"* edited by Bonnie Kime Scott (Newark: University of Delaware Press, 1988), 73–78.

3. Yeats, *Prefaces and Introductions: Uncollected Prefaces and Introductions by Yeats to Works by Other Authors and to Anthologies Edited by Yeats*, edited by William H. O'Donell (London: Macmillan, 1988), 147–50.

4. Deirdre Toomey, "The Story-Teller at Fault: Oscar Wilde and Irish Orality," in *Wilde the Irishman*, edited by Jerusha McCormack (New Haven: Yale Univ. Press, 1998), 25.

5. Zimmermann, 12.

6. Yeats quotes the entire ballad in "Popular Ballad Poetry of Ireland," *Uncollected Prose 1*, 148–49.

7. Seán O Suilleabháin, *A Handbook of Irish Folklore* (Detroit: Singing Tree, 1970), 545.

8. Roy F. Foster, *Modern Ireland 1600–1972* (London: Penguin, 1988), 5.

9. P. W. Joyce, *A Concise History of Ireland* (New York: Longmans, 1905), 86, 27.

10. P. W. Joyce, *A Social History of Ancient Ireland* (London: Longmans, 1920), 29.

11. Zimmermann, 178–79.

12. P. W. Joyce, *Social History*, 540–41.

13. Zimmermann, 208.

14. John Carr, *The Stranger in Ireland* (1806), quoted in Zimmermann, 133. See also Delargy, *Gaelic Story-Teller*, 20.

15. Delargy, *Gaelic Story-Teller,* 28–29, 25.

16. Zimmermann, 204–5.

17. Gearóid Ó Tuathaigh, "The Distressed Society: The Struggle for Emancipation and Independence, 1801–1918," in *The Irish World: The History and Cultural Achievements of the Irish People,* edited by Brian de Breffny (London: Thames and Hudson, 1977), 186.

18. Zimmermann, 213.

19. Ibid., 198.

20. Terry Eagleton, *Heathcliff and the Great Hunger: Studies in Irish Culture* (New York: Verso, 1995), 23. Eagleton discusses the Famine as contested ground for historians (22–26) and as surprisingly underrepresented in literary expression (12–15).

21. William Wilde, *Census of Ireland* (1851), I, Part 5 (1956), 242; in Evans, *Irish Folk Ways,* 295, and Zimmermann, 273.

22. Declan Kiberd, "Irish Literature and Irish History," in *The Oxford History of Ireland,* edited by Roy F. Foster (Oxford: Oxford Univ. Press, 1992), 232.

23. Kevin Danaher, *In Ireland Long Ago* (Cork: Mercier, 1967), 141–42; see also Joseph Theodoor Leerssen, *Mere Irish and Fíor-Ghael: Studies in the Idea of Irish Nationality, Its Development and Literary Expression Prior to the Nineteenth Century* (Amsterdam: John Benjamins, 1986), 190.

24. *State Papers of Henry VIII, Vol. II (1532–7)* (London: George Eyre and Andrew Spottiswoode, 1834), 215.

25. Terry Moylan, ed. *The Age of Revolution: 1776 to 1815 in the Irish Song Tradition* (Dublin: Lilliput, 2000), 1.

26. Leerssen, *Remembrance,* 157–60, 178.

27. K. Theodore Hoppen, *Election, Politics, and Society in Ireland 1832–1885* (Oxford: Clarendon, 1984), 424–29.

28. Kiberd, "Irish Literature," 231.

29. Louis Le Roux, *Patrick Pearse* (Dublin: Talbot, 1932), 43. See also Zimmermann, 354.

30. Leerssen specifically links the writings of Pearse and other nationalists to Ireland's bardic past (*Mere Irish,* 257).

31. Declan Kiberd, "The War against the Past," in *The Uses of the Past: Essays on Irish Culture,* edited by Audrey S. Eyler and Robert F. Garratt (Newark: Univ. of Delaware Press, 1988), 37, and "Irish Literature," 268. Gibbons, *Transformations in Irish Culture,* 16. Eagleton more ambiguously refers to the post-Famine era as "a weightless moment precariously balanced between the ancient and the avant-garde, a condition of absolute loss which nevertheless brims with unborn potential" (*Heathcliff,* 280). See also Eric Hobsbawm and Terence Ranger, *The Invention of Traditions* (Cambridge: Cambridge Univ. Press, 1984).

32. Zimmermann, 273; Kiberd, "Irish Literature," 260.

33. Evans, *Irish Folk Ways,* 282; A. M. Sullivan, *The New Ireland* (1877), 65, in Evans, *Irish Folk Ways,* 295.

34. Ong, 68.

35. Zimmermann, 308.

36. Thomas Gallagher, *Paddy's Lament: Ireland 1846–1847: Prelude to Hatred* (New York: Harcourt, 1982), 122.

37. Delargy, *Gaelic Story-Teller,* 9, 10.

38. E. Estyn Evans, *Irish Heritage: The Landscape, the People and Their Work* (Dundalk: Dundalgan, 1944), 54, 174, and "Introduction: The Irish—Fact and Fiction," in de Breffny, 15.

39. P. W. Joyce, *Concise History,* 203, 219.

40. Symposia outside Ireland have come to emulate this practice: Zack Bowen has sung regularly at the Miami J'yce conference; Bernard Benstock and Michael O'Shea wrote the "Dublimerick cycle," a series of limericks based on *Dubliners* that was performed in Miami, February 1995, in tribute to Bernard Benstock.

41. Yeats, "Bardic Ireland," in *Uncollected Prose 1,* 163–64.

42. See, for example, Foster, *Modern Ireland,* 28; Danaher, *In Ireland,* 142; and Kiberd, "Irish Literature," 232.

43. In Zimmermann, who cites others who also made this analogy, 363–64.

44. See Declan Kiberd, introduction to *Ulysses* (London: Penguin, 2000), xiv–xv, xxv.

45. Such commentators included the Russian filmmaker Sergei Eisenstein, who contemplated turning *Ulysses* into a film in the 1930s (S. M. Eisenstein, *Selected Works, Vol. II: Towards a Theory of Montage,* edited by Michael Glenny and Richard Taylor. Translated by Michael Glenny [London: BFI Publishing, 1991], 194). In addition, Joyce discussed a possible film of *Ulysses* with Warner Brothers, and both Louis Zukofsky and Stuart Gilbert wrote film scripts of it and submitted them to Joyce (see Alan Spiegel, *Fiction and the Camera Eye: Visual Consciousness in Film and the Modern Novel* [Charlottesville: Univ. of Virginia Press, 1976], 74–75). Eisenstein was also a missed opportunity for Beckett, who wrote to him in March 1936, asking "to be considered for admission to the Moscow State School of Cinematography" so he could study with him. Jay Leyda reproduces Beckett's letter, which, he says, Eisenstein never answered because it "was lost in the shuffle" (*Eisenstein 2: A Premature Celebration of Eisenstein's Centenary,* translated by Alan Y. Upchurch et al. [Calcutta: Seagull, 1985], 59).

46. Knowlson, *Damned,* 138.

47. Letter to Thomas MacGreevy, 18 October 1932 (Trinity College Dublin); quoted in John Pilling, *Beckett Before Godot* (Cambridge: Cambridge Univ. Press, 1997), 80. Eisenstein also links Homer with Mallarmé, 163–64.

48. Barbara Hardy, *Tellers and Listeners: The Narrative Imagination* (London: Athlone, 1975), x.

49. Fritz Senn, "Kyklonomastics," *JJQ* 36, no. 3 (Spring 1999): 490.

50. Homer, *The Odyssey,* translated by Robert Fitzgerald (Garden City: Anchor Doubleday, 1963), 8:543–48.

51. Senn, 487.

52. Senn offers an insightful analysis of this failure.

53. Daphne Vivian Fielding, *Those Remarkable Cunards: Emerald and Nancy* (New York: Atheneum, 1968), 9. It was in Cunard's London house that Yeats's *At the Hawk's Well* was first

staged in 1916. A few days later a second staging for the benefit of a war charity was held, with Queen Alexandra in attendance, in Lady Islington's drawing-room (Joseph Hone, *W. B. Yeats 1865–1939* [London: Macmillan, 1967]), 297.

54. According to Bair, Beckett was uncomfortable with most of the other visitors and soon "stopped going altogether, visiting privately instead" ("'No-man's-land,'" 17).

55. Samuel Beckett, *Eleuthéria*, translated by Michael Brodsky (New York: Foxrock, 1995), 15.

56. Zimmermann, 346–47.

57. In Kevin Whelan, "Immoral Economy: Interpreting Erskine Nicol's *The Tenant*," in *America's Eye: Irish Paintings from the Collection of Brian P. Burns*, edited by Adele M. Dalsimer and Vera Kreilkamp (Boston: Boston College Museum of Art, 1996), 60.

58. Eyal Amiran, *Wandering and Home: Beckett's Metaphysical Narrative* (University Park: Penn State Univ. Press, 1993), 33.

59. Declan Kiberd, *Inventing Ireland: The Literature of the Modern Nation* (London: Cape, 1995), 535.

60. Israel Shenker, "Moody Man of Letters," *New York Times*, 6 May 1956, sec. 2, 1. The phrase is often quoted, for example, in Cronin, 310, and Gluck, 24.

61. Harrington, *Irish Beckett*, 1.

62. This is Fitzgerald's title for Book Thirteen of his *Odyssey* translation, the chapter in which Odysseus returns home to Ithaca.

63. Leerssen, *Remembrance*, 209.

64. Joyce, "The Soul of Ireland," review of Lady Gregory, *Poets and Dreamers: Studies and Translations from the Irish* (1903), *OCPW*, 74.

65. Joyce to Arthur Power, quoted in *JJ2*, 505. See Seamus Deane on Joyce's kinship with the cultural Revivalists ("Joyce the Irishman," in *The Cambridge Companion to James Joyce*, edited by Derek Attridge [Cambridge: Cambridge Univ. Press, 1995]), 31–53.

66. Jackson and Costello, 398.

67. Joyce "abandoned Pearse's Gaelic League classes on discovering that his teacher (who would later cure this fault) could not praise Irish without denigrating the English language" (Kiberd, introduction to *Ulysses*, xiii). He took to heart Pearse's subsequent advice: "If Irish literature is to live and grow, it must get into contact on the one hand with its own past and on the other with the mind of contemporary Europe" (in Kiberd, "Irish Literature," 247).

68. Kiberd, "Irish Literature," 271.

69. Nicholas Grene, "Torrents of Talk," *Irish Review* 11 (Winter 1991–92): 140–43.

70. Jackson and Costello, xiv.

71. From his obituary in the Paris edition of the *Chicago Tribune*, in ibid., 422.

72. Con Curran, in ibid., 224.

73. Bauerle, *Joyce Songbook*, xix.

74. Joseph Kelly offers a rich discussion of the relationship between Stanislaus Joyce and his brother ("Stanislaus Joyce, Ellsworth Mason, and Richard Ellmann: The Making of James Joyce," *Joyce Studies Annual* 3 [Summer 1992], 98–140.)

75. Jackson and Costello, 268.

76. Mary and Padraic Colum suggest that the venture might well have succeeded (*Our Friend James Joyce* [Garden City: Doubleday, 1958]), 70–71.

77. Jackson and Costello, 74, 119.

78. In the words of the *Freeman's Journal*'s reviewer (29 August 1904; in *JJ2,* 168).

79. Erik Schneider, "Joyce in Concert: The *Meistersinger* Performance in Trieste," *JJQ* 38, no. 3–4 (Spring–Summer 2001): 495–97.

80. Yeats, "Popular Ballad Poetry of Ireland," *Uncollected Prose 1,* 147.

81. See Erik Schneider.

82. See Ira Nadel, "Joyce and Blackmail," *Journal of Modern Literature* 22, no. 2 (Winter 1998–99): 219.

83. See Hodgart and Worthington, 1–12. Moore's *Irish Melodies* (1807–34) were themselves largely recreations, verses set to Irish airs, rather than "folk" recordings (see Terence de Vere White, "The Melodies," in *Tom Moore: The Irish Poet* [London: Hamish Hamilton, 1977]), 69–83. Crediting the work of Senn, Elaine Newell, Weldon Thornton, and Zack Bowen, Bauerle totals up the number of musical titles in Joyce's writings at nearly fifteen hundred (*Joyce Songbook,* xvii).

84. Hardy, 265–76.

85. Colum and Colum, 22.

86. Ibid., 50.

87. Bauerle, *Joyce Songbook,* xviii.

88. Arthur Power, *Conversations with James Joyce* (New York: Barnes and Noble, 1974), 50.

89. The song he performed was his version of Yeats's "Who Goes with Fergus" (*The Collected Poems of W. B. Yeats* [London: Macmillan, 1956]), 48–49.

90. Jack MacGowran, "Interview with Jack MacGowran," 175.

91. Knowlson, *Damned,* 28.

92. Deirdre Bair, *Samuel Beckett: A Biography* (London: Vintage, 1990), 8, 14, 20–21.

93. Knowlson, *Damned,* 45.

94. Miron Grindea, "Beckett's Involvement with Music," in Bryden, 184.

95. Knowlson, *Damned,* 102.

96. In Mel Gussow, *Conversations with and about Beckett* (New York: Grove, 1996), 121–22.

97. Knowlson, *Damned,* 102.

98. Bair, *Samuel Beckett,* 500.

99. Knowlson, *Damned,* 185.

100. MacGowran, "Interview," 175. Billie Whitelaw also said that, in performing Beckett, the crucial thing was to get the rhythm right (*Billie Whitelaw . . . Who He?* [London: Hodder and Stoughton, 1995], 78).

101. Knowlson, *Damned,* 240.

102. Yet as Murphy's will indicates, Beckett apparently felt the need to flush such influences out of his system: "With regard to the disposal of these my body, mind and soul, I desire that they be burnt and placed in a paper bag and brought to the Abbey Theatre . . . and without pause into

what the great and good Lord Chesterfield calls the necessary house, where their happiest hours have been spent, on the right as one goes down into the pit, and I desire that the chain be there pulled upon them, if possible during the performance of a piece, the whole to be executed without ceremony or show of grief" (*Murphy, SB1,* 161).

103. Ronald Hayman, *Samuel Beckett* (London: Heinemann, 1980), 67.

104. Knowlson, *Damned,* 45.

2. *Dubliners:* "Scrupulous Meanness" Versus Expansive Performance

1. Hardy notes that "while the Dubliners live, they talk and tell, and after they are dead they become parts of other people's stories, like Parnell, Emily Sinico, and Michael Furey" (207).

2. Hepburn, 189. Bowen discusses Joyce's use of music in "Araby," "Eveline," "After the Race," "The Boarding House," and "A Mother" (*Musical Allusions,* 11–23).

3. See the discussion of this moment in Hodgart and Worthington, 1–2.

4. See Hepburn, 192–93, for a discussion of such moments in "Araby."

5. Jackson and Costello, 185.

6. Caroline Norton, *The Poems of the Hon. Mrs. Norton* (Philadelphia: Uriah Hunt, 1846), 186–89.

7. "The Lass That Loves a Sailor," by English songwriter Charles Dibdin (1745–1814), is reprinted by both Don Gifford, *Joyce Annotated: Notes for Dubliners and A Portrait of the Artist as a Young Man* (Berkeley: Univ. of California Press, 1982), 51, and by Robert Scholes and A. Walton Litz in their edition, *Dubliners: Text, Criticism, and Notes* (New York: Viking, 1971), 471. *Finnegans Wake* reprises it as "the lass that lured a tailor" (297.28–29), "ye seal that lubs you lasers" (324.9), and "the lass that toffs a tailor" (440.30).

8. See Terence Brown, in his edition of *Dubliners* (*D2,* 255n. 9). Hugh Kenner agrees that Eveline makes the right choice, that what she refuses "was just what her father would have said it was, the patter of an experienced seducer" ("Molly's Masterstroke," *JJQ* 10, no. 1 [Fall 1972]), 21.

9. Ellmann quotes a poem that Mick Hart wrote in his attempt to cadge money and drink (*JJ2,* 366).

10. P. W. Joyce, *Social History,* 577. Breathnach also comments on the "honoured place occupied by the harper in the political and cultural life of Gaelic Ireland" (66).

11. Leerssen, *Remembrance,* 81.

12. *Music from the Works of James Joyce.* Liner notes by Zack Bowen and Kevin McDermott (Sunphone Records, 2003). The song is alluded to numerous times in *Ulysses* and *Finnegans Wake.*

13. Jean-Michel Rabaté, "Silence in *Dubliners,*" in *James Joyce: New Perspectives,* edited by Colin McCabe (Bloomington: Indiana Univ. Press, 1982), 62.

14. Rejecting the common interpretation of the "soft wet substance," Margot Norris argues that it represents excrement (*Joyce's Web: The Social Unraveling of Modernism* [Austin: Univ. of Texas Press, 1992]), 132–34.

15. R. B. Kershner summarizes *The Bohemian Girl* and discusses its relevance to the plot of "Eveline" (*Joyce, Bakhtin, and Popular Culture: Chronicles of Disorder* [Chapel Hill: Univ. of North Carolina Press, 1989], 63–68). See Bowen's discussion of the link between Eveline and Maria based on their having this opera in common (*Musical Allusions,* 12). Joyce alludes to the song several times in *Finnegans Wake,* including "he dreamed that he'd wealthes in mormon halls," "you dreamt that you'd wealth in marble arch," and "I'll dreamt that I'll dwealth mid warblers' walls when throstles and choughs to my sigh hiehied" (*FW,* 64.4–5, 264.34–35, 449.17–19).

16. Stephen Watt, *Joyce, O'Casey, and the Irish Popular Theater* (Syracuse: Syracuse Univ. Press, 1991), 3; Seamus Reilly, "James Joyce and Dublin Opera, 1888–1904," in Knowles, 3–31. Jackson and Costello call *The Bohemian Girl* and Benedict's *The Lily of Killarney* "the most popular Dublin opera" of the time (207).

17. Quoted in Scholes and Litz, *Dubliners,* 484, and Bowen, *Musical Allusions,* 17. See also Bauerle, *Joyce Songbook,* 162–63, and Gifford, *Joyce Annotated,* 80–81.

18. Bauerle, *Joyce Songbook,* 161.

19. According to Stanislaus Joyce, Mr. Duffy is "a portrait of what my brother imagined I should become in middle age" (*MBK,* 160).

20. *A Painful Case,* John Lynch, director and producer (RTE, 1983).

21. See Patrick A. McCarthy, "Joyce's Silent Readers," in Scott, 74. McCarthy also notes that Stephen, exiting 7 Eccles Street in *Ulysses,* intones the 113th Psalm "*secreto*" (*U,* 651), which suggests that Stephen is retreating not just *from* Bloom but deliberately *into* isolation (78).

22. In the RTE film, the literalizing of this passage creates an unfortunate cartoonish talking-train effect. And, as the train passes, a voiceover of Mrs. Sinico declares explicitly, "I loved you, Mr. Duffy."

23. Warren Beck's phrase, in *Joyce's Dubliners: Substance, Vision, and Art* (Durham: Duke Univ. Press, 1969), 256.

24. Hardy, 214–15.

25. Kershner, 133.

26. According to Stanislaus Joyce, cited by Ellmann, *LJJ3,* 348n 5. Here is the song:

Oh, ye dead! oh, ye dead! whom we know by the light you give
From your cold gleaming eyes, though you move like men who live,
　　Why leave you thus your graves
　　In far-off fields and waves
Where the worm and the sea-bird only know your bed
　　To haunt this spot, where all
　　Those eyes that wept your fall,
And the hearts that bewailed you, like your own, lie dead?

It is true, it is true, we are shadows cold and wan;
And the fair and the brave whom we loved on earth are gone;

But still thus ev'n in death,
So sweet the living breath
Of the fields and the flow'rs in our youth we wander'd o'er,
That ere, condemn'd, we go
To freeze 'mid Hecla's snow,
We would taste it a while, and think we live once more!

Moore's note tells the story of a mountain in "Ireland where the ghosts of persons who have died in foreign lands walk about and converse with those they meet, like living people" (Thomas Moore, *Moore's Poems with Notes by Thomas Moore* (Chicago: The Henneberry Company, n.d.), 245–46. Joyce said that "the 2nd verse of this should be sung almost in a whisper" (*LJJ3*, 344), as presumably he sang it.

27. Kevin Whelan, "The Memories of 'The Dead,'" in Andrew and Gibbons, 70. Moore's prominence is made overt in Huston's film of *The Dead* by having someone say, "There's no doubt that Moore's the one genius of Irish music."

28. Leerssen, *Remembrance*, 177.

29. Hart, 16.

30. Bowen, *Musical Allusions*, 12–13.

31. Barry, 26.

32. Schwarz, "Gabriel Conroy's Psyche," in Schwarz's edition of *The Dead* (Boston: St. Martin's, 1994), 107.

33. Myra Russel, "*Chamber Music*: Words and Music Lovingly Coupled," in Knowles, 63.

34. Richard Nelson and Shaun Davey, *James Joyce's The Dead, American Theatre* 17, no. 7 (September 2000): 49–68.

35. Norris, *Joyce's Web*, 115. Like Maria in "Clay," the film's Aunt Julia sings this stanza twice, rather than go on to the even more difficult second stanza:

May life to her prove full of sunshine and love,
full of love, yes! yes! yes!
Who would not love her
Sweet star of the morning! shining so bright,
Earth's circle adorning, fair creature of light,
Fair creature of light.

The song is reprinted in, for example, Gifford, *Joyce Annotated*, 118–19; Schwarz's edition of *The Dead*, 35; and Bowen, *Musical Allusions*, 19. The lyrics to "Arrayed for the Bridal" are by George Linley (1798–1865). Luke Gibbons sees its theme as "a bride jilted on her wedding day," which links it to the other performances of erotic betrayal in the story ("'The Cracked Looking Glass' of Cinema: James Joyce, John Huston, and the Memory of 'The Dead,'" in Andrew and Gibbons, 137).

36. Huston's film of *The Dead* literalizes the eros/thanatos link by depicting Aunt Julia on her deathbed dressed as a bride while Gabriel is thinking of her imminent death. In "'Who Killed Julia Morkan?'" Norris makes a strong case for Julia Morkan as a great artist who is martyred by her country and church (*Joyce's Web*, 97–118).

37. Michel Poizat says of such a setting, which creates a particularly effective architectural, aesthetic, and psychological space in both Joyce's story and Houston's film, that "the history and role of the staircase in operatic stage direction would make for a very interesting little study all by itself" (*The Angel's Cry: Beyond the Pleasure Principle in Opera,* translated by Arthur Denner [Ithaca: Cornell Univ. Press, 1992], 32).

38. Hepburn discusses Joyce's offstage male singers, not only Michael Furey and Bartell D'Arcy, but also Simon Dedalus in "The Sirens" chapter of *Ulysses* (200–201). "The Lass of Aughrim" has many versions. Joyce, apparently having learned the song from Nora, sang it constantly in 1904, and when he returned to Ireland in 1909 Nora's mother, in a gesture of welcome, sang it to him while he sat, deeply moved by the experience, at her kitchen table in Galway. He wrote to Nora: "The tears are in my eyes and my voice trembles with emotion when I sing that lovely air. It was worth coming to Ireland to have got it from your poor, kind mother." In a curious echo of Maria's failure to sing the second stanza of "I Dreamt that I Dwelt in Marble Halls," however, Joyce writes that "she does not like to sing me the last verses in which the lovers exchange their tokens" (*LJJ2*, 242, 240). See also Bauerle, *Joyce Songbook,* 177, and Bowen, *Musical Allusions,* 21–22. According to Ellmann, Nora sang the following stanzas to Joyce:

If you'll be the lass of Aughrim
As I am taking you mean to be
Tell me the first token
That passed between you and me.

O don't you remember
That night on yon lean hill
When we both met together
Which I am sorry now to tell.

The rain falls on my yellow locks
And the dew it wets my skin;
My babe lies cold within my arms;
Lord Gregory, let me in.

(*LJJ2*, 240n. 4, and *JJ2*, 286.) Donagh MacDonagh reprints this version almost verbatim (20). He also reconstructs the following lines from the Child Collection:

Oh, if you be the lass of Aughrim
As I suppose you not to be

Come tell me the last token
Between you and me.

Oh Gregory, don't you remember
One night on the hill
When we swapped rings off each other's hands
Sorely against my will?
Mine was of the beaten gold,
Yours was but block tin.

("The Lass of Aughrim or the Betrayal of James Joyce," in Harmon, *The Celtic Master,* 22.)

For a detailed historical analysis of the song, see Hugh Shields, "The History of *The Lass of Aughrim,*" in *Irish Musical Studies 1: Musicology in Ireland,* edited by Gerard Gillen and Harry White (Dublin: Irish Academic, 1990), 58–73.

39. Barry, 2.

40. Kevin Rockett, Luke Gibbons, and John Hill, *Cinema and Ireland* (London: Routledge, 1988), 262.

41. Pius X decreed that the church choir was an essential part of the liturgy and hence barred to women. A month later the Pope banned the use of churches for concerts, thereby ending a valuable source of income for women musicians. Joyce, whose mother was thus barred from singing in the church choir (Jackson and Costello, 251), expressed his contempt for these actions in a December 1904 letter: "In conclusion I spit upon the image of the tenth Pius" (*SLJJ,* 49). Bloom refers to Julia in the past tense in *Ulysses* (155). Norris sees a causal link between the Pope's decree, Julia's singing, her haggard look, and her death (*Joyce's Web,* 114–17).

42. Norris, *Joyce's Web,* 117.

43. Ibid., 115.

44. Huston comments that he finds Aunt Julia's singing "funny and dear and ever so sad" (*John Huston and the Dubliners: The Making of The Dead,* Lilyan Sievernich, director [Liffey Films, 1987]). In the play *James Joyce's The Dead,* Aunt Julia sings well at first; when she weakens, Aunt Kate joins her, and the two sing effectively together.

45. Hart reproduces "The Grief of a Girl's Heart" (37–38) from Lady Augusta Gregory's *Poets and Dreamers: Studies and Translations from the Irish* (New York: Oxford Univ. Press, 1974), 261–62. See Barry's detailed analysis of the ballad's function in Huston's film (57–66).

46. For discussions of the Gregory Clause, see Christine Kinealy, *This Great Calamity: The Irish Famine 1845–52* (Dublin: Gill and MacMillan, 1994), 216–27, and Gibbons, "'Cracked Looking Glass,'" 132–33.

47. A fourth major change is the addition of a bathroom scene between Freddy and Gabriel. A rare Irishman who cannot perform in front of others, Freddy asks Gabriel to leave so that he can urinate.

48. Norris, *Joyce's Web,* 108.

49. Hart, 13. The allusion is appropriate in a way: Lady Gregory wrote letters of introduction that enabled Joyce, like Gabriel, to become a paid reviewer for the Dublin *Daily Express* (*JJ2,* 107–8).

50. Hart, 12.

51. This change is analogous to the utterly inappropriate "Naughty Girls" number, which is lifted from "The Boarding House" (*D,* 76), that Mary Jane and Aunts Julia and Kate absurdly perform in *James Joyce's The Dead.* Curiously, Denis Donoghue deems Cathleen Delany's screechy singing as Aunt Julia praiseworthy, "a choice instance of finesse. Huston presented her as the ruin of a once fine voice and still enough of a musician to know what a better performance of the aria would be" ("Huston's Joyce," *New York Review of Books,* 3 Mar. 1988, 19), and Barry is agnostic on the subject, finding the singing neither praiseworthy nor atrocious, and therefore an instance of the film's irresolution and uncertainty (20). My view accords with that of Norris, "Who Killed Julia Morkan?" (in *Joyce's Web*), and Marjorie Howes, "Tradition, Gender, and Migration in 'The Dead,' or: How Many People Has Gretta Conroy Killed?" in Andrew and Gibbons, 149–71.

52. Hart, 12.

53. Barry, 61.

54. Whelan, "Memories of 'The Dead,'" 82. As Barry notes, the film's Lily, unlike Joyce's, seems ubiquitous, and her more prominent presence foregrounds class issues beyond Joyce's treatment of them in this story (21, 60–62, 66).

55. Hart, 12–13. Ruth Bauerle also focuses on Gretta's "centrality" ("Date Rape, Mate Rape: A Liturgical Interpretation of *The Dead,*" in Scott, 113). Huston, however, says that his intention was to foreground Gabriel rather than Gretta: "The story's about a man being revealed to himself. . . . And the discovery of what one is is a soul-shaking experience" (*Huston and Dubliners*).

56. Beginning with Harry Levin, numerous critics argue that Gabriel's most important role is to represent "what Joyce might have become, had he remained in Ireland" (Joyce, *The Portable James Joyce* [New York: Viking, 1966], 18).

57. Ong, 11.

58. Herbert Howarth discusses the powerful and pervasive influence of the oral tradition that was brought into the home by servants and nurses: "Perhaps no single influence ate so deep into the minds of the politicians and writers of Ireland as the stories of their nurses, told them at the most impressionable age" (*The Irish Writers, 1880–1940: Literature Under Parnell's Star* [London: Rockliff, 1958], 8–9). See also Gibbons, "'Cracked Looking Glass,'" 143. Lily, moreover, is linked not only to orality but also to rural Ireland and the Famine by being the one who serves the potatoes, a point Huston's film underscores when she complains of having to watch them while admitting the arriving guests. Bloom reprises the Irish potato in *Ulysses* by carrying one in his pocket throughout the day.

59. See Gibbons, "Identity without a Centre: Allegory, History and Irish Nationalism," *Cultural Studies* 6, no. 3 (Oct. 1992): 358–75.

60. Leerssen, *Mere Irish,* 172.

61. Vincent P. Pecora, *Self and Form in Modern Narrative* (Baltimore: Johns Hopkins Univ. Press, 1989), 243. In "Date Rape," Bauerle goes even farther, arguing that Gabriel's speech is utterly "inhospitable," and is, in fact, "rapacious" (116). One curious change in *James Joyce's The Dead* is the decision to have Miss Ivors stay for the speech, lead the toast for the "Three Graces," and then join in Freddy's rousing song, "Now why can't we have a voice too / Why can't he have a voice or him or him?" (63), which sounds like a political statement; but in the play's dramatic context it is merely a riposte to a neighbor complaining about the party's noise.

62. Hart, 32.

63. Rockett, Gibbons, and Hill, 263.

64. Ibid.

65. Depending on the version (and there are many), the ballad depicts Lord Gregory *or* his mother refusing to admit the lass, whom he has seduced or raped and impregnated, and her baby, who, she laments, "lies cold within my arms." She then drowns herself (see *JJ2,* 286n), and in some versions Lord Gregory consequently commits suicide. MacDonagh argues that "the story of *The Lass of Aughrim* is the story of James Joyce" (22). See also Bauerle, "Date Rape," and Vincent J. Cheng, *Joyce, Race, and Empire* (Cambridge: Cambridge Univ. Press, 1995), 142–47.

66. Kershner, 144.

67. Bauerle sees this analogy appearing as early as the Lily episode: in one version of "The Lass of Aughrim," "The Lass asks Gregory to remember yet a third occasion [of sex between them], in her father's hall, 'when you had your will of me and that was the worst of all.'" Gabriel encounters Lily in the hall, which is her father's provenance since he is the caretaker, and in the gendered exchange Gabriel thrusts a coin at the reluctant, ineffectively resistant young woman (*D,* 228). In addition, if Gregory metamorphoses into Gabriel, then the lass reappears as Gretta, whose element is rain and snow and who is the object of male lust ("Date Rape," 115–18). Yet as Barry rightly notes, in Gretta's memory it is she who abandons Michael Furey to his death in the rain and cold (62–63).

68. Yeats, for one, links them in his play, *Purgatory:* "long ago/Men that had fought at Aughrim and the Boyne" (*The Collected Plays of W. B. Yeats* [London: Macmillan, 1969], 183).

69. J. G. Simms, *Jacobite Ireland 1685–91* (London: Routledge, 1969), 227.

70. Foster, *Modern Ireland,* 150.

71. According to Brown, Aughrim means "horse's back" in Irish, and the "Great Disaster" there in 1691 "broke the back of Gaelic civilization"(*D2,* 315n. 79). Bauerle maintains that Gabriel's "rejection of all association with Galway" represents a breach "in the Irish law of hospitality [since] it was in Galway that Warden Thomas Lynch was so offended by his son's offense to guests that he hanged the son!" thus making his name a word for vigilante "justice" ("Date Rape," 117).

72. Huston's *The Dead* makes a Joycean joke by having Mr. Duffy (the same or another) appear as a Morkan party guest.

73. Barry rightly praises the film for resisting the temptation to depict the ghost that haunts Gretta: "One of Huston's most reticent acts of fidelity to Joyce's 'The Dead' is that he allows it to remain a story in which the most powerful character, Michael Furey, does not put in an appearance"

(23). The tact demonstrated was even greater than Barry acknowledges since the "dark and mysterious shape" appears in the script of the film (Hart, 34).

74. Hart, 16.

75. Ibid., 17.

76. In Huston's film, only the camera makes this journey.

3. Stephen Dedalus's *Non Serviam:* Patriarchal and Performative Failure in *A Portrait of the Artist as a Young Man*

1. Roger McHugh, "A Setting for Stephen Dedalus," *Arts in Ireland* 2, no. 1 (1973): 32.

2. In *Finnegans Wake* Joyce mockingly alludes to his nickname as "Sunny Twimjim" (211.6).

3. Jackson and Costello, 76.

4. Bernard Benstock, *James Joyce* (New York: Ungar, 1985), 8.

5. In James H. Delargy, ed. *Irish Folk-Tales, Collected by Jeremiah Curtin* (Dublin: Talbot, 1956), 171.

6. Zimmermann, 437.

7. Zimmermann cites several storytellers who would begin with this phrase (487, 488, 493).

8. In a letter to Joyce written decades later, John Joyce remembered such occasions fondly: "Do you recollect the old days . . . when you were Babie Tuckoo, and I used to take you out in the Square and tell you all about the moo-cow that used to come down from the mountain and take little boys across?" (*LJJ3,* 31 Jan. 1931, 212).

9. Substituting "place" for "grave," Joyce's version suppresses allusions to death that emerge later. Similarly undisturbing at first, "the red and the green are, until the Christmas dinner scene, completely compatible in Stephen's mind" (Bowen, *Musical Allusions,* 35).

10. See, for example, the description of Joycean musical and storytelling evenings in Carol Loeb Shloss, *Lucia Joyce: To Dance in the Wake* (New York: Farrar, 2003), 52–53.

11. Hélène Cixous finds a similar process of development ruled by imperatives in *Finnegans Wake:* "Orthodoxy and security are to be found in 'the howtosayto itiswhatis hemustwhomust worden schall' (p. 223)" (*The Exile of James Joyce,* translated by Sally A. J. Purcell [New York: David Lewis, 1972], 296).

12. In his satirical poem "The Holy Office" Joyce similarly represents himself:

> I stand the self-doomed, unafraid,
> Unfellowed, friendless and alone,
> Indifferent as the herring-bone.

(*The Critical Writings of James Joyce,* edited by Ellsworth Mason and Richard Ellmann [New York: Viking, 1970], 152).

13. Like Huston's movie of "The Dead," Joseph Strick's film of *Portrait* is more overtly political than Joyce's fiction. The latter film begins with a written text: "Ireland 1885. Ruled by Britain but moving towards independence under the leadership of Charles Stewart Parnell, a Protestant nationalist supported by the Catholic majority of his country." Shortly thereafter a second, and last, text appears: "1891. Parnell has fallen from power. Named as the secret lover of Mrs. Kitty O'Shea in a divorce suit, he was vilified and abandoned by most of his supporters and forced from politics in disgrace. For the time, the independence movement is badly damaged." In addition, where Joyce has Stephen vaguely hear voices and then imagine the return of Parnell's body (*PA*, 25), Strick depicts priests, whom Stephen and we overhear, whispering about Parnell's lust and pride, and his death resulting from "inflammation of the brain."

14. Stephen first hears the defiant assertion on the retreat: the preacher declares that Lucifer's fall resulted from "the sin of pride, the sinful thought conceived in an instant: *non serviam: I will not serve*" (*PA*, 134). In *Ulysses* Stephen repeats his *non serviam* in defiance of the vision summoned up by his "intellectual imagination": his mother's corpse urging him to repent (*U*, 541).

15. Stephen's defiant words would seem to have even greater resonance for Beckett, who intertextually deploys them in "Home Olga," his acrostic homage to Joyce, in whom "there's more than Homer knows how to spew" (*SB3*, 8). In *Finnegans Wake* Joyce parodies Stephen's credo as "the bruce, the coriolano, and the Ignacio" (228.10–11).

16. Kershner, 167.

17. An older Stephen recalls that he had twice been unjustly pandied, but he also acknowledges "that he had often escaped punishment" (*PA*, 181).

18. Given Stephen's flight from such performances, it is appropriate that Joyce has him, while mortifying his senses after his anguished confession, neither sing nor whistle (174).

19. Jackson and Costello, 209; see also Seamus Deane's notes to *A Portrait of the Artist as a Young Man* (Harmondsworth: Penguin, 1992), 293n. 31. Jackson and Costello also note the talent for mimicry of Joyce's mother (260).

20. Because Irish street singers had to capture a crowd with their first line, they often began with "Come all ye," which became synonymous with street ballads (Danaher, *In Ireland*, 145). John Joyce's biographers suggest that the song was one that he commonly sang during his family's many moves (Jackson and Costello, 218). It was also a favorite of Joyce's, one he sang often (Colum and Colum, 51). Shields, *Narrative Singing*, offers an extensive discussion of the genre.

21. Like Shem the Penman, Simon has "a plaintiff's tanner vuice" (*FW*, 182.22–23).

22. Oliver St. John Gogarty's phrase, quoted in Cixous, 38.

23. In *Finnegans Wake*, Joyce, referring to his father as "his farfamed fine Poppamore, Mr Humhum, whom history, climate and entertainment made the first of his sept and always up to debt," recalls and parodies this catalogue: "a blighty, a reeky, a lighty, a scrapy, a babbly, a ninny, dirty seventh among thieves and always bottom sawyer, till nowan knowed how howmely howme could be" (173.22–29).

24. Joyce himself attended Irish classes with George Clancy (the original of Davin) that were given by Padraic Pearse (*Portrait*, ed. Deane, 309n. 28, 317n. 123).

25. Stephen feels similar contempt for Moore as he views "the droll statue of the national poet of Ireland" (*PA,* 209).

26. *Moore's Poems,* 497–98. *Finnegans Wake* recalls both the song and Simon's responsibility for their singing it: "the light of other days dire dreary darkness; our awful dad" (136.20–21).

27. Norris, *Joyce's Web,* 56.

28. In *Finnegans Wake* Joyce depicts Shem the Penman infested by "the foxtrotting fleas, the lieabed lice, . . . the buzz in his braintree, . . . the rats in his garret, the bats in his belfry, the budgerigars and bumbosolom beaubirds" (180.18–28). See Norris, *Joyce's Web,* 68.

29. *Joyce's Web,* 56–57.

30. Bowen, *Bloom's Old Sweet Song,* 85. Interpretation and evaluation of the villanelle have long been a matter of critical dispute. See, for example, Charles Rossman, "Stephen Dedalus' Villanelle," *JJQ* 12 (Spring 1975): 281–93; Bernard Benstock, "The Temptation of St. Stephen: A View of the Villanelle," *JJQ* 14, no. 1 (Fall 1976): 31–38; Robert Scholes, "Stephen Dedalus, Poet or Esthete?" in Joyce, *A Portrait of the Artist as a Young Man: Text, Criticism, and Notes,* edited by Chester G. Anderson (New York: Viking, 1968), 468–80; and Bowen, "Stephen's Villanelle: Antecedents, Manifestations, and Aftermath," in *Bloom's Old Sweet Song,* 85–90.

31. Noting this detail, Norris also comments that Stephen had earlier tried to write a poem about Parnell "on the back of one of his father's second moiety notices" and that the vampire poem in "Proteus" is written on a strip of paper torn from the bottom of Deasy's letter to the newspaper about hoof and mouth disease. Stephen's art, she comments, "is literally inscribed in the textualization of Ireland's political and economic life. Stephen can only write on the back or in the margins of texts of British commercial power" (*Joyce's Web,* 19).

32. Bowen speculates that "Stephen is probably trying to establish himself with E.C. as a singer of touching ballads of antiquity rather than a singer of popular faddistic songs" (*Musical Allusions,* 42).

33. *Portrait,* ed. Deane, xvi.

34. Whelan, "Memories of 'The Dead,'" 62.

35. Strick's *Portrait* makes Stephen far less complexly performative than Joyce does. Joyce renders Stephen's relationship to art ambiguous and dubious, raising questions as to whether he could ever succeed as an artist. But the movie's flattened and simplified Stephen has virtually no artistic dimension.

36. Frank Budgen, *James Joyce and the Making of Ulysses* (London: Grayson, 1934), 107.

4. Vying for Artistry in *Ulysses*

1. Beckett shared Stephen's (and Joyce's) antipathy toward Britain, Catholicism, and Ireland. See, for example, Bair, *Samuel Beckett,* 517.

2. Victor Turner, *Dramas, Fields, and Metaphors: Symbolic Action in Human Society* (Ithaca: Cornell Univ. Press, 1974), 233.

3. The Gabler edition has "alone" instead of "above" (*Ulysses: The Corrected Text,* edited by Hans Walter Gabler with Wolfhard Steppe and Claus Melchior [New York: Random, 1986], 1.250).

4. Haines does miss the allusion: "—That [saying] about the cracked lookingglass of a servant being the symbol of Irish art is deuced good" (*U,* 16). The passage in Wilde reads, "I can quite understand your objection to art being treated as a mirror. You think it would reduce genius to the position of a cracked looking-glass" ("The Decay of Lying," in *The Works of Oscar Wilde* (London: Spring Books, 1977), 835. Norris also discusses this linkage (*Joyce's Web,* 63).

5. Douglas Hyde, *Love Songs of Connacht* (New York: Barnes and Noble, 1969), 31.

6. Leerssen, *Mere Irish,* 252.

7. Gabler's text then adds, "Why had they chosen all that part?" (2.45), which makes no sense.

8. Walsh, *Bloom* typescript, 88.

9. Shari Benstock, "The Dynamics of Narrative Performance: Stephen Dedalus as Storyteller," *ELH* 49, no. 3 (Fall 1982): 716.

10. Zimmermann, 248.

11. Zimmermann, 468; Kevin Danaher, "Stories and Storytelling in Ireland," in *Automobile Association Handbook of Ireland* (1970), 27.

12. Delargy, *Gaelic Story-Teller,* 32.

13. Toomey, 33.

14. Leerssen, *Remembrance,* 195.

15. Ellmann says that Joyce admired the speech but also significantly improved it (*JJ2,* 91).

16. Shari Benstock infers this last point from the fact that the plum seller's cry is heard as the funeral cortege passes Nelson's pillar on O'Connell street at 11:30 (91); it would likely still be in the air when Stephen walks up that street to the *Freeman's Journal*'s office an hour later (Shari Benstock, 718).

17. For an extended analysis of Stephen's inner narrative of this visitation that he does not make, see ibid., 712–18.

18. Earlier, in the classroom, Stephen had analogized himself to "the fiery Columbanus," who like Joyce and Stephen had left Ireland to "civilize" the continent (28).

19. Bowen, *Bloom's Old Sweet Song,* 87.

20. Apparently written by Gogarty (Bauerle, *Joyce Songbook,* 209).

21. The film's early reviews ranged from Ellmann's denigration ("The epic contracts into a domestic comedy") to Judith Crist's praise for its having "classic scope, a grandeur and a throbbing humanism, an intense dramatic power" ("A Superb Screen Translation of Joyce's *Ulysses,*" *New York Herald Tribune-Washington Post* [16 Mar. 1967]: 5). For a summary of the early reviews, see Norris, *Ireland into Film: Ulysses* (Cork: Cork Univ. Press, 2004), 47–68.

22. Mary Lowe-Evans, *Crimes against Fecundity: Joyce and Population Control* (Syracuse: Syracuse Univ. Press, 1989), 27.

23. Blake's name for a god jealous of the joy of his own creation; see Don Gifford and Robert J. Seidman, *Notes for Joyce: An Annotation of James Joyce's Ulysses* (Berkeley: Univ. of California Press, 1989), 192.

24. Anon., *Saint Andrew Daily Missal,* Bruges, Belgium: Abbey of St. Andrew, 1958.

25. Walsh, *Bloom* typescript, 68–69, 88, 95.

26. Walsh's *Bloom* literalizes this link by interpolating a shot of a drunken Simon playing the piano before "an obviously bored/embarrassed/ashamed," Stephen and Dilly (typescript, 2004, 83).

27. Bowen, *Bloom's Old Sweet Song,* 110.

28. Bowen, *Musical Allusions,* 164.

29. The Joyce family coat of arms, which John Joyce found in Burke's *General Armory* (1884), reads: "argent an eagle displayed gules charged on the breast with a bar gemel ermine" (Jackson and Costello, 129).

30. Lenehan is still measuring his audience: he offers this praise only after his ribald jokes at Bloom and Molly's expense fail to induce M'Coy to join his laughter (225). In "Cyclops," playing to a very different audience, Lenehan incites the Citizen to violent anti-Semitism by misinforming him that Bloom has gone to "gather in the shekels" he has supposedly won from betting on Throwaway in the Gold Cup (321).

31. His daughter Milly works in photography, for which she is said to have a "hereditary taste" (148); Bloom anticipates engaging in the "intellectual pursuit" of "snapshot photography" (667).

32. Bowen, *Musical Allusions,* 48–49.

33. The smell of Gerty MacDowell's perfume again triggers Bloom's memory of that night (357).

34. Bowen, *Musical Allusions,* 93.

35. Hardy, 257–58.

36. In "Penelope," Molly too recalls "Waiting" (706), suggesting that, unsatisfied by Boylan, she remains hopeful of better things to come when Bloom returns fully to her "waiting always waiting to guiiiide him toooo me waiting nor speeeed his flying feet" (708). "In Old Madrid," another waiting song of love, similarly shifts from an association with Boylan to one with Bloom (264, 709, 732).

37. Bauerle suggests that Molly's recollection of "Goodbye, Sweetheart, Goodbye" in "Penelope" (724) "is her farewell to Boylan and her affirmation of Bloom" (*Joyce Songbook,* 362). If that is the case, it anticipates the similar, and more prominent, role played by "Love's Old Sweet Song."

38. Norris, *Ireland into Film,* 63.

39. Zimmermann, 453.

40. Delargy, *Gaelic Story-Teller,* 37.

41. Zimmermann, 380, 381, 466, 471.

42. As has long been demonstrated, the list of Molly's "lovers" (724) cannot survive close scrutiny. Kenner's "Molly's Masterstroke" and David Hayman's "The Empirical Molly" (in

Approaches to Ulysses: Ten Essays, edited by Thomas F. Staley and Bernard Benstock [Pittsburgh: Univ. of Pittsburgh Press, 1970], 103–35) are especially persuasive that Molly is engaged in her first affair, which goes a long way toward explaining both what is special for her and Bloom about 16 June 1904 and her extraordinary monologue about this day.

43. As host, Bloom anticipates the role of Earwicker in *Finnegans Wake,* who presides over a public house and plays host in numerous ways, including at his own wake.

44. Gifford, *Notes for Joyce,* 480.

45. See Bowen, *Bloom's Old Sweet Song,* 18–19, and Bauerle, *Joyce Songbook,* 533–37.

46. Bowen suggests that this poem expresses Stephen and Bloom's mutual victimization (*Musical Allusions,* 324–28).

47. Harry Blamires, *The New Bloomsday Book* (New York: Routledge, 1996), 226.

48. See Kenner, "Molly's Masterstroke." Kenner persuasively argues that Molly, nervous about her first affair, seeks to "postpone, perhaps evade, the physical moment: certainly reduce it" (26).

49. In Strick's film of *Ulysses,* Bloom's analogous action is tossing into the waste bin the gift basket that Boylan brought Molly.

50. See Bowen's discussion of the relationship between *The Odyssey* and the adventures of Sinbad the Sailor (*Bloom's Old Sweet Song,* 96–100).

51. *Finnegans Wake* enumerates what Bloom might have ordered, "iggs for the brekkers come to mournhim, sunny side up with care" (12.14–15), and then elaborately parodies Molly's willingness to serve her husband breakfast in bed: "She'd cook him up blooms of fisk and lay to his heartsfoot her meddery eygs, yayis, and staynish beacons on toasc and a cupenhave so weeshy-washy of Greenland's tay or a dzoupgan of Kaffue mokau an sable or Sikiang sukry or his ale of ferns in trueart pewter and a shinkobread" (199.15–20).

52. In fact, Molly "made him pull out and do it on me" (694) to ensure that Boylan did not impregnate her.

53. The waterfall four miles northwest of Algeciras (Gifford and Seidman, *Notes for Joyce,* 517).

54. Bowen, *Bloom's Old Sweet Song,* 10.

55. Here are the song's first stanza and chorus:

Once in the dear dead days beyond recall,
When on the world the mists began to fall,
Out of the dreams that rose in happy throng
Low in our hearts love sang an old sweet song;
And in the dusk where fell the firelight gleam
Softly it wove itself into our dream.
Just a song at twilight, when the lights are low,
And the flick'ring shadows softly come and go,
Tho' the heart be weary, sad the day and long,

Still to us at twilight comes
Love's old song, comes Love's old, sweet song.

(In Bowen, *Bloom's Old Sweet Song,* 138.) *Finnegans Wake* calls it "life's old sahatsong" (110.24).

5. Vying for Center Stage in Beckett's Early Plays

1. Whelan, "Memories of 'The Dead,'" 68.

2. Gluck, 41. She finds Joyce's influence pervasive in Beckett's early writings (44–69).

3. The loss of the native language and culture is a traditional bardic theme. For example, Leerssen offers this translation from a long seventeenth-century poem on the related declines of Irish nobility and literacy: "The Irish do not even understand the Irish language, they speak it carelessly, they do not read it with any propriety; they abandon it, and leave honour behind . . . If you ask them to read verses in their own sweet mother tongue it is a waste of time, because they cannot" (*Mere Irish,* 233–34).

4. Bloom seems not to realize that his watch has ceased functioning until "Nausicaa," when he mentions it several times (345, 353, 356, 360).

5. Abel, 136.

6. Ibid., 135.

7. Gluck cites several passages in *Finnegans Wake* that allude to Beckett or suggest his influence on it (27–28).

8. Knowlson, *Damned,* 602; Brater, 161; Knowlson, *Damned,* 602–3.

9. James Knowlson, "Beckett as Director: The Manuscript Production Notebooks and Critical Interpretation," *Modern Drama* 30, no. 4 (Dec. 1987): 453.

10. Billie Whitelaw comments that Beckett "is very particular and meticulous and insists that it be right." In James Knowlson, "Practical Aspects of Theatre, Radio and Television: Extracts from an Unscripted Interview with Billie Whitelaw. A Television Recording Made on 1 February 1977 for the University of London Audio-Visual Centre." *Journal of Beckett Studies* 3 (Summer 1978): 89.

11. Young, 138.

12. Jackson and Costello, 381.

13. Brater, 5.

14. Shenker, 3.

15. Quoted in Knowlson, *Damned,* 319. Lawrence Harvey suggests that Beckett's "Home Olga," his acrostic poem to Joyce for his birthday in 1932, was "an admirer's farewell to the master" (296), but Joyce accepted it as an offering and it led to a temporary reconciliation after a breech caused by his daughter Lucia's fixation on Beckett.

16. Beckett to Alan Schneider, 11 January 1956 (*No Author,* 8).

17. This line appears in the film but not the published script.

18. Dougald McMillan and Martha Fehsenfeld, *Beckett in the Theatre: The Author as Practical Playwright and Director* (New York: Riverrun, 1988), 69.

19. Knowlson, *Damned,* 372.

20. Alan Schneider, "Waiting for Beckett," *Chelsea Review* 2 (Autumn 1958): 3–20. Reprinted in *Beckett at 60: A Festschrift* (London: Calder, 1967), 40. Lahr was more successful when he subsequently played the role in New York, with E. G. Marshall replacing Tom Ewell as Didi.

21. Jonathan Croall, *The Coming of Godot: A Short History of a Masterpiece* (London: Oberon, 2005), 22–23.

22. Knowlson, *Damned,* 350. See also Peter Hall on his production of the first English language *Godot,* "Peter Hall looks back at the original *Godot,*" http://samuel-beckett.net/PeterHall Godot.html, 1955. "Controversial" was a common label for *Godot* in the early years. It is, for example, the word used by the anonymous review in the *San Quentin News,* for the play that "enthusiastically captivated" more than a thousand attendees at a special performance ("San Francisco Group Leaves S.Q. Audience Waiting for Godot," *San Quentin News* 28 [28 Nov. 1957]: 1).

23. "Pantomime" became "TV" in Schneider's film of the play.

24. See Brater, 142–43. Joyce's first play, *A Brilliant Career* (1900), "a rehash of ingredients borrowed, unconsciously I am sure" from various Ibsen plays (*MBK,* 115), particularly *An Enemy of the People,* and which Joyce destroyed, was not specifically about the Famine but it apparently depicted "the devastating effects of a plague," which was one of the Famine's consequences (Lowe-Evans, 13).

25. William Wilde, *Irish Popular Superstitions;* quoted in Zimmermann, 209. Richard Dormer, who played Lucky in Peter Hall's 2005 production of *Godot* in Bath, says that, for him, Lucky's speech evokes the horrors of the famine (Croall, 47).

26. Karl Marx, "The Eighteenth Brumaire of Louis Bonaparte," *The Marx-Engels Reader,* edited by Robert C. Tucker (New York: Norton, 1978), 594–617.

27. Kiberd, "War against the Past," 35.

28. Zimmermann, 274.

29. Eric Bentley, "The Talent of Samuel Beckett," *New Republic* 134, no. 7 (14 May 1956): 20.

30. Abel, 84.

31. Perhaps in order to suggest that Pozzo may have been performing shortly before setting forth, Beckett changed the line when he directed the 1976 Schiller-Theater production: "He gave Pozzo a less mysterious and more solid bourgeois character by having him speculate in a new bit of dialogue that he must have left his watch at home 'on the Steinway'" (McMillan and Fehsenfeld, 63). The Gate Theatre film of *Godot* retains this change.

32. William Carleton, *Tales and Sketches,* in Zimmermann, 215.

33. "A kind of French dance resembling a cotillion," according to the *OED,* but perhaps also an allusion to the Irish custom in which "fighting often followed dancing" (Reg Hall, "Heydays Are Short Lived: Change in Music-Making Practice in Rural Ireland, 1850–1950," in *Crosbhealach an Cheoil 1996: The Crossroads Conference: Tradition and Change in Irish Traditional Music,* edited by Fintan Vallely (Dublin: Whinstone Music, 1999), 77.

34. This list of Lucky's dances coincides with that offered by Mick Moloney as likely to be in the repertoire of an Irish musician's dance music (*Far from the Shamrock's Shore: The Story of Irish-American Immigration through Song* [New York: Crown, 2002], 1).

35. Zimmermann, 537.

36. See Eric D. Smith, "'I Have Been a Perfect Pig': A Semiosis of Swine in 'Circe,'" *Joyce Studies Annual* 13 (Summer 2002), 129–46.

37. Catherine Curran, "Changing Audiences for Traditional Irish Music," in *Crosbhealach an Cheoil 1996: The Crossroads Conference: Tradition and Change in Irish Traditional Music,* edited by Fintan Vallely (Dublin: Whinstone Music, 1999), 57.

38. Delargy, *Gaelic Story-Teller,* 24.

39. Beckett, in McMillan and Fehsenfeld, 67.

40. P. W. Joyce, *Social History,* 457–58.

41. Brater, 13.

42. Working with Rick Cluchy, "Beckett points out that the actor's gestures, changes of position and movements are never to coincide with the spoken word on the tape" (McMillan and Fehsenfeld, 299).

43. Gontarski, *Endgame,* xix.

44. John Pentland Mahaffy, *The Principles of the Art of Conversation* (London: Macmillan, 1887), vii.

45. Bair, *Samuel Beckett.* He added that they "were actually himself and Suzanne as they were in the 1950's—when they found it difficult to stay together but impossible to leave each other" (468).

46. In Ruby Cohn, *Back to Beckett* (Princeton: Princeton Univ. Press, 1973), 152.

47. For purposes of this study, I date Beckett's plays from the year of initial performance *or* publication, whichever came first. With *Krapp* the dates are the same.

48. Zimmerman, 365.

49. Knowlson's revised text of *Krapp* follows Beckett's production practice: eliminating the clownish garb, much of the opening business, and his walk that was "a kind of shuffling dance," as well as Krapp's singing of "Now the Day Is Over."

50. See Bair, *Samuel Beckett,* 350–52; Knowlson, *Damned,* 318–20.

51. Beckett did, however, revise *Krapp* to make it less overtly self-referential. Bair writes that it "is one of the most openly autobiographical of his writings, and one which he worked over with painstaking precision in an attempt to disguise these traces" (*Samuel Beckett,* 490). For example, just as Beckett removed the Irish accent from Mouth in *Not I,* he omitted a reference to Krapp's birthplace (Dublin) and specific dates that corresponded roughly to those of his own life. Beckett also made Krapp less focused on his sexual needs.

52. Knowlson, *Theatre Workbook,* 26. It remains, however, in *CSPSB* (59, 62) and *SB3* (225, 229).

53. Marcel Mihalovici, *Krapp; ou, La dernière bande* (Paris: Heugel, 1961). Mihalovici, working with Beckett, also wrote music for *Cascando.* (See "My Collaboration with Samuel Beckett," *Beckett at 60: A Festschrift* [London: Calder, 1967], 20–22).

54. Beckett, letter to Jean Reavey (August 1962), Harry Ransom Center, Univ. of Texas at Austin.

55. Knowlson, *Theatre Workbook 1,* 128–29, 135.

56. Ibid., 127.

57. Kalb, 55.

58. Hardy, 59.

59. Beckett, in McMillan and Fehsenfeld, 298.

60. Pierre Chabert, in Knowlson, *Theatre Workbook 1,* 95. Chabert's discussion of *Krapp* as a musical score appears in McMillan and Fehsenfeld, 289–91.

61. Alan Schneider, *Rockaby* documentary, D. A. Pennebaker and Chris Hegedus (Buffalo: State Univ. of New York, 1981).

62. Beckett to Jean Martin (who played Krapp under Beckett's direction in 1970). In Knowlson, *Theatre Workbook 1,* 81.

63. Ibid., 87; McMillan and Fehsenfeld reproduce a slightly different version of this comment (288–89).

64. Ibid., 128.

65. See Cohn, *Just Play,* 10.

66. In Ronald Hayman, "Martin Held Talks to Ronald Hayman," *Times Saturday Review,* 25 Apr. 1970, I.

67. In John Fletcher, *About Beckett: The Playwright and the Work* (London: Faber, 2003), 190.

68. James Knowlson and John Pilling, *Frescoes of the Skull: The Later Prose and Drama of Samuel Beckett* (New York: Grove, 1980), 108. *Happy Days* was first published and performed in 1961; Knowlson and Pilling were writing in 1979.

69. Knowlson, *Damned,* 426.

70. Carey Perloff, "Three Women and a Mound," in Oppenheim, 164.

71. In Martha Fehsenfeld, "Beckett at Work," *The Beckett Circle* 2, no. 1 (Summer 1979): 4.

72. Zimmermann, 444.

73. Something similar happens often in the radio plays. Both Mrs. Rooney in *All That Fall* and Henry in *Embers* allude to sounds that occur after rather than before they speak, as if they were summoning the sounds rather than commenting on them.

74. Gontarski implies as much when he writes, "Winnie herself by now perhaps may be buried (by the mound of Time) to her lips" ("Beckett's Voice Crying in the Wilderness, from 'Kilcool' to *Not I,*" *Papers of the Bibliographical Society of America* 74 (First Quarter 1980), 27.

75. Knowlson, *Damned,* 433.

76. Beckett, letter to Kay Boyle (7 October 1961), Harry Ransom Center, Univ. of Texas at Austin.

77. Brater, 80.

78. Curiously, while the scene also remains in the Grove centenary edition, the note is gone.

79. See Bair, *Samuel Beckett,* 481–82, Knowlson, *Damned,* 429–30, and Cronin, 520.

80. Gontarski, *Shorter Plays,* xviii.

81. Cohn, *Beckett Canon,* 281.

82. Gontarski, *Shorter Plays,* xix.

83. In Martin Esslin, "Samuel Beckett and the Art of Broadcasting," *Encounter* 45, no. 3 (Sept. 1975): 44.

84. Gontarski, *Shorter Plays,* xviii.

85. Alan Schneider, "'Any Way You Like, Alan': Working with Beckett," *Theatre Quarterly* 5, no. 19 (Sept.–Nov. 1975): 28.

86. Gontarski, *Shorter Plays,* xix.

87. Knowlson and Pilling, 117.

88. Kershner, 262.

89. Knowlson and Pilling, 30, 116–20, 137.

90. In ibid., 114.

91. Alan Schneider, *Entrances,* 342.

92. Beckett letter to George Devine, 3 Sept. 1964, in *Disjecta: Miscellaneous Writings and a Dramatic Fragment,* edited by Ruby Cohn (London: John Calder, 1983), 112.

93. Ibid., 111.

6. Performers and Antiperformers in Beckett's Dramaticules

1. For Beckett's directing of *Endgame,* see McMillan and Fehsenfeld, 201–36.

2. Davis is quoted in Brater, 36; see Gontarski, *Shorter Plays,* xxvii. Unsurprisingly, it is Joyce's work rather than Beckett's that has been staged as musicals: "James Joyce's *The Dead,*" for example, and, despite Stephen Joyce's efforts to block it, *Molly Bloom: A Musical Dream,* at the 2000 Edinburgh Festival.

3. Leerssen, *Remembrance,* 195.

4. Ong, 33.

5. David Hayman, "A Meeting in the Park and a Meeting on the Bridge: Joyce and Beckett," *JJQ* 8, no. 4 (Summer 1971): 382.

6. Brater, 3.

7. Gontarski, *Shorter Plays,* xx.

8. Gussow, 49.

9. Bair argues, however, that "there was a noticeable difference in Beckett's attitude toward productions of his plays, depending on the country of performance" and, on the basis of numerous interviews with actors, directors, and others associated with production, she details the differences in Beckett's behavior during rehearsals in England, Germany, and France (*Samuel Beckett,* 591).

10. Gontarski, *Shorter Plays,* xxiv.

11. Alec Reid, "Impact and Parable in Beckett: A First Encounter with *Not I,*" *Hermathena* 141 (Winter 1986): 12.

12. Gontarski, *Shorter Plays,* xv.

13. Ibid.

14. Ibid., xxiii.

15. James C. C. Mays, "Esse Est Percipi: Beckett's Plays," *Irish Review* 1 (1986): 42.

16. Bair, *Samuel Beckett,* 513.

17. Ibid., 628.

18. Whitelaw, 120.

19. Cronin, 551.

20. In Mel Gussow, *Conversations with and about Beckett* (New York: Grove, 1996), 22.

21. Whitelaw, 151.

22. In Kalb, 17.

23. Ibid., 60.

24. In Reid, "Impact and Parable," 12.

25. Asmus, in Kalb, 183.

26. Ibid., 98.

27. Brater, 3.

28. Charles R. Lyons, *Samuel Beckett* (New York: Grove, 1983), 104.

29. Brater, 39.

30. Knowlson, *Damned,* 20.

31. Ibid., 433.

32. Stanley E. Gontarski, *Samuel Beckett's Happy Days: A Manuscript Study* (Columbus: Ohio State Univ. Libraries, 1977), 33.

33. In McMillan and Fehsenfeld, 201.

34. James C. C. Mays makes a similar point: "Beckett's writing is more theatrical than dramatic, in that it is essentially performative. . . . The Beckett actor never quite loses himself in the part, which is what makes the part distinctively theatrical" ("Samuel Beckett [1907–89]," *The Field Day Anthology of Irish Writing,* vol. 3 [Derry: Field Day, 1991], 235.

35. Beckett's reduction of characters to body parts suggests an echo of *Ulysses,* as Eisenstein describes it: "*Ulysses* blatantly gives the name of a dismembered part of the body to each chapter. These random parts of the body—whether limbs or innards . . . make for a thematic unity by symbolizing the subject matter and the image of the chapter to which they correspond" (195).

36. See Kristin Morrison, *Canters and Chronicles: The Use of Narrative in the Plays of Samuel Beckett and Harold Pinter* (Chicago: Univ. of Chicago Press, 1983), 115–16; Knowlson and Pilling, 121–22; and Ruby Cohn, *A Beckett Canon* (Ann Arbor: Univ. of Michigan Press, 2001), 290.

37. Gontarski, *Shorter Plays,* xxviii.

38. The instinct was there even earlier: after starting out as a man, Winnie in *Happy Days* became W before she was given a name.

39. Katharine Worth, *The Irish Drama of Europe from Yeats to Beckett* (Atlantic Highlands, N.J.: Humanities, 1978), 253, 250–51.

40. Gontarski, *Shorter Plays,* xvi.

41. Charles R. Lyons, "Beckett's Fundamental Theatre: The Plays from *Not I* to *What Where*." In *Beckett's Later Fiction and Drama: Texts for Company,* edited by James Acheson and Kateryna Arthur (New York: St. Martin's, 1987), 81. Lyons is referencing Hamm's narrative in *Endgame,* but the insight holds for the later plays as well.

42. Cohn, *Beckett Canon,* 295.

43. Patrick Magee's Joe exaggerates his contrasting reactions to the voiceover and the silences, flinching visibly each time Voice begins to speak.

44. Hayles, 78.

45. Zilliacus, 190.

46. Knowlson, *Damned,* 522.

47. Brater, 24.

48. In Gussow, 34. See also Knowlson, *Damned,* 521–22.

49. See, for example, two reviews in the *Sunday Times:* J. W. Lambert, "Faces of Humanity" (21 Jan. 1973): Arts 29, and Harold Hobson, "Table Talk" (11 Feb. 1973): Arts 28.

50. Quoted in Bair, *Samuel Beckett,* 622. In its conception and early version, *Not I* was among Beckett's most Irish and autobiographical works. It emerged from the drafts only as Beckett established artistic distance from his material, which, as the title proclaims, is its subject.

51. As in *Rough for Radio II.*

52. Knowlson and Pilling, 198.

53. Regarding *All That Fall,* Harmon writes that Beckett "was opposed to any kind of adaptation for the stage; its quality, he said, depended on its '*coming out of the dark.*' In the same letter he defined *Act Without Words* as primitive theater: it could not be made into a film" (*No Author,* 320). Yet Beckett later praised Whitelaw's *Not I,* "both stage and TV, [as] an unforgettable technical achievement" (423).

54. Zimmermann, 313.

55. Whitelaw, 132.

56. Anon., "Kindred Spirits." *Sunday Times* (London), 14 Jan. 1973, 28.

57. In "The Day of the Rabblement" (1901), Joyce both affirms Ibsen's supreme dramatic achievement and implies that he is to be anointed Ibsen's successor. In *Stephen Hero,* Joyce calls Ibsen "the first among the dramatists of the world" (45), presumably more for his moral integrity and iconoclasm than for his masterful construction of plot and dramatic situations. Yet his review of Ibsen's *When We Dead Awaken* (1900), though largely laudatory, is more balanced, criticizing what Joyce came to consider Ibsen's romanticizing of character and situation and his lack of realism (*4D,* 71). See Klaus Reichert on Joyce's view of Ibsen, "The European Background of Joyce's Writing," in Attridge, 62–70.

58. Many of Beckett's later plays fall into two contrasting groups: those that are far more intelligible when read (*Play, Not I, A Piece of Monologue*) and those that make little sense except in performance (*Film, Ghost Trio, . . . but the clouds . . . , Quad, What Where*).

59. Cohn, *Beckett Canon,* 317.

60. Bair, *Samuel Beckett,* 625.

61. "Shades" is also the last word of Yeats's "The Tower" (*Collected Poems,* 225), the poem from which Beckett took the title ". . . *but the clouds.* . . ." Cohn stresses Joyce and Beckett's shared Irish cosmopolitanism and details Beckett's echoes of "The Dead" (*Samuel Beckett: The Comic Gamut* [New Brunswick: Rutgers Univ. Press, 1962]), 33–34.

62. Ellmann, who comments that "Most of Yeats's late work in verse and drama contained elements that were congenial to Beckett," enumerates many of Beckett's echoes of Yeats's plays (*4D,* 100).

63. "Metronome" is Beckett's word (in Walter D. Asmus, "Practical Aspects of Theatre, Radio and Television: Rehearsal Notes for the German Première of Beckett's *That Time* and *Footfalls* at the Schiller-Theater Werkstatt, Berlin," translated by Helen Watanabe. *Journal of Beckett Studies* 2 [Summer 1977]: 85). Apparently Beckett often brought a metronome to rehearsals and used it to create his dramatic music (Lois Gordon, *The World of Samuel Beckett 1906–1946* [New Haven: Yale Univ. Press, 1996], 34). Rehearsing *Happy Days* at the Royal Court, Beckett placed a metronome on the floor and said, "This is the rhythm I want" (in Croall, 88).

64. Gussow, 101–2.

65. Whitelaw, 142.

66. Knowlson and Pilling, 221.

67. Whitelaw, 143.

68. Knowlson and Pilling, 227.

69. Whitelaw, 224.

70. Kalb, 10.

71. Whitelaw, in Alan Schneider, *Rockaby* documentary.

72. Alan Schneider, *Rockaby* documentary.

73. The only locale mentioned is the Isle of Swans in Paris, where Beckett and Joyce often walked together.

74. The play does, however, take its place in a French tradition of "impromptus" by such writers as Molière, Giraudoux, and Ionesco.

75. Kalb, 60.

76. Kalb enumerates many of the other questions raised but not answered in *Ohio Impromptu* and offers an excellent analysis of the work in performance (48–62).

77. In Martha Fehsenfeld, "Beckett's Late Works: An Appraisal," *Modern Drama* 25, no. 3 (Sept. 1982), 360.

78. Knowlson, *Damned,* 593.

79. Cohn, *Beckett Canon,* 370.

80. Whitelaw, 125.

81. Beckett, in Gussow, 42.

82. In Gontarski, *Shorter Plays,* 409, 415. Brater also discusses this adaptation (160–63).

83. Brater suggests that Beckett eliminates green because it represents "Dante's color for hope" (161).

84. Ibid., 162.

85. Bim and Bom were the names of popular Russian comedians. Beckett alludes to them in *Murphy,* the manuscript of *Godot,* and *How It Is* (McMillan and Fehsenfeld, 62).

86. "First without words" was cut from the productions on which Beckett worked (Gontarski, *Shorter Plays,* 416).

87. Cronin, 554.

88. Ibid., 556.

89. Brater, 162.

90. See Ruby Cohn, "Inexhaustible Alan," in *Beckett Translating/Translating Beckett,* edited by Alan Warren Friedman, Charles Rossman, and Dina Sherzer (University Park: Pennsylvania State Univ. Press, 1987), 227–32.

Coda: Stage(d) Endings

1. For an extensive analysis of the paucity of funerals in modern literature, see my *Fictional Death and the Modernist Enterprise* (Cambridge: Cambridge Univ. Press, 1995), 127–40.

2. Norris notes that Strick's film of *Ulysses* depicts two imagined possibilities: Stephen meeting a young woman and walking off with her as he departs Bloom's house and a professorial Stephen in bed with Molly (*Ireland into Film,* 52, 69).

3. Jonathen Kalb, "The Mediated Quixote: The Radio, Television and Film Plays of Samuel Beckett," in *The Cambridge Companion to Beckett,* edited by John Pilling (Cambridge: Cambridge Univ. Press, 1994), 131.

Bibliography

Abel, Lionel. *Metatheatre: A New View of Dramatic Form.* New York: Hill and Wang, 1963.

Amiran, Eyal. *Wandering and Home: Beckett's Metaphysical Narrative.* University Park: Penn State Univ. Press, 1993.

Andrew, Dudley, and Luke Gibbons, eds. "The Theater of Irish Cinema." *Yale Journal of Criticism* 15, no. 1 (Spring 2002): 23–58.

Anon. "1. The Play's the Thing," "2. Memos of a First-Nighter," "3. San Francisco Group Leaves S.Q. Audience Waiting for Godot." *San Quentin News* 28 (28 Nov. 1957): 1, 3.

———. *Saint Andrew Daily Missal* (1814). Bruges, Belgium: Abbey of St. Andrew, 1958.

———. "Kindred Spirits." *Sunday Times* (London), 14 Jan. 1973, 28.

Asmus, Walter D. "Practical Aspects of Theatre, Radio and Television: Rehearsal Notes for the German Première of Beckett's *That Time* and *Footfalls* at the Schiller-Theater Werkstatt, Berlin," translated by Helen Watanabe. *Journal of Beckett Studies* 2 (Summer 1977): 82–95.

Attridge, Derek, ed. *The Cambridge Companion to James Joyce.* Cambridge: Cambridge Univ. Press, 1995.

Bair, Deirdre. "'No-man's-land, Hellespont or vacuum': Samuel Beckett's Irishness." *Crane Bag* 1, no. 2 (1977): 14–20.

———. *Samuel Beckett: A Biography* (1978). Revised edition. London: Vintage, 1990.

Barkentin, Marjorie, with Padraic Colum. "Ulysses in Nighttown. Adapted from James Joyce." In *The Off-Broadway Theatre. Seven Plays,* edited by Richard A. Cordell and Lowell Matson, 335–405. New York: Random, 1959.

Barry, Kevin. *Ireland into Film: The Dead.* Cork: Cork Univ. Press, 2001.

———, ed. *The James Joyce Songbook.* New York: Garland, 1982.

Beck, Warren. *Joyce's Dubliners: Substance, Vision, and Art.* Durham: Duke Univ. Press, 1969.

Beckett, Samuel. *The Collected Shorter Plays of Samuel Beckett.* New York: Grove, 1984.

———. *Disjecta: Miscellaneous Writings and a Dramatic Fragment,* edited by Ruby Cohn. London: John Calder, 1983.

———. *Dream of Fair to Middling Women,* edited by Eoin O'Brien and Edith Fournier. Dublin: Black Cat, 1992.

———. *Eleuthéria.* Translated by Michael Brodsky. New York: Foxrock, 1995.

———. Letter to Kay Boyle. 7 Oct. 1961. Harry Ransom Center, Univ. of Texas at Austin.

———. Letter to Jean Reavey. August 1962. Harry Ransom Center, Univ. of Texas at Austin.

———. *Samuel Beckett: The Grove Centenary Edition.* 4 vols. Series editor Paul Auster. New York: Grove, 2006.

Beckett, Samuel, et al. *Our Exagmination Round His Factification for Incamination of Work in Progress.* New York: New Directions, 1962.

Benstock, Bernard. *James Joyce.* New York: Ungar, 1985.

———. "The Temptation of St. Stephen: A View of the Villanelle." *JJQ* 14, no. 1 (Fall 1976): 31–38.

Benstock, Shari. "The Dynamics of Narrative Performance: Stephen Dedalus as Storyteller." *English Literary History* 49, no. 3 (Fall 1982): 707–38.

Bentley, Eric. "The Talent of Samuel Beckett." *New Republic* 134, no. 7 (14 May 1956): 20–21.

Ben-Zvi, Linda. "Samuel Beckett, Fritz Mauthner, and the Limits of Language." *PMLA* 95, no. 2 (Mar. 1980): 183–200.

Blamires, Harry. *The New Bloomsday Book.* New York: Routledge, 1996.

Bowen, Zack R. *Bloom's Old Sweet Song: Essays on Joyce and Music.* Gainesville: Univ. of Florida Press, 1995.

———. *Musical Allusions in the Works of James Joyce: Early Poetry Through Ulysses.* Albany: State Univ. of New York Press, 1974.

Boyd, Michael. "Joyce into Beckett: Prolegomena to Any Future Fictions." In *The Reflexive Novel: Fiction as Critique,* 118–45. Lewisburg: Bucknell Univ. Press, 1983.

Brater, Enoch. *Beyond Minimalism: Beckett's Late Style in the Theater.* New York: Oxford Univ. Press, 1987.

Breathnach, Breandán. *Folk Music and Dances of Ireland.* Dublin: Mercier, 1980.

Bryden, Mary, ed. *Samuel Beckett and Music.* New York: Oxford Univ. Press, 1998.

Bucknell, Brad. *Literary Modernism and Musical Aesthetics: Pater, Pound, Joyce, and Stein.* Cambridge: Cambridge Univ. Press, 2001.

Budgen, Frank. *James Joyce and the Making of Ulysses.* London: Grayson, 1934.

Bunting, Edward. *Ancient Music of Ireland* (1840). Cork: Cork Univ. Press, 1983.

Carey, Phyllis, and Ed Jewinski, eds. *Re: Joyce'n Beckett.* New York: Fordham Univ. Press, 1992.

Cheng, Vincent J. *Joyce, Race, and Empire.* Cambridge: Cambridge Univ. Press, 1995.

Cixous, Hélène. *The Exile of James Joyce,* translated by Sally A. J. Purcell. New York: David Lewis, 1972.

Cohn, Ruby. *Back to Beckett.* Princeton: Princeton Univ. Press, 1973.

———. *A Beckett Canon.* Ann Arbor: Univ. of Michigan Press, 2001.

———. *Just Play: Beckett's Theater.* Princeton: Princeton Univ. Press, 1980.

———. *Samuel Beckett: The Comic Gamut.* New Brunswick: Rutgers Univ. Press, 1962.

Colum, Mary, and Padraic Colum. *Our Friend James Joyce.* Garden City: Doubleday, 1958.

Conrad, Joseph. *Great Short Works of Joseph Conrad.* New York: Harper, 1967.

Crist, Judith. "A Superb Screen Translation of Joyce's 'Ulysses.'" *New York Herald Tribune-Washington Post,* 16 Mar. 1967, 5.

Croall, Jonathan. *The Coming of Godot: A Short History of a Masterpiece.* London: Oberon, 2005.

Cronin, Anthony. *Samuel Beckett: The Last Modernist.* New York: Da Capo, 1999.

Curran, Catherine. "Changing Audiences for Traditional Irish Music." In *Crosbhealach an Cheoil 1996: The Crossroads Conference: Tradition and Change in Irish Traditional Music,* edited by Fintan Vallely, 56–63. Dublin: Whinstone Music, 1999.

Danaher, Kevin. *In Ireland Long Ago.* Cork: Mercier, 1967.

———. "Stories and Storytelling in Ireland." In *Automobile Association Handbook of Ireland* (1970), 26–27.

De Breffny, Brian, ed. *The Irish World: The History and Cultural Achievements of the Irish People.* London: Thames and Hudson, 1977.

Delargy, James H. *The Gaelic Story-Teller. With Some Notes on Gaelic Folk-Tales.* London: Proceedings of the British Academy, 31 (1945); Chicago: Univ. of Chicago Press, 1969.

———, ed. *Irish Folk-Tales, Collected by Jeremiah Curtin* (1941–42). Dublin: Talbot, 1956.

Doherty, Francis. "*Krapp's Last Tape:* The Artistry of the Last." *Irish University Review* 12, no. 2 (Autumn 1982): 191–204.

Donoghue, Denis. "Huston's Joyce." *New York Review of Books,* 3 Mar. 1988, 18–19.

Driver, Tom F. "Beckett by the Madeleine." *Columbia University Forum* 4, no. 2 (Summer 1961): 21–25.

Eagleton, Terry. *Heathcliff and the Great Hunger: Studies in Irish Culture.* New York: Verso, 1995.

———. "Staging the Famine." *Irish Reporter* 19 (Third Quarter 1995): 12–13.

Eisenstein, S. M. *Selected Works. Vol. II: Towards a Theory of Montage,* edited by Michael Glenny and Richard Taylor, translated by Michael Glenny. London: BFI Publishing, 1991.

Elliott, C. Robert. *The Power of Satire: Magic, Ritual, Art* (1960). Princeton: Princeton Univ. Press, 1970.

Ellmann, Richard. *Eminent Domain: Yeats among Wilde, Joyce, Pound, Eliot and Auden.* London: Oxford Univ. Press, 1970.

———. *Four Dubliners: Wilde, Yeats, Joyce, and Beckett.* London: Hamish Hamilton, 1987.

———. *James Joyce* (1959). Revised edition. New York: Oxford Univ. Press, 1983.

———. *Oscar Wilde.* New York: Knopf, 1988.

Esslin, Martin. "Samuel Beckett and the Art of Broadcasting." *Encounter* 45, no. 3 (Sept. 1975): 38–46.

———. *Mediations, Essays on Brecht, Beckett, and the Media.* London: Methuen, 1980.

———. *The Theatre of the Absurd* (1961). Revised edition. London: Vintage, 2004.

Evans, E. Estyn. *Irish Folk Ways.* New York: Routledge, 1989.

———. *Irish Heritage: The Landscape, the People and Their Work.* Dundalk: Dundalgan, 1944.

Fehsenfeld, Martha. "Beckett at Work." *Beckett Circle* 2, no. 1 (Summer 1979): 4.

———. "Beckett's Late Works: An Appraisal." *Modern Drama* 25, no. 3 (Sept. 1982): 355–62.

Feist, Gene. *James Joyce's Dublin.* New York: Samuel French, 1991.

Fielding, Daphne Vivian. *Those Remarkable Cunards: Emerald and Nancy.* New York: Atheneum, 1968.

Fletcher, John. *About Beckett: The Playwright and the Work.* London: Faber, 2003.

Fletcher, John, and John Spurling. *Beckett, the Playwright.* London: Methuen, 1985.

Foster, Roy F. *Modern Ireland 1600–1972.* London: Penguin, 1988.

———, ed. *The Oxford History of Ireland.* Oxford: Oxford Univ. Press, 1992.

Friedman, Alan Warren. *Fictional Death and the Modernist Enterprise.* Cambridge: Cambridge Univ. Press, 1995.

Friedman, Alan Warren, Charles Rossman, and Dina Sherzer, eds. *Beckett Translating/Translating Beckett.* University Park: Pennsylvania State Univ. Press, 1987.

Gallagher, Thomas. *Paddy's Lament: Ireland 1846–1847: Prelude to Hatred.* New York: Harcourt, 1982.

———. "Identity without a Centre: Allegory, History and Irish Nationalism." *Cultural Studies* 6, no. 3 (Oct. 1992): 358–75.

———. *Transformations in Irish Culture.* Cork: Cork Univ. Press, 1996.

Gifford, Don. *Joyce Annotated: Notes for Dubliners and A Portrait of the Artist as a Young Man.* 2nd edition. Berkeley: Univ. of California Press, 1982.

Gifford, Don, with Robert J. Seidman. *Notes for Joyce: An Annotation of James Joyce's Ulysses* (1974). Berkeley: Univ. of California Press, 1989.

Gilbert, Stuart. *James Joyce's Ulysses: A Study* (1931). New York: Knopf, 1952.

Glassie, Henry. *Passing the Time in Ballymenone: Culture and History of an Ulster Community.* Philadelphia: Univ. of Pennsylvania Press, 1982.

Gluck, Barbara Reich. *Beckett and Joyce: Friendship and Fiction.* Lewisburg: Bucknell Univ. Press, 1978.

Gmelch, Sharon, ed. *Irish Life and Traditions.* Syracuse: Syracuse Univ. Press, 1986.

Goffman, Erving. *The Presentation of Self in Everyday Life.* New York: Doubleday, 1990.

Gontarski, Stanley E. "Beckett's Voice Crying in the Wilderness, from 'Kilcool' to *Not I.*" *Papers of the Bibliographical Society of America* 74 (First Quarter 1980): 27–47.

———. *Crapp's First Tapes: Beckett's Manuscript Revisions of Krapp's Last Tape.* Philadelphia: Temple Univ. Press, 1977.

———. *The Intent of Undoing in Samuel Beckett's Dramatic Texts.* Bloomington: Indiana Univ. Press, 1985.

———. *Samuel Beckett's Happy Days: A Manuscript Study.* Columbus: Ohio State Univ. Libraries, 1977.

———, ed. *The Theatrical Notebooks of Samuel Beckett, Volume II: Endgame.* London: Faber, 1993.

———, ed. *The Theatrical Notebooks of Samuel Beckett, Volume IV: The Shorter Plays.* London: Faber, New York: Grove, 1999.

Gordon, Lois. *The World of Samuel Beckett 1906–1946.* New Haven: Yale Univ. Press, 1996.

Gregory, Lady Augusta. *Poets and Dreamers: Studies and Translations from the Irish.* New York: Oxford Univ. Press, 1974.

Grene, Nicholas. "Torrents of Talk." *Irish Review* 11 (Winter 1991–92): 140–43.

Gussow, Mel. *Conversations with and about Beckett.* New York: Grove, 1996.

Hale, Jane Alison. *Beckett's Dramatic Perspective.* West Lafayette, Ind.: Purdue Univ. Press, 1987.

Hall, Peter. "Peter Hall Looks Back at the Original *Godot.*" 1955. http://samuel-beckett.net/PeterHallGodot.html.

Hall, Reg. "Heydays Are Short Lived: Change in Music-Making Practice in Rural Ireland, 1850–1950." In *Crosbhealach an Cheoil 1996: The Crossroads Conference:*

Tradition and Change in Irish Traditional Music, edited by Fintan Vallely, 77–81. Dublin: Whinstone Music, 1999.

Hardison, O. B., Jr. *Christian Rite and Christian Drama in the Middle Ages: Essays in the Origin and Early History of Modern Drama.* Baltimore: Johns Hopkins Univ. Press, 1969.

Hardy, Barbara. *Tellers and Listeners: The Narrative Imagination.* London: Athlone, 1975.

Harmon, Maurice, ed. *The Celtic Master: Contributions to the First James Joyce Symposium Held in Dublin, 1967.* Dublin: Dolmen, 1969.

———. *No Author Better Served: The Correspondence of Samuel Beckett and Alan Schneider.* Cambridge: Harvard Univ. Press, 1998.

Harrington, John P. *The Irish Beckett.* Syracuse: Syracuse Univ. Press, 1991.

Hart, Clive. *Joyce, Huston, and the Making of The Dead.* Princess Grace Irish Library. Lectures: 5. Gerrards Cross: Colin Smythe, 1988.

Harvey, Lawrence E. *Samuel Beckett: Poet and Critic.* Princeton: Princeton Univ. Press, 1970.

Hayles, N. Katherine. "Voices out of Bodies, Bodies out of Voices: Audiotape and the Production of Subjectivity." In *Sound States: Innovative Poetics and Acoustical Technologies,* edited by Adelaide Morris, 74–96. Chapel Hill: Univ. of North Carolina Press, 1997.

Hayman, David. "The Empirical Molly." In *Approaches to Ulysses: Ten Essays,* edited by Thomas F. Staley and Bernard Benstock, 103–35. Pittsburgh: Univ. of Pittsburgh Press, 1970.

———. "A Meeting in the Park and a Meeting on the Bridge: Joyce and Beckett." *JJQ* 8, no. 4 (Summer 1971): 372–84.

Hayman, Ronald. "Martin Held Talks to Ronald Hayman." *Times Saturday Review,* 25 Apr. 1970, I.

———. *Samuel Beckett.* London: Heinemann, 1980.

Healy, James N., ed. *Ballads from the Pubs of Ireland.* Cork: Mercier, 1966.

Hemingway, Ernest. *Death in the Afternoon.* New York: Scribner's, 1960.

Hobsbawm, Eric, and Terence Ranger. *The Invention of Traditions.* Cambridge: Cambridge Univ. Press, 1984.

Hobson, Harold. "Table Talk." *Sunday Times,* 11 Feb. 1973, Arts 28.

Hodgart, Matthew J. C., and Mabel P. Worthington. *Song in the Works of James Joyce.* New York: Columbia Univ. Press, 1959.

Hofheinz, Thomas C. *Joyce and the Invention of Irish History: Finnegans Wake in Context.* Cambridge: Cambridge Univ. Press, 1995.

Homan, Sidney. *Beckett's Theaters: Interpretations for Performance.* Lewisburg: Bucknell Univ. Press, 1984.

———. *Filming Beckett's Television Plays: A Director's Experience.* Lewisburg: Bucknell Univ. Press, 1992.

Homer. *The Odyssey,* translated by Robert Fitzgerald. Garden City: Anchor Doubleday, 1963.

Hone, Joseph. *W. B. Yeats 1865–1939.* London: Macmillan, 1967.

Hoppen, K. Theodore. *Election, Politics, and Society in Ireland 1832–1885,* 424–29. Oxford: Clarendon, 1984.

Howarth, Herbert. *The Irish Writers, 1880–1940: Literature Under Parnell's Star.* London: Rockliff, 1958.

Hyde, Douglas. *Love Songs of Connacht* (1893). New York: Barnes and Noble, 1969.

Jackson, John Wyse, and Peter Costello. *John Stanislaus Joyce: The Voluminous Life and Genius of James Joyce's Father.* London: Fourth Estate, 1997.

Johnson, Paul. *The Birth of the Modern: World Society 1815–1830.* New York: HarperCollins, 1991.

Jordan, Neil. *Michael Collins: Screenplay and Film Diary.* New York: Penguin, 1996.

Joyce, James. *The Critical Writings of James Joyce,* edited by Ellsworth Mason and Richard Ellmann. New York: Viking, 1970.

———. *The Dead,* edited by Daniel R. Schwarz. Boston: St. Martin's, 1994.

———. *Dubliners.* New York: B. W. Huebsch, 1916.

———. *Dubliners,* edited by Terence Brown. New York: Penguin, 1992.

———. *Dubliners: Text, Criticism, and Notes,* edited by Robert Scholes and A. Walton Litz. New York: Viking, 1971.

———. *Exiles.* New York: Viking, 1961.

———. *Finnegans Wake.* New York: Viking, 1939.

———. *The Letters of James Joyce,* vol. 1, edited by Stuart Gilbert (1957); vols. 2 and 3, edited by Richard Ellmann. New York: Viking, 1966.

———. *Occasional, Critical, and Political Writing,* edited by Kevin Barry. Oxford: Oxford Univ. Press, 2000.

———. *The Portable James Joyce* (1946), edited by Harry Levin. New York: Viking, 1966.

———. *A Portrait of the Artist as a Young Man.* New York: B. W. Huebsch, 1916.

———. *A Portrait of the Artist as a Young Man: Text, Criticism, and Notes,* edited by Chester G. Anderson. New York: Viking, 1968.

———. *A Portrait of the Artist as a Young Man,* edited by Seamus Deane. Harmondsworth: Penguin, 1992.

———. *Selected Letters,* edited by Richard Ellmann. London: Faber, 1975.

———. *Stephen Hero,* edited by Theodore Spencer. London: Jonathan Cape, 1991.

———. *Ulysses.* Shakespeare and Company: Paris, 1922.

———. *Ulysses: The Corrected Text,* edited by Hans Walter Gabler with Wolfhard Steppe and Claus Melchior. New York: Random, 1986.

Joyce, P. W. *A Concise History of Ireland.* New York: Longmans, 1905.

———. *A Social History of Ancient Ireland.* London: Longmans, 1920.

Joyce, Stanislaus. *The Complete Dublin Diary of Stanislaus Joyce,* edited by George Harris Healey. Ithaca: Cornell Univ. Press, 1971.

———. *My Brother's Keeper: James Joyce's Early Years,* edited by Richard Ellmann. New York: McGraw-Hill, 1964.

Junker, Mary. *Beckett: The Irish Dimension.* Dublin: Wolfhound, 1995.

Kalb, Jonathan. *Beckett in Performance.* Cambridge: Cambridge Univ. Press, 1991.

Kelly, Joseph. "Stanislaus Joyce, Ellsworth Mason, and Richard Ellmann: The Making of James Joyce." *Joyce Studies Annual* 3 (Summer 1992): 98–140. Austin: Univ. of Texas Press.

Kenner, Hugh. *Dublin's Joyce.* London: Chatto, 1955.

———. "Molly's Masterstroke." *JJQ* 10, no. 1 (Fall 1972): 19–28.

———. *The Stoic Comedians: Flaubert, Joyce, Beckett.* Berkeley: Univ. of California Press, 1962.

Kershner, R. B. *Joyce, Bakhtin, and Popular Culture: Chronicles of Disorder.* Chapel Hill: Univ. of North Carolina Press, 1989.

Kiberd, Declan. Introduction to *Ulysses,* ix–lxxxix. London: Penguin, 2000.

———. *Inventing Ireland: The Literature of the Modern Nation.* London: Cape, 1995.

———. "Irish Literature and Irish History." In *The Oxford History of Ireland,* edited by Roy F. Foster, 230–81. Oxford: Oxford Univ. Press, 1992.

———. "The War against the Past." *The Uses of the Past: Essays on Irish Culture,* edited by Audrey S. Eyler and Robert F. Garratt, 24–54. Newark: Univ. of Delaware Press, 1988.

Kinealy, Christine. *This Great Calamity: The Irish Famine 1845–52.* Dublin: Gill and MacMillan, 1994.

Knowles, Sebastian D. G., ed. *Bronze by Gold: The Music of Joyce.* New York: Garland, 1999.

Knowlson, James. "Beckett as Director: The Manuscript Production Notebooks and Critical Interpretation." *Modern Drama* 30, no. 4 (Dec. 1987): 451–65.

———. *Damned to Fame: The Life of Samuel Beckett.* New York: Simon and Schuster, 1996.

———. "Practical Aspects of Theatre, Radio and Television: Extracts from an Unscripted Interview with Billie Whitelaw. A Television Recording Made on 1 February 1977 for the University of London Audio-Visual Centre." *Journal of Beckett Studies* 3 (Summer 1978): 85–90.

———, ed. *Happy Days: Samuel Beckett's Production Notebook.* London: Faber, 1985.

———, ed. *Light and Darkness in the Theatre of Samuel Beckett.* London: Turret, 1972.

———, ed. *The Theatrical Notebooks of Samuel Beckett, Volume III: Krapp's Last Tape.* London: Faber, 1989.

———, ed. *Theatre Workbook 1. Samuel Beckett: Krapp's Last Tape* (1980). Revised edition. London: Faber, 1992.

Knowlson, James, and John Pilling. *Frescoes of the Skull: The Later Prose and Drama of Samuel Beckett.* New York: Grove, 1980.

La Jeunesse, Ernest Horry. *Recollections of Oscar Wilde,* edited by Percival Pollard. London: J. W. Luce, 1906.

Lambert, J. W. "Faces of Humanity." *Sunday Times,* 21 Jan. 1973, Arts 29.

Lanters, José. *Missed Understandings: A Study of Stage Adaptations of the Works of James Joyce.* Amsterdam: Rodopi, 1988.

Leerssen, Joseph Theodoor. *Mere Irish and Fíor-Ghael: Studies in the Idea of Irish Nationality, Its Development and Literary Expression Prior to the Nineteenth Century.* Amsterdam: John Benjamins, 1986.

———. *Remembrance and Imagination: Patterns in the Historical and Literary Representation of Ireland in the Nineteenth Century.* Cork: Cork Univ. Press, 1997.

Le Roux, Louis. *Patrick Pearse.* Dublin: Talbot, 1932.

Leyda, Jay, ed. *Eisenstein 2: A Premature Celebration of Eisenstein's Centenary,* translated by Alan Y. Upchurch et al. Calcutta: Seagull, 1985.

Lloyd, David. "Writing in the Shit: Beckett, Nationalism, and the Colonial Subject." *MFS* 35, no. 1 (Spring 1989): 71–86.

Lowe-Evans, Mary. *Crimes against Fecundity: Joyce and Population Control.* Syracuse: Syracuse Univ. Press, 1989.

Lyons, Charles R. "Beckett's Fundamental Theatre: The Plays from *Not I* to *What Where.*" In *Beckett's Later Fiction and Drama: Texts for Company,* edited by James Acheson and Kateryna Arthur, 80–97. New York: St. Martin's, 1987.

———. *Samuel Beckett.* New York: Grove, 1983.

Lyons, F. S. L. *Ireland since the Famine: 1850 to the Present.* London: Weidenfeld and Nicolson, 1971.

MacGowran, Jack. "Interview with Jack MacGowran" (20 Apr. 1971). In *Yeats, Joyce, and Beckett: New Light on Three Modern Irish Writers,* edited by Kathleen McGrory and John Unterecker. Lewisburg: Bucknell Univ. Press, 1976.

———. "MacGowran on Beckett: Interview by Richard Toscan." *Theatre Quarterly* 3, no. 11 (July–Sept. 1973): 15–22.

Mahaffy, John Pentland. *The Principles of the Art of Conversation.* London: Macmillan, 1887.

Martin, Timothy. *Joyce and Wagner: A Study of Influence.* Cambridge: Cambridge Univ. Press, 1991.

———, ed. *Joyce and Opera.* Special issue of *JJQ* 38, no. 1–2 (Fall 2000–Winter 2001).

Marx, Karl. "The Eighteenth Brumaire of Louis Bonaparte." *The Marx-Engels Reader,* edited by Robert C. Tucker, 594–617. New York: Norton, 1978.

Mays, James C. C. "Esse Est Percipi: Beckett's Plays." *Irish Review* 1 (1986): 34–44.

———. "Samuel Beckett (1907–89)." In *The Field Day Anthology of Irish Writing,* vol. 3, 233–38. Derry: Field Day, 1991.

McCabe, Patrick. *The Butcher Boy.* London: Picador, 1992.

McHugh, Roger. "A Setting for Stephen Dedalus." *Arts in Ireland* 2, no. 1 (1973): 28–32.

McMahon, Sean, ed. *The Poolbeg Book of Irish Ballads.* Dublin: Poolbeg, 1991.

McMillan, Dougald, and Martha Fehsenfeld. *Beckett in the Theatre: The Author as Practical Playwright and Director.* 3 vols. New York: Riverrun, 1988.

McMullan, Anna. *Theatre on Trial: Samuel Beckett's Later Drama.* New York: Routledge, 1993.

Mercier, Vivian. *The Irish Comic Tradition.* Oxford: Clarendon, 1962.

Mihalovici, Marcel. *Krapp; ou, La dernière bande.* Paris: Heugel, 1961.

———. "My Collaboration with Samuel Beckett." In *Beckett at 60: A Festschrift,* 20–22. London: Calder, 1967.

Moloney, Mick. *Far from the Shamrock's Shore: The Story of Irish-American Immigration through Song.* New York: Crown, 2002.

Moore, Thomas. *Irish Melodies (1807–34).* Philadelphia: Oliver Ditson, 1893.

———. *Moore's Poems with Notes by Thomas Moore.* Chicago: Henneberry Company, n.d.

Morrison, Kristin. *Canters and Chronicles: The Use of Narrative in the Plays of Samuel Beckett and Harold Pinter.* Chicago: Univ. of Chicago Press, 1983.

Moylan, Terry, ed. *The Age of Revolution: 1776 to 1815 in the Irish Song Tradition.* Dublin: Lilliput, 2000.

Nadel, Ira. "Joyce and Blackmail." *Journal of Modern Literature* 22, no. 2 (Winter 1998–99): 215–23.

Nelson, Richard, and Shaun Davey. *James Joyce's The Dead. American Theatre* 17, no. 7 (Sept. 2000): 49–68.

Norris, Margot. *Ireland into Film: Ulysses.* Cork: Cork Univ. Press, 2004.

———. *Joyce's Web: The Social Unraveling of Modernism.* Austin: Univ. of Texas Press, 1992.

———. "Updating *Ulysses:* Joseph Strick's 1967 Film." *JJQ* 41, no. 1–2 (Fall 2003–Winter 2004): 79–87.

Norton, Caroline. *The Poems of the Hon. Mrs. Norton.* Philadelphia: Uriah Hunt, 1846.

O'Brien, Conor Cruise. "Irishness." In *Writers and Politics,* 97–100. New York: Pantheon, 1965.

O'Brien, Eoin. *The Beckett Country: Samuel Beckett's Ireland.* Dublin: Black Cat, 1986.

O'Casey, Sean. *Juno and the Paycock.* In *Modern Irish Drama,* edited by John P. Harrington, 204–54. New York: Norton, 1991.

Ong, Walter J. *Orality and Literacy: The Technologizing of the Word.* London: Routledge, 2002.

Oppenheim, Lois, ed. *Directing Beckett.* Ann Arbor: Univ. of Michigan Press, 1994.

O Suilleabháin, Seán. *A Handbook of Irish Folklore.* Detroit: Singing Tree, 1970.

Pater, Walter. *The Renaissance: Studies in Art and Poetry.* London: Macmillan, 1914.

Pecora, Vincent P. *Self and Form in Modern Narrative.* Baltimore: Johns Hopkins Univ. Press, 1989.

Peillon, Michel. "Irish Festivities in Comparative Perspective." *Maynooth Review* 6, no. 2 (May 1982): 39–59.

Pierce, David. *James Joyce's Ireland.* New Haven: Yale Univ. Press, 1992.

Pilling, John. *Beckett before Godot.* Cambridge: Cambridge Univ. Press, 1997.

———. *Samuel Beckett.* London: Routledge, 1976.

———, ed. *The Cambridge Companion to Beckett.* Cambridge: Cambridge Univ. Press, 1994.

Poizat, Michel. *The Angel's Cry: Beyond the Pleasure Principle in Opera,* translated by Arthur Denner. Ithaca: Cornell Univ. Press, 1992.

Power, Arthur. *Conversations with James Joyce.* New York: Barnes and Noble, 1974.

Rabaté, Jean-Michel. "Silence in *Dubliners.*" In *James Joyce: New Perspectives,* edited by Colin McCabe, 45–72. Bloomington: Indiana Univ. Press, 1982.

Rappaport, Roy A. *Ritual and Religion in the Making of Humanity.* Cambridge: Cambridge Univ. Press, 1999.

Rathjeu, Friedhelm. *In Principle, Beckett Is Joyce.* Thirteenth International James Joyce Symposium, Dublin, June 1992, Edinburgh: Split Pea, 1994.

Reid, Alec. *All I Can Manage, More than I Could: An Approach to the Plays of Samuel Beckett.* Dublin: Dolmen, 1968.

———. "Impact and Parable in Beckett: A First Encounter with *Not I.*" *Hermathena* 141 (Winter 1986): 12–21.

Rockett, Kevin. "Something Rich and Strange: James Joyce, Beatrice Cenci and the Volta." *Film and Film Culture* 3 (2004): 21–34.

Rockett, Kevin, Luke Gibbons, and John Hill. *Cinema and Ireland.* London: Routledge, 1988.

Rossman, Charles. "Stephen Dedalus' Villanelle." *JJQ* 12 (Spring 1975): 281–93.

Ryan, Noelle. *Samuel Beckett: Early Days in Foxrock.* Foxrock: Local History Club, 1982.

Schechner, Richard. *Performance Theory* (1977). Revised edition. New York: Routledge, 2003.

Schneider, Alan. "'Any Way You Like, Alan': Working with Beckett." *Theatre Quarterly* 5, no. 19 (Sept.–Nov. 1975): 27–38.

———. "Directing Beckett." *New York Times,* 18 Dec. 1977, sec. 2: 5.

———. *Entrances. An American Director's Journey.* New York: Viking Penguin, 1986.

———. "Waiting for Beckett." *Chelsea Review* 2 (Autumn 1958): 3–20. Reprinted in *Beckett at 60: A Festschrift,* 34–52. London: Calder, 1967.

Schneider, Erik. "Joyce in Concert: The *Meistersinger* Performance in Trieste." *JJQ* 38, no. 3–4 (Spring–Summer 2001): 495–97.

Scott, Bonnie Kime, ed. *New Alliances in Joyce Studies: "When It's Aped to Foul a Delfian."* Newark: Univ. of Delaware Press, 1988.

Senn, Fritz. "Kyklonomastics." *JJQ* 36, no. 3 (Spring 1999): 485–506.

Shenker, Israel. "Moody Man of Letters." *New York Times,* 6 May 1956, 2:1, 3.

Shields, Hugh. "The History of *The Lass of Aughrim.*" In *Irish Musical Studies 1: Musicology in Ireland,* edited by Gerard Gillen and Harry White, 58–73. Dublin: Irish Academic, 1990.

———. *Narrative Singing in Ireland: Lays, Ballads, Come-All-Yes and Other Songs.* Dublin: Irish Academic, 1993.

Shloss, Carol Loeb. *Lucia Joyce: To Dance in the Wake.* New York: Farrar, 2003.

Simms, J. G. *Jacobite Ireland 1685–91.* London: Routledge, 1969.

Smith, Eric D. "'I Have Been a Perfect Pig': A Semiosis of Swine in 'Circe.'" *Joyce Studies Annual* 13 (Summer 2002): 129–46.

Spenser, Edmund. "A View of the Present State of Ireland." *The Works of Edmund Spenser,* vol. 10, edited by Edwin Greenlaw, Charles Grosvenor Osgood, Frederick Morgan Padelford, Ray Heffner. Baltimore: Johns Hopkins Univ. Press, 1949.

Spiegel, Alan. *Fiction and the Camera Eye: Visual Consciousness in Film and the Modern Novel.* Charlottesville: Univ. of Virginia Press, 1976.

State Papers of Henry VIII, Vol. II (1532–7). London: George Eyre and Andrew Spottiswoode, 1834.

Thornton, Weldon. *Allusions in Ulysses: A Line-by-Line Reference to Joyce's Complex Symbolism.* New York: Simon and Schuster, 1973.

Thuente, Mary Helen. *The Harp Re-strung: The United Irishmen and the Rise of Irish Literary Nationalism.* Syracuse: Syracuse Univ. Press, 1994.

Toomey, Deirdre. "The Story-Teller at Fault: Oscar Wilde and Irish Orality." In *Wilde the Irishman,* edited by Jerusha McCormack. New Haven: Yale Univ. Press, 1998.

Turner, Victor. *Dramas, Fields, and Metaphors: Symbolic Action in Human Society.* Ithaca: Cornell Univ. Press, 1974.

Tymoczko, Maria. *The Irish Ulysses.* Berkeley: Univ. of California Press, 1994.

Walsh, Sean. *Bloom.* Typescript of the film, 2004.

Watt, Stephen. *Joyce, O'Casey, and the Irish Popular Theater.* Syracuse: Syracuse Univ. Press, 1991.

Weaver, Jack W. *Joyce's Music and Noise: Theme and Variation in His Writings.* Gainesville: Univ. Press of Florida, 1998.

Whelan, Kevin. "Immoral Economy: Interpreting Erskine Nicol's *The Tenant.*" In *America's Eye: Irish Paintings from the Collection of Brian P. Burns,* edited by Adele M. Dalsimer and Vera Kreilkamp, 57–67. Boston: Boston College Museum of Art, 1996.

White, Terence de Vere. *Tom Moore: The Irish Poet.* London: Hamish Hamilton, 1977.

Whitelaw, Billie. *Billie Whitelaw . . . Who He?* London: Hodder and Stoughton, 1995.

Wilde, Oscar. "The Decay of Lying." In *The Works of Oscar Wilde,* 825–43. London: Spring Books, 1977.

———. *The Picture of Dorian Gray,* edited by Donald L. Lawlor. New York: Norton, 1988.

Wilmer, S. E., ed. *Beckett in Dublin.* Dublin: Lilliput, 1992.

Woods, Armin, and Stefan Köhl. *Famous Irish Songs: With the Lyrics, the Score and Guitar Support.* New York: Bergh Publishing, 1989.

Woolf, Virginia. "Modern Fiction." In *The Common Reader,* 150–58. New York: Harvest, 1953.

Worth, Katharine. "Beckett and the Radio Medium." In *British Radio Drama,* edited by John Drakakis, 191–217. Cambridge: Cambridge Univ. Press, 1981.

———. *The Irish Drama of Europe from Yeats to Beckett.* Atlantic Highlands, N.J.: Humanities, 1978.

Yeats, W. B. *The Collected Plays of W. B. Yeats.* London: Macmillan, 1969.

———. *The Collected Poems of W. B. Yeats.* London: Macmillan, 1956.

———. *Prefaces and Introductions: Uncollected Prefaces and Introductions by Yeats to Works by Other Authors and to Anthologies Edited by Yeats,* edited by William H. O'Donell. London: Macmillan, 1988.

———. *Uncollected Prose: 1: 1886–96,* edited by John P. Frayne. *2: 1887–1939,* edited by John P. Frayne and Colton Johnson. New York: Columbia Univ. Press, 1970, 1976.

Young, Jordan R. *The Beckett Actor: Jack MacGowran, Beginning to End.* Beverly Hills: Moonstone, 1987.

Zilliacus, Clas. *Beckett and Broadcasting: A Study of the Works of Samuel Beckett for and in Radio and Television.* Abo: Abo Akademi, 1976.

Zimmermann, Georges Denis. *The Irish Storyteller.* Dublin: Four Courts, 2001.

Productions

Araby. Dennis Courtney, director. American Street Productions, 1997.

Beckett Directs Beckett: Waiting for Godot; Krapp's Last Tape; Endgame. San Quentin Drama Workshop, Univ. of Maryland, College Park, 1990–92.

Beckett on Film: 19 Films x 19 Directors. Michael Colgan and Alan Moloney, producers. Blue Angel Films, 2000.

Beginning to End. Patrick Garland, director; adapted by Jack MacGowran and Samuel Beckett. BBC 1, 1965.

Bloom. Sean Walsh, director. Odyssey Pictures, 2004.

The Dead. John Huston, director. Vestron Video, 1987.

Eh Joe. Samuel Beckett, director. SDR TV, 1966.

Embers. David Clark, director; Katharine Worth, producer. Univ. of London Audio-Visual Center, 1959.

Endgame. American Repertory Theatre, 1984. Tony Coe, director and producer. Open Univ., BBC, 1989.

Exiles. (1) Harold Pinter, director; London 1970; (2) Vincent Dowling, producer. Abbey Theatre, RTE, 1982.

Film. (1) Alan Schneider, director; with Buster Keaton. Evergreen Productions, 1965; (2) Max Wall, director. BBC, 1979.

Happy Days. Samuel Beckett, director. Schiller-Theater, Berlin, 1971.

James Joyce's The Dead. Richard Nelson, director. Belasco Theatre, New York, 1999; Kennedy Center, Washington, DC, 2000.

John Huston and the Dubliners: The Making of "The Dead." Lilyan Sievernich, director. Liffey Films, 1987.

Krapp's Last Tape. (1) Samuel Beckett, director; Théâtre d'Orsay, Paris, 1970; (2) Alan Schneider, director; D. A. Pennebaker, producer; with Jack MacGowran. New York, 1971.

Michael Collins. Neil Jordan, director. Warner Brothers, 1996.

Music from the Works of James Joyce. Liner notes by Zack Bowen and Kevin McDermott. Sunphone Records, 2003.

Not I. (1) Anthony Page, director; with Billie Whitelaw. Royal Court, 1973; (2) Tristram Powell, director; with Billie Whitelaw. BBC, 1977.

A Painful Case. John Lynch, director and producer. RTE, 1983.

Play. (1) George Devine and Samuel Beckett, directors. Old Vic Theatre, 1964; (2) Alan Schneider, director. New York, 1964; (3) Jean-Marie Serreau and Samuel Beckett, directors. Paris: Pavillon de Marsan: 1964.

A Portrait of the Artist as a Young Man. Joseph Strick, director. Mystic Fire, 1977.

Quad. (1) SDR TV, 1982; (2) John Reilly, director and producer. Peephole Art, Global Village, 1988.

Rockaby, Footfalls, Eh Joe. Walter D. Asmus, director. Films for the Humanities and Sciences, 1988.

Rockaby documentary. Alan Schneider, director; Daniel Labielle, producer; with Billie Whitelaw. D. A. Pennebaker and Chris Hegedus. Buffalo: State University of New York, 1981.

Shades: Not I, Ghost Trio, . . . but the clouds. . . . RTE, 1977.

Ulysses. Joseph Strick, director. Mystic Fire Video, 1967.

Waiting for Godot. (1) Alan Schneider, director; Jack Kuney, producer. Miami and New York, 1956. (2) Jules Irving, director. San Francisco Actor's Workshop, San Quentin Prison, 1957. (3) Alan Schneider, director. WNTA TV, 1961.

What Where. (1) SDR TV, 1985. (2) John Reilly, producer and director; Stanley E. Gontarski, theater director. Peephole Art, Global Village, 1988.

Words and Music. David Clark, director; Katharine Worth, producer. Univ. of London Audio-Visual Center, 1961.

Index

Fictional characters' names are not inverted and are followed by (fict.). Chapters of Joyce's books are identified by *D* for *Dubliners* and *U* for *Ulysses* such as "Circe" (*U*/Joyce).

Page numbers in italics denote illustrations.